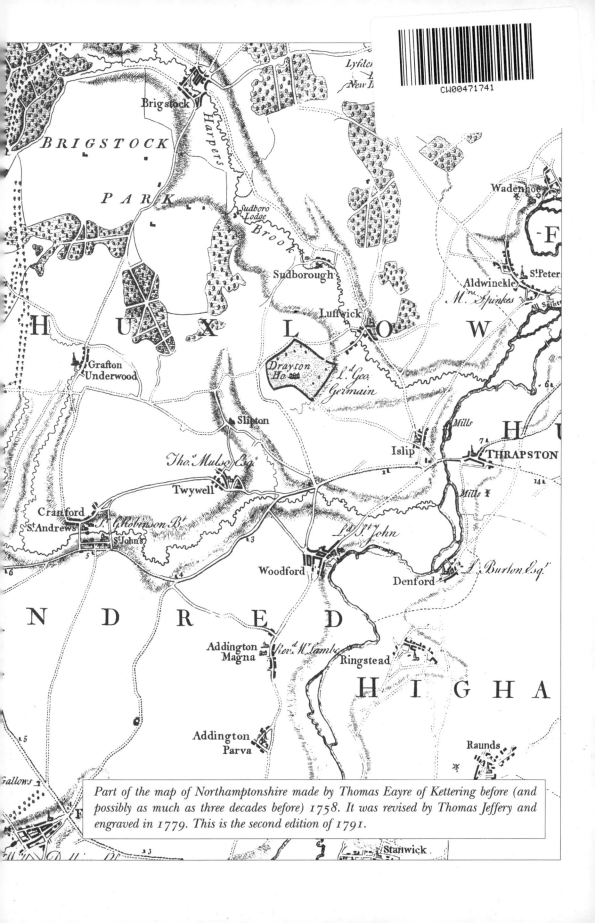

Part of the map of Northamptonshire made by Thomas Eayre of Kettering before (and possibly as much as three decades before) 1758. It was revised by Thomas Jeffery and engraved in 1779. This is the second edition of 1791.

A HISTORY OF
KETTERING

Market Place and church, c.1900.

A HISTORY OF
KETTERING

R.L. Greenall

Phillimore

2003

Published by
PHILLIMORE & CO. LTD
Shopwyke Manor Barn, Chichester, West Sussex, England

ISBN 1 86077 254 4

Printed and bound in Great Britain by
MPG BOOKS
Bodmin, Cornwall

In affectionate memory of
Fred Moore
Frank Thompson
and
Tony Ireson
who loved every brick, stone and story of old Kettering

CONTENTS

LIST OF ILLUSTRATIONS

Frontispiece: Market Place and church, *c.*1900

ACKNOWLEDGEMENTS

Warm thanks are expressed to the staff of Kettering Art Gallery and Museum; and to the following for their unfailing helpfulness over many years – Terry Bracher and Colin Eaton at Northamptonshire Libraries and Information Service, Abington Street Library, Northampton, and to John Burden, Derrick Bond and Andrea Pettingale and their colleagues over many years at Kettering Library; to Patrick King, Rachel Watson, Sarah Bridge and their colleagues at Northamptonshire Record Office. My thanks also go to the Minister and Deacons of Fuller Church for access to their archives; to William Campbell; to the late J.L.Carr for conversations on Kettering over a number of years; to Frank Faulds and his wife; to Peter Taylor for the use of his maps; and to the late Ernest Timpson, who showed me round Perfecta Works and proved a mine of information on the town's nonconformist and industrial history. To others I express appreciation below.

PICTURE ACKNOWLEDGEMENTS

Grateful acknowledgements are made to the following for permission to reproduce illustrations in their keeping: Mr J.S. Althorpe for the use of the photographs of the late Fred Moore, 23, 38, 44, 48, 54, 59, 68, 71, 72, 74, 75, 76, 78, 79, 85; Mrs R. Cave for Gotch family photographs, 31, 37, 89; Kettering Civic Society, 3, 34, 95, 100; Kettering *Evening Telegraph*, 68, 86; Audrey Mitchell, 97; Northamptonshire Libraries and Information Service collections at Northampton, 5, 9, 13, 16, 17, 18, 25, 27, 29, 32, 33, 35, 49, 52, 55, 60, 64, 67, 77, 81, 90, 91, 92 and Kettering, 21, 36, 41, 51, 65; Northamptonshire Record Office; Joyce and Maurice Palmer, frontispiece, 66, 83, 87, 88, 94; the late Frank Thompson, 80, 86. The following are from the author's collection: 1, 2, 6, 7, 19, 24, 39, 40, 42, 43, 45, 46, 47, 50, 53, 56, 57, 58, 61, 62, 63, 69, 70, 73, 82, 84, 93, 96 and 98.

FOREWORD

In this year of 2003 it is 112 years since Frederick William Bull, a local solicitor with antiquarian interests, published his *A Sketch of the History of the Town of Kettering Together with Some Account of its Worthies*. Seventeen years later, in 1908, he added his *Supplement to the History of the Town of Kettering Together with a Further Account of its Worthies*. Whilst not providing a 'joined up' account of the rise and fluctuations in the history of the town, Bull was a scholarly and accurate researcher and his books provide subsequent writers with a splendid quarry to work. In our own time, a number of works on Kettering have been published, though most concentrate on its recent history or are collections of pictures. Bearing in mind the sources which have become available to historians since Bull's era and the way perspectives on the past have changed, it is perhaps time to attempt a new history of the town.

Some local histories are written by insiders, some by outsiders. This is by an outsider, who, by a happy accident, became involved with Kettering and its past. No stranger can ever claim to know a place in the same way as those born or brought up there. Natives have the sort of intimate knowledge acquired through education and experiences, or retailed by family, friends and neighbours no stranger can ever acquire, though there is a time-limit on how far back such knowledge stretches. On the other hand, the outside researcher perhaps can see the place more comparatively, recognise its singularities and is sometimes in a position to unearth historical information from a wider range of sources than are available within the town. Not all Kettering's secrets are in Kettering.

A happy way to bring together these sources of knowledge is (or was) through adult education courses in local history, where a tutor brings material from the archives and class members discuss what had been found and contribute their own knowledge, experience and carefully preserved material – old photographs, pamphlets, letters and other valuable ephemera – often not found in the archives. This is where this book has its origins. The writer first became interested in the history of Kettering, teaching, at fairly regular intervals since 1970, courses promoted by the Workers' Educational Association and the University of Leicester

Department of Adult Education on the history of the town (and other subjects). Other tutors in this work, such as John Steane and Douglas Clinton, led research groups which produced unpublished work on the parish records and a range of other sources, which has, as far as possible, been incorporated into this book. Members of these groups included the following: Jane Brown, the late Gladys Creasey, Raymond Dorr, John Inns, Maureen Loake, the late Fred Moore, David Moseley, June Scouse, John Skillington and the late Frank Thompson. Mr Clinton was one of a group who worked on the history of the parish church and was largely responsible for drafting *A History of Kettering Parish Church*, which the Kettering Civic Society published in 1977.

Amongst the collectors who were generous in allowing the author to work on their material were the late Fred Moore and the late Frank Thompson. Both had amassed extensive collections of photographs, printed sources (including scarce pamphlets) and a certain amount of manuscript material. Fred, in particular, amongst other things, rescued from the dustbin a collection of legal papers relating to the Gotch bankruptcy trial of 1857, a major event in Victorian Kettering.

It is sometimes difficult to recruit groups in adult education. In Kettering this has never been a problem. There exists a great interest in how the town evolved and in the abiding character of the place. To strangers, this may seem difficult to comprehend. Kettering is not what people often think of when they think of an 'historic' town. Professor Pevsner did not consider it was worth lingering over and it is the sort of place (rather like South Wigston in Leicestershire) which would have made Professor Hoskins shudder. It has few outstanding buildings (though it has, or had, plenty of interesting ones). Outwardly Kettering is a Victorian industrial town which lost its identity when it lost its staple trade. But a town's history is always much more than the signals old buildings send out. Kettering is more interesting than its outward appearance promises.

Although only imperfectly aware of it at the time, arriving in the town in 1970 was to make contact at the point when Victorian Kettering, which had survived the changes of the 20th century remarkably well, was in some danger of being swept away. Footwear was in serious decline, the Liberal party had quit the stage of history, the once-mighty Kettering Co-operative movement was having to change or decline. The Borough Council, like nearly every other Council in the land, was seriously into 'urban renewal' which involved, *inter alia*, destruction of much of old Kettering. Architects and planners were in thrall to Brutalism; set in concrete, one might say. In the rush for modernity there was a danger of stripping the place of its character. Another change also materialised. The long-debated reform of local government brought the old, compactly urban Borough of Kettering to an end and re-invented it as the new Borough of Kettering consisting of old Kettering, four nearby small towns and 22 parishes stretching away to the edges of Market Harborough and Corby. There was logic in this. England was becoming a motorised society; Kettering had been spreading out beyond the old borough boundary for years. So, is today's Kettering a continuation of the past or something new? It is, of course, both. The historian and the sociologist (and we are all amateur sociologists now) need to remind themselves of the essential truth of the words of the late J. Enoch Powell: 'Human society is a layered-cake. No two generations have lived in the same world, though they live side by side and converse as freely as if they have'. One hopes what follows will help to clarify Kettering conversations.

LEICESTER, 2003

PART ONE

Pre-Industrial Kettering:
The Legacy of the Past

One

LOCAL AND REGIONAL SETTING

Kettering lies in the middle of Middle England, fifty miles or so east of Birmingham and seventy or so north from London. Within the county of Northampton, it lies on the cross-country road (the A43) which runs from Oxford through Brackley and Northampton to Stamford, Kettering itself being 10 miles from Northampton and 20 from Stamford. It also lies where two once-important roads from London, the A6 via Bedford and the A5 and A508 via Newport Pagnell and Wellingborough, converge and then proceed on to Market Harborough, Leicester, Derby and Manchester or to Uppingham, Oakham and beyond.

Nationally, Kettering is a low-profile sort of place, never having had a recognisable claim to fame, though its most important product was once trampled underfoot on several continents as well as in Britain. Even that claim to fame has now all but passed as the making of shoes has declined to almost nothing. Readers of contemporary fiction might recollect that the boring parents of the heroine of Helen Fielding's comic novel *Bridget Jones's Diary* live in Kettering and have friends in Grafton Underwood, but for the purposes of the novel they might be located anywhere, the story being premised on the idea that, for 30-somethings, there is no life beyond London.

For most of its thousand-year existence Kettering was a typically-sized Northamptonshire parish of 2,617 acres, though since local government

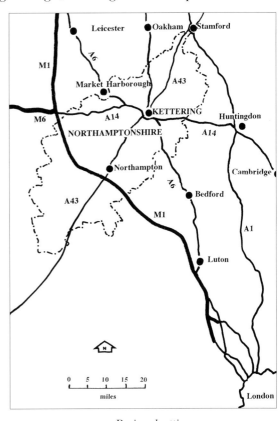

1 *Regional setting.*

3

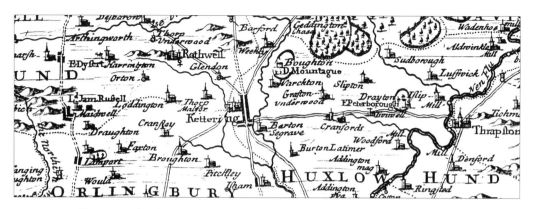

2 *Kettering and its district in 1712, from John Morton's* Natural History of Northamptonshire.

re-organisation in the 1970s contemporary Kettering now consists of a territory with a total acreage of 58,000 and a population of about 72,000. Kettering town is located on a flat-topped ridge, composed mainly of Northampton sand, at around 250 feet above sea level. On either side of this ridge the land falls steeply, to the Ise on the east and to the Slade on the west, both of which flow south through clay-floored valleys and join the River Nene at Irthlingborough. The Nene then finds its way to the sea via Peterborough.

Kettering's agricultural land, now largely built over, was once known as 'rich turnip land'; the subsoil is iron and limestone. In Roman times iron was smelted from the ironstone on an extensive scale in and around Kettering, and the industry revived after railway cuttings exposed that mineral source again in the years after 1851. The limestone produces some of the finest building material available; between Kettering and Stamford (the former Forest of Rockingham) and between Irthlingborough and Peterborough are handsome stone villages with some of the best medieval churches in the country, built from the enduring oolitic limestone. Corby apart, this is a countryside largely untouched by industry. It contained many country estates, some of which are still in the hands of the families which founded them. Closest to Kettering in their connections are Rockingham Castle, still the home of the Watsons, and Boughton House, one of the homes of the Dukes of Buccleuch, descendants of the Montagus of Boughton. The two families were joint lords of the manor of Kettering.

If Kettering has a rural hinterland, for two centuries its main business was industry. The town is one of the chain of small industrial towns along the A6, from Desborough to Rushden, which (with Northampton and Wellingborough) constituted the boot and shoe-making area of Northamptonshire. Although footwear has withered, the outward spread of these towns, with their new housing estates (and who can fail to cherish Desbeau Park, Desborough?), 'Enterprise Parks', 'Leisure Villages', 'out of town' supermarkets and new roads to serve them, is seemingly inexorable.

Two

THE ORIGINS OF KETTERING

The Anglo-Saxon Chronicle recounts, in graphic terms, how, in the year 921, Edward the Elder, King Alfred's son, marched up to Towcester with his army and forced the Danes of Northampton to accept his overlordship. He then proceeded north (possibly through Kettering) and compelled the Danes of Stamford to do the same. Now absorbed into the kingdom of England, English local government replaced Danish and, at some point between 921 and 1010, a county of Northampton came into being, and was divided into administrative sub-districts called hundreds. The hundreds were districts originally liable to render a hundred hides, the basic unit of tax, though the hidation came to be modified thereafter. At what we would call the parish level, other important developments were also taking place. Planned townships (nucleated villages together with their field systems) were brought into being. We are accustomed to think that the landscape and pattern of English rural settlement was essentially an organic, evolutionary thing. Recent archaeological and historical research has demonstrated that while that is true of some parts of the country it is not for this part of the Midlands. At some time between 921 and the year 956, the date of the earliest documentary reference to it, the settlement we call Kettering came into existence, and it did so as an act of planning. Its first streets, tenements, arable fields and township boundaries were systematically laid out. By whom? No one knows for sure, but it must have been the Crown through the local lords and their administrators. Whoever did it, the project was on an enormous scale. When William the Conqueror came to the throne in 1066 he found a country with a well-established administrative and economic system *in situ.*

There appear several inter-related reasons for the great early 10th-century settlement planning. The first is that the creation of nucleated settlements with their field systems was the basis of a system of taxation for the needs of the Crown, created by the war against the Danes and in anticipation of future demands for government spending. Another was the transformation of agriculture from being basically pastoral to a system dedicated to the production of cereals, for which much of the soils of the Midlands were well-suited. It was for this reason that the open field system, based on the

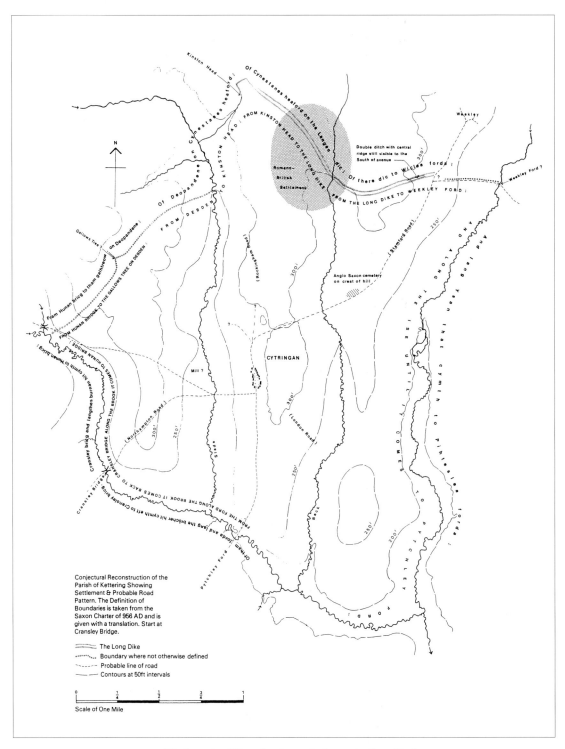

3   *The bounds of Kettering in 956, drawn by Peter Taylor.*

rotation of crops on two, and later, three great fields, one half or one third lying fallow each year, was laid out. Each year, after harvest, the arable land became open or common for the pasturing of animals, particularly sheep, whose dung manured the land and maintained its fertility. It seems certain that the transformation of the agrarian system was effected to provide food for a growing population, and this involved the drawing together of the hitherto scattered farmsteads of the Anglo-Saxons into villages. There may also have been an element of defence in early nucleation. The origin of the place-name Kettering apparently baffled English place-name scholars in the 1930s, but it seems clear that it means 'the place (or territory) of Ketter's people or kinsfolk', and whilst the name is unusual it is not unique: there is a Ketteringham in Norfolk.

The system was manorial. The charter of 956 recites the granting by King Eadwig (or Edwy) 'by divine ordinance indefatigable King of the English' to one of his thanes, Aelfsige, 'ten cassati for ever' at 'Cytringan', with the right to bequeath the manor to his successors. The charter sets out the bounds of Aelfsige's Cytringan and they were to remain the bounds of Kettering until the incorporation of Barton Seagrave in the late 20th century:

> Cransley Bridge along the brook until it [the boundary] comes to Humbridge; from Humbridge to the gallows tree on Deben; from Deben to Kinston Head; from Kinston Head to the long dyke; from the long dyke to Weekley ford along the Ise until it comes to Pytchley ford; from the ford along the brook until it comes back to Cransley bridge.

Aelfsige and his heirs do not appear to have held the estate very long because, in 972, King Edgar granted 'Kyteringas' by charter to the recently re-founded monastery of Peterborough, still referred to by its old name, *Medeshamstede*. In what was probably an anti-monastic reaction the estates of the abbey were attacked. As the *Ely History* tells it, 'After the death of King Edgar in 975, Leofri, son of Bixi, an enemy to God and deceiver of his fellow-men, by rapine and violence despoiled the convent of Medeshamstede of its possessions in Burch, Undele and Kettering, the lands lying waste without tillage or culture for two years'. Leofric was compelled to return Kettering to the abbot and it remained one of the manors with which the Abbey of Peterborough was endowed until its dissolution by King Henry VIII in 1538. An intriguing question is, was the granting of the manor of Kettering to the Abbey of Peterborough in the 10th century something new, or the restoration of a connection which went back before the onset of the Danish invasions?

The manor and village of Kettering certainly pre-dated the church and the ecclesiastical parish, perhaps by as long as a century. The district was re-christianised after the pagan Danish interregnum through the minster system, central churches with resident priests who evangelised their districts. Eventually village churches were built and the parochial system adopted, a parish being an area containing enough tithe payers to maintain a full-time

4   *Anglo-Saxon funerary urns, photographed by F.W. Bull in 1903.*

priest. In the case of Kettering and most other villages and towns in
Northamptonshire the bounds of the manor and of the parish were and are
the same. This is not necessarily true of other parts of England. Which, if
any, was the mother church of Kettering? Rothwell, Geddington and Brigstock
were all once minsters, but there is no evidence as to an ancient relationship of Kettering with any of these exists. It is more likely that Kettering was
linked with the greatest local Christain power-centre of all – the Abbey of
Peterborough. The earliest reference to Kettering having a church is in the
Black Book of Peterborough of about 1125 which records enigmatically that
'the church of the village is at the altar of the abbey church of Burg'. Not
until 1146 does a Peterborough charter makes specific mention of
'Ketteringge with the church and the mill and all its appurtenances'. The
present parish church is a complete rebuild of the 15th century; apart from
one or two pieces of masonry in the outer wall of the south aisle and the
east wall no evidence of the older church it replaced survives. The assumption
has to be that the original church was built a generation or two after the
Conquest, probably as a result of a church extension policy on the part of
the Abbey.

Because it did not exist as a village earlier than the tenth century, in a way, there is perhaps no need to seek the origins of Kettering further. But there is a long and rich history of human settlement before late-Saxon nucleation. In the Anglo-Saxon centuries there were family farmsteads scattered thinly in the landscape, though archaeology has not revealed much evidence of them in the town or fields of Kettering, and probably never will, given the fact that much of the land is now built over, and all that is usually found are scatters of pottery fragments. Brown and Foard, however, suggest that two furlong names in the old open-field, *Walcotes* and *Sharlcotes*, offer clues to at least two scattered settlement sites awaiting discovery. Between 1900 and 1904 much interest was generated in Kettering by the discovery of an extensive early Anglo-Saxon burial site on high ground along the Stamford Road. Some 80 to 90 burial urns containing the ashes of cremated corpses, some skeletons and items such as part of a

Roman Remains at Kettering.

Lord Dalkeith's Generous Gift.

ROMAN-BRITISH OBJECTS FROM KETTERING.
(Reproduced by kind permission of the Society of Antiquaries.)
1, Bronze knife handle of dog; 2, Embossed bronze plate, late Celtic style;
3, Bone pin, axehead top; 4, 5, Bronze pins, incomplete, with claw settings in
the head; 6, Bronze pin, moulded head; 7, Crescent brooch, enamelled; 8, 10,
Finger rings with setting; 8, Gilt brooch with conical setting of glass—this
type sometimes found in Anglo-Saxon graves; 11, 13, Brooches, first century;
12, Metal spoon, stem wanting; 14, Lozenge pendant, enamelled.

5 *Romano-British finds from the collection donated by the Earl of Dalkeith to Kettering Museum, illustrated in the* Northampton Independent, *3 February 1912.*

cruciform brooch and fragments of glass were also found. In 1929 excavations in the area yielded up more inhumations, 16 burial urns and bronze ornaments. Two other sites revealed single Anglo-Saxon graves, one on Windmill Avenue and one of 1806 on the west side of the valley of the Ise, the body accompanied by a spear-head. These are all indications of early Anglo-Saxon settlement in the district, and a further clue to an even earlier English presence lies in the place-name Weekley, the 'Wic-' prefix being seen by place-name scholars as an indication of *feodorati*, Anglo-Saxon mercenaries brought in to boost the defences of the Empire, probably in the second half of the fourth century.

The major ancient monument in the parish is the large unwalled Roman settlement which lies under the northern part of the town and extends into Weekley and Geddington parishes. Evidence of considerable iron-smelting has been found and the settlement was occupied until the fourth century AD. In addition, within the older part of the modern town centre, when excavating the foundations of the Temperance Hall in Gold Street in 1864, workmen discovered the remains of an ancient furnace, together with pieces of slag, identified as Roman. This part of Northamptonshire was one of the three great centres of iron-working in Roman Britain, the others being the Weald of Kent and Sussex and the Forest of Dean in Gloucestershire. The making of iron seems to have been carried on in Rockingham Forest down to the time of Domesday Book and beyond, and was probably discontinued because of the cutting down of trees needed for charcoal or because alternative uses of the woodland were adopted. As an industry, iron-making was not to return to Northamptonshire until shortly after the Great Exhibition of 1851.

It is now clear that Roman Britain was far more extensively settled and populous than used to be thought. The Kettering-Weekley industrial area was linked to a Roman Road (Gartree) which ran from Leicester to Irchester. Excavation in advance of proposed ironstone quarrying at Weekley in 1970-71 revealed evidence of continuous occupation from the later Iron Age into the Roman era in a series of ditched enclosures covering quite an extensive area. Adjacent to the Iron-Age site was found a later Roman villa, all of which, taken with other archaeological discoveries in the area, indicate much Iron-Age and Roman activity in the district. The question is, was there continuity of human settlement from the Roman and earlier settlement into the Anglo-Saxon era? The answer is probably not. It seems clear that in the later Romano-British era there was a catastrophic fall in population and economic activity, probably on a greater scale than the economic decline of the later Middle Ages. The Dark Ages remain remarkably dark in the Kettering area. No literary evidence exists for what happened in the immediate post-Roman era and the early centuries of the Anglo-Saxon settlement, and the archaeological evidence is fragmentary.

Scattered archaeological evidence from before the Iron Age is imprecisely recorded. Worked flints, Bronze-Age pottery and material from Bronze-Age burials have been collected but not enough to form any clear pattern of development. The most enigmatic monument dating from before the 10th century is what seems from air photographs to be three sides of a large enclosure. The dyke which marked a section of the bounds of Kettering in the charter of 956 is part of this, but what the enclosure was, and from when it dates have not yet been explained.

Nor, for that matter, is there more than fragmentary evidence from the time of the establishment of the Anglo-Saxon kingdoms and the conversion to Christianity in the seventh and eighth centuries. The present Northamptonshire area became part of the Midland kingdom of Mercia, nearby Irthlingborough being one of the places the Mercian Council is known to have met. In the second half of the seventh century Christianity was established. The abbey of Medeshamstede was founded by Peada of Mercia, and, according to the Anglo-Saxon Chronicle, his brother and successor, Wulfhere, saw the monastery consecrated and richly endowed in the time of its first abbot, Seaxwulf. In the next generation, Medeshamstede was

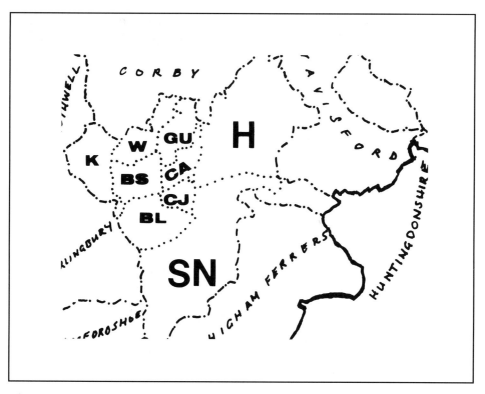

6 *Until hundreds fell into disuse in the 19th century, Kettering was part of the hundred of Huxloe. However, that was formed from three ancient hundreds – Huxloe, Suthnaveslund and Northnaveslund, which were part of the eight hundreds claimed by Peterborough Abbey. With Kettering, the following were included in Northnaveslund: Warkton, Cranford, Barton Seagrave, Grafton and Burton. Were they once an Anglo-Saxon estate or soke?*

instrumental in spreading the Gospel to the Outer Mercians and monastic offshoots were planted at Brixworth, Oundle and Castor, all of which later became minsters. There is some evidence that what later became Northamptonshire was divided into three large local administrative units based on the royal estate centres of Kings Sutton in the south, Northampton in the centre and Oundle in the north, evidence for the latter being a reference in Bede's *The Ecclesiastical History of the English Nation* (written about 731) to events '*in provincia Undulum*' – 'in the province of Oundle'. It is possible that Kettering was part of this province.

After more than a century of existence, the monastery of Medeshamstede was destroyed by Danish invaders in 870. Four years later the king of Mercia was driven out and his kingdom fell under Danish control. The Northamptonshire district, as far south as Watling Street, came under the control of Danish armies who fortified Stamford and Northampton, probably creating burhs (towns) there for the first time. Apart from that, little is known about the subsequent century. The site of the Mercian monastery of Medeshamstede lay waste until 963, when, as the Anglo-Saxon Chronicle records, following the firm establishment of the English kingdom, Aethelwold, bishop of Winchester, asked King Edgar to give him all the monasteries which the heathen had destroyed because he wished to restore them, and the King granted his request. After restoring Ely, Aethelwold came to Medeshamstede 'and found nothing but old walls and wild woods'. However, he found hidden in the old walls, so the Chronicle says, documents about the original endowments and privileges of Medeshamstede. King Edgar, after examining the documents allegedly found, re-granted all the old rights, exemptions and lands which hitherto pertained and Aethelwold duly re-established the abbey of St Peter at 'Burch' (or 'Burg'). It is from this era that the Kettering charter dated 976 originates, though in fact it exists only in a 12th-century version.

These re-founded monasteries not only had estates but extensive jurisdictions or 'liberties'. The abbey of Peterborough was given the eight hundreds of Oundle which ran from Nassaburgh, in which Peterborough was situated, south-west down the valley of the River Nene as far as the Ise. At its south-west corner lay North Navereslund hundred, in which Kettering was located. Were the Eight Hundreds of Oundle a re-creation of the old Anglo-Saxon 'Province of Oundle'? Had Kettering been linked to Medeshamstede in pre-Danish times? It seems possible.

At the time of Domesday Book Kettering was within the hundred of Navereslund, which had originally been two hundreds, North and South Navereslund. Many of the planned townships of the early 10th century were originally part of older and much larger units, or *sokes*. In time, some evolved into hundreds. At the time of Domesday a few sokes still survived – for example, Finedon and Rothwell. The latter had 10 dependencies all of which later became separate townships and ecclesiastical parishes. Seven of these became the hundred of Rothwell. Kettering, despite its close proximity, was not one of one of Rothwell's dependencies in 1086. If North Navereslund was created out of a soke, no evidence exists for this, nor is there any for an ecclesiastical connection with an ancient minster (some of the main soke centres, such as Rothwell, also having minster churches). The pre-956 antecedents of Kettering therefore remain obscure. It is possible that North and South Navereslund are a later version of the territory of the Iron-Age hill fort at Irthlingborough, but this is no more than informed archaeological speculation.

Three

MANOR, MARKET AND CHURCH: MEDIEVAL KETTERING

The Manor

In Domesday Book Kettering is listed under the estates of the Abbey of St Peter of Burg and the entry reads:

> The same church holds 10 hides in Cateringe [Kettering]. Land for 16 ploughs. In lordship there is 1 (plough), and 1 female slave; and (there are) 31 villagers with 10 ploughs. 2 mills at 20 shillings; 107 acres of meadow, and 3 acres of woodland. It was worth £10 (in the time of King Edward the Confessor); now (it is worth) £11.

The '10 hides' (the units of taxation) are presumably the same as the ten *cassati* Aelfsige had in 956. The information about mills, meadows (essential for the growing of hay for feeding the animals) and the wood is self-explanatory, and so is the modest increase in the overall value since 1066, Kettering having avoided being the scene of any violence by or against the Conqueror. The 31 villagers were the peasant farmers, each having a virgate of land, later to be referred as a yardland. As long as the open-field system remained in use farms were described in yardlands, and so in Kettering the term remained in use until 1804. In the great re-planning of the early 10th century there was a direct relationship between hidation and virgates, so many virgates to the hide: in the case of Kettering this was four. This is not clear in the Domesday reference but it is in a Peterborough charter of *c*.1125 which clearly states that there were 40 yardlands, and the same number of yardlands appear in an account roll of 1310.

The peasant's virgate or yardland was distributed around the open-field in *lands*, long narrow strips. These strips were in large blocks known as *furlongs* (nothing to do with our racing furlong of 220 yards). The most significant fact about lands and furlongs is that the lands of the peasants were laid out in a regular way, a tenurial cycle, furlong by furlong. Not all furlongs were the same size, but the tenurial cycle was the same. It was a system that could not have evolved through custom and practice, though for many centuries it was maintained by custom and practice. It clearly was planned, firstly in the early 10th century and maybe re-planned later as the amount of land under the plough increased until it could increase no more. As late as the 1720s there were still 40 yardlands (with some other irregular parts added) with a still discernible tenurial cycle of lands in each furlong

7   *The present manor house (now Kettering & District Museum) and church. The house has developed from the medieval 'noble hall'.*

in Kettering. We know this because there exists an immensely detailed map of the parish in the 1720s. In the course of time some farmers came to occupy more than one yardland and others less, usually a half or a quartern, but the yardland total stayed more or less the same. The acreage of the yardland could vary from manor to manor, but it was usually around 30 acres.

In the manorial system the land was granted to the manorial lord (the Abbot of Peterborough) by the King in return for the lord's service, and the lord granted land to the customary tenants, the villeins, and to the cottagers, in return for payment in money, in kind and in service, in the form of daywork on his manorial demesne, a farm or grange of some 300 acres or so. Some demesnes were in the form of dispersed land-holdings but in Kettering the demesne was of the concentrated kind, and is clearly shown in Ralph Treswell's map of 1587.

The working of the system is set out very clearly in a charter of *c.*1125, recorded in the *Black Book of Peterborough.* 'In Kateringes which is assessed at 10 hides 40 villani hold 40 virgates [or yardlands]. And these men for the lord's work plough in spring 4 acres for each virgate. And besides this they find plough teams [carucas] three times in winter, three times for spring ploughing, and once in summer. And they have twenty-two plough teams wherewith they work. And all of them work 3 days a week. And besides this they render per annum for each virgate of custom 2 shillings and eleven pence halfpenny. And they all [together] render 50 hens and 640 eggs. And besides this Aelgericus holds 13 acres and renders 16 pence and has 2 acres of meadow. And there is here one mill with a miller and he pays 20 shillings. And 8 cotsetas [cottagers] each holding 5 acres. They work once a week and twice a year make malt. Each of them gives a penny for a goat and if he has a she-goat a half-penny. And there is one shepherd and one swineherd who holds 8 acres. And in the demesne of the manor are 4 plough teams with 32 oxen [8 per team] 12 cows with 10 calves and 2 unemployed animals, and

3 draught cattle and 300 sheep, and 50 pigs and as much meadow over as is worth 16 shillings. The Church of the village is at the altar of the abbey church of Burg. For the love feast of St Peter they give 4 rams and 2 cows, or 5 shillings. The returns from the estate of Kettering are £26 yearly'. Kettering's manorial economy was part of a bigger system in which all the manors belonging to Peterborough contributed to the needs and requirements of the monastery. In Northamptonshire, in addition to Kettering, the Abbey's manors were Irthlingborough, Stanwick, Clapton, Luddington, Polebrook, Ashton, Warmington, Oundle, Biggin and Cottingham. There were another 17 in the immediate vicinity of Peterborough, two in Leicestershire and Rutland and seven in Lincolnshire. Monasteries such as Peterborough were among the largest and certainly the most permanent medieval corporations.

In common with any well-managed corporation, annual accounts had to be rendered from each part of the business. For 1292 we have the *Compotus*, published by Charles Wise in a Latin-English version (Wise was schoolmaster of Warkton and a considerable antiquarian). The Kettering demesne farm, or grange, was managed by a bailiff appointed by the abbot, and a reeve, chosen by the villeins. The two of them prepared annual accounts which were transcribed on a roll, together with accounts from other manors. These are set down in minute detail. First, all the arrears, rents, dues, recognizances, fines, perquisites and other receipts which made up the monetary income of the manor; second, all the expenses, 'necessary', 'small' and 'outsider' are listed, together with stipends, liveries, allowances and the cost of corn and livestock purchased; and third is a carefully balanced account of the produce and outgoings of the grange and of the customary day's work.

About sixty years earlier, in the time of the abbacy of Walter de St Edmunds (1233-46), 'a noble hall faced with stone, a new sheepfold and a new cowshed were erected' in Kettering. It is not clear from the *Compotus* who lived in the 'noble hall'. Apparently it was not the bailiff because expenses are recorded for his visits. Possibly it was the Abbey steward, because, although records are made of the provender provided for the horses of other visitors and for the visits of the '*custos maneriorum*', there are none for visits of the steward. The grange was managed by the bailiff, Roger de Myriden, but he was also bailiff of the Western group of Abbey manors of Warmington, Ashton, Biggin Grange, Stanwick, Irthlingborough and Oundle, and merely rode in and out of Kettering on business. The day-to-day running of the farm must have been in the hands of Henry the reeve.

The working of the demesne farm was analysed some years ago in an unpublished essay by R.A. Martin. The farm was basically a cereals-and-sheep one of around 360 acres. In 1292 the arable crops were, in descending order of acreage, oats (131 acres), white wheat, barley, dragium (drage, a medieval type of wheat), beans and peas, and corn (a mere four and three quarter acres). The spring-sown crops were oats, barley and dragium, the rest were winter-sown. That year, just over 260 acres were under the plough, the rest lay fallow. There were three fields and the lord's meadows. In the course of the three-year cycle, each field would have four, possibly five, ploughings.

If we consider only its domestic consumption, the farm was self-sufficient in all but oats. But pursuing its function as a supplier to the monastery, it bought in large quantities of oats (about six times its own production), of corn (about five times) and of barley (about four times). The oats were used on the farm as provender for the farm horses and those of visitors, and some went to feed calves, cows and some sheep. One hundred and sixty-four quarters were sent to 10 other manors and 562 quarters were sent to the Abbey. White wheat and corn were used for bread making, and much of it given in allowances to the employees as part of their wages. Beans and peas were used as feed for pigs and ewes, though three bushels went as pottage for the household. None went off the farm. Some barley was used as feed for pigs, fowls and pigeons. The rest of the barley and all of the dragium was used for malting.

Medieval Market Town

By this time Kettering had been a market town for upwards of sixty years. In 1227 a charter from Henry III granted to the abbot of Peterborough the right to hold a weekly market on a Friday, which continues to this day. The researches of Glenn Foard into the rentals and surveys of Peterborough Abbey demonstrate that agricultural Kettering was originally laid out on the north-south axis of the present High Street, expanding later into Northall, Silver Street, Bakehouse Hill and Wadcroft. Here was where the virgaters had their houses and yards. The laying out of a market, three centuries later, north-west of the church led to Kettering's changing shape. In addition to the Market Place, Sheep Street, and Parkstile Lane (the present Market Street) were laid out. Before 1300 Newland was added. With the coming of the market the character of the place changed. Before long there were more non-farmers, with holdings of under eight acres, than virgaters. The surnames of some of the 46 people paying tax to the crown in 1301 indicate the movement of people into Kettering from the area around – John de Leycester, Robert de Geytington, Henry de Okele, Henry Tannsor, Thomas de Clendon, Thomas de Alwolton, Simon de Lincoln. The area served by Kettering's market was probably constant over the centuries, drawing people from the same villages as it does now. However, Kettering market was in competition with a more ancient one, Rothwell. Although by the later 17th century Kettering had emerged victorious and Rothwell's market shrank away, it is not clear on existing evidence how Kettering's market stood in relation to Rothwell's in the Middle Ages.

Kettering's history was influenced by its proximity to the royal forest of Rockingham. In Norman and Angevin times the royal forests in

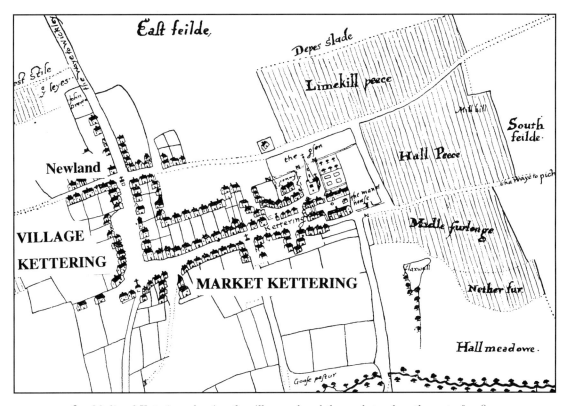

8   *Medieval Kettering, showing the village end and the market end on the map of 1587.*

Northamptonshire were in a state of steady expansion, so much so that a very high proportion of the county came under the law of the forest. At one time Rockingham Forest stretched from the Welland to the Nene and from Stamford and Wansford to Northampton, so Kettering then was within it. As late as the perambulation of 1286 these remained its bounds, the Forest being divided for administrative purposes into the bailiwicks of Rockingham, Brigstock and Cliffe. However, in the 13th century large areas were disafforested, because of land shortages for a growing population and the granting of land within the forest to his subjects by the sovereign. In 1299, new Perambulations were made of the forests for Edward I and these were confirmed at Lincoln in 1301, disafforesting all land outside these bounds. The perambulation of 1299 makes it clear that the forest came right up to the northern edge of Kettering parish, along the banks of the Ise and including the villages of Geddington (where the king had a hunting lodge) and Warkton within it. Over the centuries, people from the southern parts of Rockingham Forest came to Kettering market, migrated there to make a living, and maybe introduced into the town some of that free-spirit often found in forest villages. With the woodland beginning in Warkton, there was always a temptation to some Kettering men to poach the deer, rabbits and game birds there.

Kettering in the later Middle Ages

By this time the manorial system was approaching four centuries of almost unvarying existence; people must have thought it would last forever. From about 900 (and possibly earlier) to 1300 the population and economy had been expanding, and market towns such as Kettering had grown richer and more populous. How populous is hard to say. For most places the headcount of the Poll Tax of 1377 offers the possibility of estimating medieval population, but the return for Kettering has not survived. One thing is certain. Kettering's population growth had peaked around 1300 and was to suffer setbacks in the second half of the 14th, 15th and early 16th centuries. Going by the experience of most other Midland towns, its population was not again to reach the size it was in the early 14th century until about the time Queen Elizabeth came to the throne, more than two centuries later.

The reasons for this contraction are that by about 1300 overpopulation and overcropping were beginning to cause rural problems. There were also outbreaks of murrain – cattle plague – in the next few years. There is even evidence of a climatic change for the worse from around 1300. The greatest cause of population and economic contraction was the sequence of visitations of the bubonic plague, first of all in 1348-9 and again on at least another three occasions before 1400, and at least another five in the following century. Little direct evidence survives for its effect in Kettering. For obvious reasons, parochial clergy with the duty to bury the dead were vulnerable, and in most places there is evidence of new clergy appointed to benefices around 1348-9. In 1349 Adam Wade, rector since 1346, was succeeded by Alan de Crophill, though there might have been another reason than the plague for this. That there was plague close by was demonstrated by Mr Groome, who examined the surviving records of the Hundred Court for Higham Ferrers for 1348-9. He found that of 51 litigants in that court, within the space of three weeks in early 1349 over a third died. The generally accepted assumption is that the plague carried off about one third of the population in the middle of the 14th century. The effects were catastrophic. Some markets and fairs were abandoned, houses and lands were left vacant for want of tenants, farm wages rose and prices fell. After 50 years of economic decline, the 1405 rental shows extensive desertion of tenements in the town, espcially in the Newland area.

One of the most important effects of the shrinkage of the economy in this period was the replacement of daywork obligations on the Abbot's demesne and customary payments by copyhold tenure and monetary rents. It is not certain when this became operative, but the practice of property and land being held by copyhold was established by the end of the 15th century and became an important feature of life in Kettering. Until the 19th century, all property in the parish, except the parson's freehold, was copyhold. With the change in tenure the importance of the lords of the manor and their courts did not end, legal title to property purchased or inherited was now established by the holder having a copy of the record of the transaction being entered in the manorial court roll. When property was so entered a fine (a fee) was payable to the lord, but once this was done then the copyholder for all practical purposes had freedom of tenure. Copyhold tenure was much prized; people were pleased to be free of irksome feudal obligations. Some copyholders became substantial holders of property, though it was never Kettering's fate to be too dominated by over-powerful property owners.

Historians of the Middle Ages rely on documents relating to royal taxation for much of their information on economic matters. In 1524 Henry VIII introduced a new tax, the Lay Subsidy. In it the names of 133 persons who paid tax in Kettering are listed, with the amount they were assessed on and how much they paid. On this basis, Kettering was the fifth richest place in Northamptonshire. Only four towns had more taxpayers listed – Northampton, Peterborough, Wellingborough and Oundle. With fewer taxpayers came Towcester, Higham Ferrers, Daventry and Brackley, a ranking which remained constant for several centuries.

The Lay Subsidy was levied on all persons with lands, moveable goods or wages to the value of one pound or more. Movable goods were defined as to include all corn, plate, stock or merchandise, corn severed from the ground, grain, household stuff and other movable goods round the house and sums of money owing. Each person was charged where he or she usually lived. No person was assessed on both lands and goods *and* wages, but on whichever category produced the most revenue for the Exchequer. For some reason (copyhold?) in Kettering nobody paid on land held; all the tax was paid on goods or wages. There were three tax bands – £20 or over, at a shilling in the pound; two pounds to £19, at sixpence in the pound; and one pound to 39 shillings, at fourpence in the pound.

Nine people were assessed at £20 or over, the two richest by far being John Lane, the Abbot's bailiff, who lived at the 'noble hall', later the 'Manor House', and Richard Alderman, a farmer possessed of land in Leicestershire as well as Northamptonshire: these were the only £100 men, and between them they paid just over a quarter of the total tax sum for Kettering. The next richest was Henry Drewry, with £30. The problem is that, in most cases, occupations are not known, but it is possible from extant wills to give the occupations of some people listed. Of the other six top-bracket payers, we know William Flecton was a farmer and Thomas Lawfford a tanner. Below them came a large group of 76 people paying tax on amounts between two pounds and £19. Among them were John Cave, bowmaker, Guy Spencer, fishmonger, William Crowne, John Fysher, Mark Hasylwood and John Donmow, husbandmen (farmers), Richard Pyndar, mercer, and Alice Eyre, Isabel Lawfford, Margery Taylor and Alyce Baker, all widows of means. Of the remaining 92 taxpayers, all assessed at 39 shillings down to one pound, we know little. There occur a few (though only a few) names of families which became well-known in later times – John and Thomas Rownton, Edward, John and Agnes Eyre, and John and Edmund Sawer, forebears of the Sawyer family. In 1524 both Sawers were assessed at the middling-range band of 40 shillings in goods and 12 pence in tax. It is generally accepted that all those who were taxed were heads of households (including women) and that probably about a third of the population was omitted for reasons of poverty. Taking this to be the case, we might calculate the population in 1524 at around 800. Assuming that the population before the Black Death was 30 per cent higher, a figure of around 1,100 suggests itself for Kettering at the peak of its medieval growth.

Another consequence of the decay of feudalism after the mid-14th century was the practice of the monastery leasing out the manorial demesne of Kettering rather than farming it in hand, as at the time of the *Compotus* of 1292. When this began is not clear but John Lane had 'the site of the manor', Hallfield and other lands from the Abbey by leases in 1528 and 1534. As we have seen Lane, the third son of William Lane of Orlingbury, was one of the two richest men in Kettering. He was succeeded by his son, also named John, as leaseholder of the manorial demesne, the two parks and of all the mills. For about a century the Lanes were Kettering's leading family. But by the early 17th century they had become armigerous and moved out to Isham and later Cosgrove.

Religion and the Church in the Middle Ages
As already observed, the early history of the Church in Kettering is unclear and probably lost forever. It is not until the early 13th century we even have a name of a priest, Master Grace, who became rector in 1219-20. By then it is possible that there had been a church and a parish for a century, though it could have been that Kettering was served by a vicar provided by Peterborough, or from a minster, in the early years. All that we have to enable us to construct some picture of medieval church life in Kettering are the list of rectors, some information from episcopal and other general sources, some late medieval wills and the fabric of the existing church.

The first point to note is that the living of Kettering was well-worth having. The rectory was never reduced to a vicarage, that is to say, the great tithes were never alienated into other hands, as happened with certain other livings. Perhaps this was because the Abbot and convent of Peterborough, who had the advowson (the right of presentation), would not countenance a reduction in the value and status of one of 'their' rectories. In 1254, according to Bridges' *History*, the living was (after deducting a pension to the Sacrist of Burgh of three marks) valued at 35 marks, a mark being two thirds of a pound: 13s. 4d. In 1535 the gross yearly income of the rectory was given in the *Valor Ecclesiasticus* as £37 3s. 11½d. The rectory of Kettering was, and long continued to be, a good one, reserved for well connected men, often of some distinction in the Church or the universities.

There is a well established list of rectors, which will not be recited here save to make some comments and draw some conclusions. Thirty or so years after Master Grace became rector, Emanuel de Sauro, a Genoese kinsman of Pope Innocent IV, obtained a Papal Indulgence to hold Kettering and other benefices, causing them to be served by vicars, he being non-resident and not in holy orders. There is no evidence that de Sauro ever set foot in England. Did the good people of Kettering suffer by such nepotism? Probably not. A succession of priests would be employed to say Mass, administer the sacrament and baptise, marry, confess and bury them. On who these vicars or stipendiary priests were, the record is silent. After 34 years of de Sauro, a local man, Master Roger de Rothwell, was given the benefice in 1284. His successor was another absentee, rector for 40 years. Master Roger Brun was given the benefice of Kettering 'with others' by Papal Indulgence to support him as Chancellor of the University of Oxford. In the same year of 1284, there is a separate record of a relaxation of one year and forty days' penance to those visiting the church of Kettering on the feasts of Saints Peter and Paul and the Assumption. Could it be that, in the 13th century, people needed a religious incentive to attend Kettering Feast?

In the words of L.P. Hartley, 'The past is a foreign country. They do things differently there'. They certainly did in the Middle Ages. Nothing illustrates this better than two 14th-century incidents, both involving considerable violence against the person and property. The papal register of 1348 records an attack on and seizure of the church of Kettering by a named list of men who were alleged to have done a considerable amount of damage, including killing a clerk, throwing down the images in the church and seizing and holding the assets of the rectory for three months. The object of their fury was John Wade, the rector, and it seems what provoked this violent incident were the circumstances of his appointment. The previous incumbent, Alan de Setrington, had been instituted in Rome in 1347, but de Setrington died there soon after. Wade was instituted as rector on his promise to pay 200 florins towards a crusade against the Turks, an undertaking he failed to honour. The leader of the gang of 21 who were involved in the attack, several of whose names indicate that they came from the vicinity, was Alan de Crophill, clerk, who seems to have been given the reservation of the benefice in 1346. Quite what happened is unclear, but Wade appears to have lost, because de Crophill succeeded him in 1349. Undoubtedly what lay behind the fury against Wade was the great value of the living, then said to be worth 40 marks a year. The other incident was a few years later. On the Saturday before the Feast of of St Martin, 9 November 1364, Hugh de Welborn took sanctuary in Kettering church after murdering Robert Songes with a knife. Again, the circumstances of the case are unclear, but in punishment de Welborn swore before the Coroner, William de Holdenby, to leave the realm penniless and go into exile via the port of Lynn.

Thereafter, there is a continuous list of rectors, some of whom are known to have been pluralists. One was Master William Grene, the last pre-Reformation rector, who had the living from 1529 to 1540. Grene, who is believed to be related to the rising Sawyer family, was canon

9   *The interior of the parish church, 15th-century Perpendicular except for the east end, which is earlier.*

residentiary of St Paul's Cathedral in London and also parson of Northchurch and of Lancaster.

In the second or third quarter of the 15th century, the parish church was almost completely rebuilt. A splendid example of the Perpendicular style, it is a big church with a tall tower and crocketed spire, 'not too short and not too long', in Pevsner's estimation. The only earlier parts are an early 14th-century doorway and the decorated east part of the chancel with the east window. The tower was probably first to be erected, to the west of the then existing nave after the demolition of its western bay, and a new nave was afterwards joined to it. One feature of this arrangement is that the tower is not square to the nave, though only the sharpest of architectural buffs would see this. It is, however, apparent on plans of the church. Who built it? Who, indeed built parish churches generally? Was there monastic involvement or funding? The tower and spire are remarkably similar to those at Oundle – another major Peterborough manor. In the absence of wills surviving from this period, we have no clues about contributors to the rebuilding, nor does the fabric bear the names of sponsors in the way that the great church at Long Melford in Suffolk does. Nonetheless, the great church still stands, as it has for five and a half centuries, magnificent in its domination of the low-rise town. Together with the layout of the streets in the old town centre, it is the most obvious legacy of the Middle Ages.

Although the structure of the building has not been seriously altered since the 15th century there is little left inside it of what it was like then, for the simple reason that two centuries of post-Reformation Protestant zeal removed most non-structural vestiges of medieval Catholicism. However, bequests to the church made in the wills of well-to-do people for the half century or so before the Reformation throw considerable light on popular piety. These reveal that there were aisle chapels with altars, images and lights to Our Lady, St Katherine, St Paul and St John the Baptist. The will of Thomas Lyne in 1512 states: 'I bequeath ten shillings for a trental [30 requiem masses] for the wealth of my soul said at Saint Paul's altar in Kettering church.' Money was left to the maintenance of the Rood (the large images of Christ on the Cross flanked by the Virgin Mary and St John the Baptist, which stood on top of the screen dividing the chancel from the nave), for 'torches' (great candles used in Catholic ritual) and for plate. Money and cloth were bequeathed for vestments: the will of John Lane in 1546 recites: 'I give two white Tunaches [tunics] of white damask & my best vestments to the altar of Saint John in Kettering Churche.' And Richard Alderman, in his will of the 33rd year of the reign of King Henry VIII (1541-2), gave 'to Kettering church a black cope & a vestment of black velvet'.

There were at least four religious guilds or brotherhoods – Our Lady, St Katherine, St John and the Sepulchre, and the wills often have the wish of the deceased to be buried in the chapel or the aisle close by their guild altar or light. In the later Middle Ages the practice was adopted of leaving money to pay for obits, the saying of Mass annually for the soul or souls of those in purgatory on the anniversary of their death, or on some other 'mind-day'. The will of William Flecton of 1528 shows how precise instructions could be:

> And also yearly for ever to keep the first Monday in clean Lent an obit for my soul & the souls of my friends & yearly to dispose of the same obit for ever ten shillings in manner and forme following, that is to say, to the parish priest there for his business & for the names of me and my friends in the bede roll twelve pence, to the parish clerk three pence, to every priest that dwelleth within the town of Kettering being present four pence, to six yeoman clerks twelve pence, to three children that sing versicles & read lessons four pence, to the bellsmen one penny, to the profit of the bells four pence, to every poor body in the alms house a penny, and half a pound of wax to burn about the hearse there & the residue of the said ten shillings to be bestowed among poor folks.

The bede roll was the list of persons to be specially prayed for.

There was also the existence of a morrow mass, or chantry, priest, paid to say the first mass of the day early in the morning, often attended by those who were travelling, then a potentially hazardous business. The morrow mass priest was a stipendiary priest whose salary was paid out of certain copyhold lands and tenements in Kettering, purchased out of bequests by the faithful in the past, which in 1545 had an annual value of 40 shillings. In addition, individual bequests in wills were made for specific mention and prayers. Sir Richard Tailor, priest of Boughton, in 1535 left 'two shillings to the morrow mass priest & he to say de profundis at the levitory for my soul & all christian souls, and if there be no morrow mass priest then the said two shillings to be given to the poor people of Kettering'. Tailor also left his surplice to Our Lady chapel in Kettering for the morrow mass priest to wear at services and when he did so the priest was to say a 'pater noster' (Our Father) and an 'Ave' (Hail Mary), 'or else at the least to say God have mercy on his soul'. Tailor also left money for a cope or a vestment of white silk ('as they shall think best') to Our Lady chapel.

In medieval times the interior of the church did not have the austere, unadorned appearance it has today. The walls would have been decorated with paintings – scenes of popular saints and the main stories of the Christian faith. The quality of these paintings can still be seen in the depiction of two angels with feathered wings in the clerestory, and the fading remains of a once-impressive painting of a saint on the wall of the north aisle. The latter was discovered about 1840 when the walls were cleaned. For many years it was believed this figure with a wallet with gilt escalloped shells and pilgrim's crook was St James of Compostella. But Canon Lindsay, in 1890, identified him as St Roch, a 14th-century French saint credited with miraculous cures of plague sufferers.

Without the survival of these wills and fragments of wall-paintings we would know little of popular religion in late medieval times. They offer no more than a glimpse into an era when all people had the same religion, and the church had power over the minds of people it was never again going to exert. All that was soon to change.

Four

THE REFORMATION AND KETTERING

The Stripping of the Altars

In 1538 the unthinkable happened. As part of the diplomatic struggle between the Pope and Henry VIII over the matter of the King's divorce from Katherine of Aragon, his wife of many years, the king renounced papal supremacy and made himself head of the Church in England. The monastic houses of England and Wales were dissolved and their assets seized by the crown. It was nothing less than a revolution which involved the severance of this country from the Catholic church, its conversion to Protestantism and the greatest redistribution of land and other property since the Norman Conquest. No place remained untouched by it. Kettering's six centuries-long connection with the Benedictine Abbey of Peterborough terminated abruptly.

Much is known of the economic consequences of this severance, almost nothing of the immediate religious aftermath. Some idea of the bewildering religious developments can be seen through the rectors of Kettering. Robert Shorton, rector from 1515 to 1529, Hussy lecturer in Divinity at the University of Oxford, became Dean of Cardinal Wolsey's Chapel and he was also Almoner to Queen Katherine. Shorton, therefore, must have found himself in a delicate position when he was appointed one of the theologians to be consulted on the question of the King's divorce. His successor as rector of Kettering was Master William Grene, who also served the Queen as private chaplain. We can assume he was one of her defenders, but it was his curate, George Clitherowe, who got himself into hot water voicing criticism of the King, Anne Boleyn and the Archbishop of Canterbury in public. Clitherowe was informed against, and it seems there were moves in Kettering to protect the curate and browbeat the informers. Clitherowe was taken off to London. As so often in these cases, how the matter was resolved is not recorded, but Clitherowe is not heard of again. Grene was succeeded in 1540 by Master Anthony Draycott, Doctor of Divinity, presented to the living by the Bishop of Peterborough, a new diocese created by Henry VIII. The great monastic church of Peterborough became its cathedral, and the last dean of the monastery became the first bishop. Dr Draycott took the oath of supremacy and renounced the Pope's authority. Well-connected nationally and locally,

Draycott was chaplain to Henry VIII and must have accepted the changes towards Protestantism in the brief reign of Edward VI. However, in Queen Mary's reign, as Chancellor of the dioceses of Lincoln and Coventry and Lichfield, he had the reputation of being a great harrier of Protestants. When Queen Mary died and Queen Elizabeth succeeded to the throne in 1559 Draycott declined to take the oath of supremacy and was deprived of his benefice the next year. All who had lived through these years faced having to accept, resist or accommodate to the religious changes which came down from above.

The new Queen was Protestant and the following year a religious settlement was instituted, with a new liturgy based on the earlier Prayer Books. The basic beliefs of the Church were later defined in the Thirty-Nine Articles, to which all clergy had to subscribe. The Mass was replaced by Holy Communion, altars were replaced by communion tables, the abolition of purgatory and the intercession of prayers for the souls of the dead were re-affirmed.Where the images of the rood had been restored, or never taken down, they were now removed and replaced by the royal arms, an illustration of how the Reformation was imposed which could scarcely have been more graphic. Wall-paintings were whitewashed over and stained-glass windows depicting the crucifixion and the saints were destroyed or removed from many churches. The new injunctions were enforced by teams of visitors who travelled to every part of the realm. Surviving churchwardens' accounts show that the removal of the new images and fittings so recently paid for was delayed in case the new regime proved impermanent; some lasted until the 1560s. But the survival of the reformed Church of England was guaranteed by the long life of Queen Elizabeth and the defeat of the internal and external supporters of a Catholic restoration.

Despite the fact that, in the long run, Northamptonshire became one of the least Catholic and most puritanical counties of England, the evidence seems to suggest that, in the first 20 years of the Reformation, the changes in religion were accepted passively. If anything, in these years, Northamptonshire seemed conservative in religious matters, only one person in the county being burned for heresy in the Marian presecution. In the first half of the reign of Queen Elizabeth there was certainly a strong Catholic presence in Northamptonshire, especially in the Kettering area, led by such landed families as the Treshams of Rushton, the Vauxes of Harrowden, the Brudenells of Deene and the Mordaunts of Drayton. Until the Pope excommunicated Queen Elizabeth in 1570 and England became inexorably involved in the international struggle between Catholic and Protestant in Europe, they trod a fine line between keeping their religion alive and staying free of persecution. So-called 'Church Catholics' occasionally conformed by going to church once a month. However, from 1570, Catholics were urged to become *recusants* (those who refused to conform). In the following decade they were stiffened in their resolve by English mission priests ordained abroad and sent to England to minister to the faithful. Elizabethan Catholics were increasingly persecuted through fines and imprisonment for 'popish recusancy' and prosecuted for treason if they were involved against the Crown. These punishments brought down the Treshams and the Vauxes; the Brudenells and the Mordaunts survived by being 'Church Catholics' and eventually abandoning Catholicism. By the mid-17th century Catholics were thin on the ground around Kettering.

At the time of Queen Mary's death it was Protestants who were thin on the ground in Northamptonshire. How then did it become a puritanical sort of place? Draycott's successor, William Todd, lasted only 15 months before he was deprived. The next rector, Anthony Burton, conformed. Rector from 1561 to 1576 his name was to be long remembered in the annals of the church in Kettering, though not for devotional reasons, as we shall see. In the episcopal visitation of 1570, Burton was cited as non-resident. The same visitation also recorded that his curate, William Wetherlye, 'haunteth unlawful games', rather than setting a godly example to his flock.

Perhaps not surprisingly the clerical profession had become debased by the processes of the Reformation. It was widely recognised that many of the parochial clergy were ill-equipped to perform their pastoral functions, especially those of expounding the scriptures and the doctrines of the new Church of England. Severe criticisms of certain bishops, including the bishop of Peterborough, were expressed by puritans. In the 1570s the practice of 'prophecyings', meetings of the clergy for prayers and sermons, which were then critically discussed, began to be held in some districts, though they were not official policy of the Church and did not have the approval of the Queen, who looked to the Archbishop of Canterbury to suppress these practices. Queen Elizabeth did not like religious change. One of the best known of the prophesyings was that led by Percival Wiburn in Northampton. When Wiburn was forced out, he was protected by puritan gentlemen and continued with his work outside the town.

There is no evidence of prophesyings in Kettering. Burton had his mind on other things, and Sir Christopher Hatton (out of rivalry with the Earl of Leicester, a supporter of puritans) was a notable anti-puritan. However, though he had influence in Kettering through his ownership of the manorial demesne, it was short-lived. In any case, if Hatton was anti-puritan, other nearby landowners, such as Sir Edward Montagu of Boughton and William Cecil, Lord Exeter, were not. They wished to see a better-educated and more godly ministry and if this meant giving support to puritan initiatives, so be it.

Although the Queen wanted a clamp-down on puritan activities, she did not have an Archbishop who was zealous enough until the appointment of Whitgift in 1583. However, the new Archbishop's zeal had the effect of unifying the puritan party. Puritans at this time were influenced by the writings of Thomas Cartwright, a former Professor of Divinity at Cambridge, who attacked episcopalian government and advocated the adoption of the presbyterian system of John Calvin, first established in Geneva, and becoming established in Scotland. Somehow, Cartwright believed that presbyterianism could be grafted on to the Church of England. However, it was clear that if it ever was, bishops would be left with little authority; the real power would lie with 'classes', boards consisting of clergy and lay 'elders'.

In the 1580s Northamptonshire was notable for the adoption of the 'classical' system, with classes in the county town, Daventry and Kettering. The leader of the latter was Thomas Stone, rector of Warkton, and he was joined by other local clergymen, though none from Kettering itself. Geared to improving clerical standards by gathering information about parochial livings in the county and by meeting for mutual examination and discipline, their aim was to improve clerical standards. The Northamptonshire classes were part of a wider movement which had friends in Parliament. Nonetheless it attracted only a minority of the clergy and the government was hostile; in 1590 classes and their leaders were suppressed. Puritan clergy such as Stone faced severe examination and were forced into submission or deprived of their livings. The clamp-down marked the end of organised puritan activity in Queen Elizabeth's reign.

It did not mark the end of puritanism. A more popular form, based on the leadership of individual clergy at parochial level began to produce a godly laity. Here surely lies the origins of Kettering's 'hot Protestantism'. Between 1584 and 1605 some 35 laymen and women were cited in the church courts for 'nonconformity', usually for 'receiving the communion irreverently', or not receiving it at all. Receiving it irreverently meant receiving it standing. Protestants deeply disliked kneeling, making the sign of the cross and other traditional devotional practices, as 'papistical'. In 1595 a number of Kettering people were prosecuted for receiving the communion at Cransley in an unorthodox fashion. Numbered among them were Henry Bridger, the Kettering schoolmaster, constantly in trouble with the ecclesiastical authorities, and Francis Wigston, who in 1605 with seven others was charged with leaving their parish in order to hear sermons. It seems that these people took their lead from their rectors. John Dammes (1576-98) was charged on two occasions with not wearing his surplice and for receiving the communion standing. David Thompson (1598-1633) was cited in 1605 for celebrating communion wearing a hat and gloves but no surplice, for preaching false doctrine and for failure to conduct services according to the Book of Common Prayer. He came close to being deprived of his living.

Market towns, with country people flocking in on market and fair days, were natural places for new religious ideas to be disseminated. Here they were able to attend sermons and lectures and purchase religious literature. Although Kettering was not a borough with a powerful mayor and corporation and its own magistrates, it did have an élite of copyholders and tradesmen. It seems clear that, in the late Elizabethan and early Stuart era, many leading figures in the town were influenced by ambitions of purging the Church of what they considered vestigial catholic doctrines and practices. As yet, however, not much credence was given to separatist ideas. Nonetheless, puritan ministers and laity were confident enough to modify church services and practices along the lines noted in defiance of the church authorities, and risk punishment for it.

Significant amongst those persuaded of the truths of the new ideas were certain squires and land owners. In the vicinity of Kettering were the Montagus of Boughton, the Ishams of Lamport, the Maunsells of Thorpe Malsor and the Pickerings of Titchmarsh, while further away there were the Knightleys of Fawsley. They gave patronage and protection to puritan ministers and, as well as being natural leaders at the local level, became in some cases active in the puritan cause in Parliament. Within Kettering, the Sawyers came out strongly in support. As the Queen neared the end of her long life, puritans hoped for much from her heir, King James VI of Scotland, who had received a stern Scots presbyterian upbringing and was known for his love of theological argument. They were not to know that he saw England as an escape from all that.

The Early History of Kettering Free Grammar School

The original foundation document has not been found. For a long time the earliest reference to the school was thought to be a document of 1626, but the researches of Mr York have established that it originated in 1577. He found a Victorian copy of the original foundation document, tucked away in a solicitor's office. It clearly states that in June 1577, by letters patent, Queen Elizabeth I, 'in consideration that Kettering was a large town and great in the number of boys and replete of youths, and that the said town might be adorned with a learned, suitable and lettered man and schoolmaster by whom the boys and youths there might be instructed and educated in good learning and fear of God', granted to Edward Watson junior, gent, Basil Lane, gent, Henry Sawyer, Thomas Sparrow, Henry Richards, William Cave, Henry Linne, Richard Meadhouse and Nicholas Alderman, the first trustees, property in the hands of the crown the rents of which would pay the salary of this schoolmaster. This property consisted of seven houses, one cottage, two shops, various barns and other buildings and some land of the manor of Kettering 'late possessions of the Monastery of Peterborough'. The grant was for 21 years and the annual rent payable was 22s. 2d. The tenants were made responsible for repairs to the property and the trustees were to nominate a schoolmaster, who had to be approved by the Bishop of Peterborough. Provision was made for what should happen if a majority of the trustees died before the lease ran out.

There was a new grant from the Crown in 1597, presumably for this reason, and a new lease granted the following year, when the original one expired. The next mention of the school is in 1626 in a document of 1653 which states that the properties the income from which funded the school were formerly part and parcel of the possessions of 'Charles the late king', but had now passed to the use of the Commonwealth of England. In 1626 the properties had been granted to Sir Lewis Watson and eight others in

10   *The old Grammar School building before the 1850s, drawn by Hugh Wallis for Bull's History of Kettering.*

trust for the school for 31 years. In 1629, as King Charles had sold his interest in the manor, at or soon after this date the endowment became vested in the trustees, who no longer had to lease the property from the State.

All this relates to the endowments of the school and the trustees who administered them, but tells us nothing about the school as a school. And indeed we know little except that there presumably was one from 1577, that it probably taught Latin and English to a small number of boys, but of the quality of the education and whether or not the school sent boys to the universities we know nothing. The significance of such schools is that they aimed to produce godliness as well as good-learning and were clearly part of the protestantisation project. Little is known of early Kettering schoolmasters. As we have seen, Henry Bridger got into trouble with the ecclesiastical authorities in the later years of the Queen's reign, but we do not have any other names until one Seaton appears in 1635 and a Mr Hewett in 1653. Whether or not the master was sometimes the rector or the curate, as was often the case elsewhere and occurred in Kettering after 1660, is not known.

Two other things might be observed. One is that to be a Free School trustee was a mark of status. The leading figure was always a Watson of Rockingham, and the names of the other eight give a check-list at any given date of Kettering's more influential men. Thus in 1626 the trust consisted of Sir Lewis Watson, Edmund Sawyer, John Sawyer, Edward Sawyer junior, Francis Sawyer, Edmund Drury, Richard Drawwater, William Glover and Henry Sparrow, a list which shows how far the Sawyer family had come to prominence in Carolean times. Secondly, Mr York demonstrates that the idea that the school was a re-founding of an older song school is probably not correct. That the morrow mass priest ran such a school before the Reformation seems certain from references in the early 16th-century wills quoted above. However, the assets of that chantry were not diverted to the use of the Free School, but passed into private hands. The School was funded by properties that passed to the Crown.

The Stripping of the Assets

In few places can the diversion of the wealth of a great monastery into lay hands be seen with greater clarity than in Ketttering. Peterborough was valued by six King's Commissioners in 1536 – Sir William Parr of Horton, uncle of Queen Catherine Parr, Sir John Tresham of Rushton, Sir Edward Montagu of Boughton, the King's Sergeant at Law, Thomas Brudenell of Deene, John Turnor, the auditor, and John Lane, the Abbey bailiff, Kettering's richest taxpayer. In the *Valor Eccliasticus* the rents accruing to the Abbey from Kettering were the highest from all the manors listed under the Abbot's Demesne, the next most valuable being Oundle. The mills were worth more than those on the other manors, and the grange of Kettering, tenanted by John Lane, was also the most valuable of the manorial farms of the Abbey. All the wealth of the monasteries went to the Crown, but because Henry VIII spent on the grand scale much of it was rapidly disposed of. Men who had made money and wanted land, or men who already had land and wanted more, found themselves in a buyers' market. It is in this period that many long-lasting landed families established themselves.

One of the first asset-strippers in Kettering was Edward Watson of Rockingham Castle. There were in fact two manors in Kettering – one being appropriated to the rectory, and the other, the Royal manor, to the Crown. Watson purchased the advowson of Kettering in 1561 and presented the living to Anthony Burton, Ll.B, who in due course also came into possession of those of South Luffenham and Cranford and a prebendary's stall in Peterborough Cathedral. Burton's gratitude to his patron (or was it a condition of his presentation?) was such that, in the following year, apparently with the assent of the Bishop of Peterborough, he granted to Edward Watson the younger, later Sir Edward Watson, a lease of the Rectory manor and its assets for a term of 60 years at an annual rent of £20. This lease would terminate in 1622. In 1565 Burton granted a second lease for 100 years to commence at the expiry of the first lease, at a yearly rental of £36. This would terminate in 1722. But in 1569 Burton granted the same Edward Watson a third lease for 80 years to commence at the expiry of the second lease. This lease, therefore, was to run until 1802. Thus, says Charles Wise, 'had one incumbent succeeded, with the assent of his Bishop, in alienating the greater part of the rectorial income from his successors for a period of 240 years'. Although the rectors of Kettering continued to be known by that title thereafter, they were rectors in name only. Burton had signed away the profits of their manorial court and the great tithes, 'top-sliced' for almost two and a half centuries by the Watson family. Resentment over this may well have been behind a case brought to the Archdeacon's court in Northampton in 1576 in which Thomas Bradshawe, Robert Pynedar, Guy Browne and Robert Lawford, churchwardens, alleged 'that they had not the 40th part of their parsonage devided to the poore as the 2 Injunctions doe command in defalt of Mr Watson'. Whether or not they ever got it is unclear.

The Rectory manor court claimed jurisdiction over the tenements in that part of Kettering bounded on the south by the churchyard, on the west by Market Hill, on the north by Parkstile Lane (now Market Street) and on the east by what is now London Road. Although this is only a small part of the town, with twelve or so properties in the Tudor and Stuart era, this is where some of the richest people lived. Certain of them could be stiff-necked. In the court roll of the Rectory manor of 1570 an order was made to distrain the goods of John Lane because of his failure on two occasions to 'render fealty' and 'pay suit and

11 *Map of the manorial 'site' or old demesne estate made by Ralph Treswell for Sir Christopher Hatton of Holdenby and Kirby. This version was used in the second volume of Bull's* History of Kettering.

service' to the court for a cottage which had come into his possession. It records that when the bailiff arrived to serve the distress warrant 'the said John with divers other base people did there and then, by force of arms, beat the said bailiff with divers rods and rescue the said distraint, not permitting the said bailiff to carry out the said distraint quietly and peaceably'. It is not clear whether this was merely a parish-pump dispute or whether it was symptomatic of some more deep-seated rivalry between Lane and Edward Watson. Wise is in no doubt it was the latter. He says it is highly probable that Lane's opposition arose from the feeling that a rival magnate from outside had settled in Kettering. The Watsons were to long outlast the Lanes. In the end, in this dispute, arbitrators drew up 'a pair of indentures' to settle the matter. But there were to be others.

The jurisdiction of the Royal manor embraced the rest of the town and fields. At first, this manor passed to the Crown, but in 1543-4 it was granted to Lord Parr of Horton, who held it until his death in 1546. It was then granted briefly to William Garrard and others, and again reverted to the Crown. The Royal manor had two parts – the 'Site' and the manorial rights. In the 28th year of her reign (1585-6), Queen Elizabeth granted to Sir Christopher Hatton and his heirs the Manor House and its garden, the Hallfield and all the demesne lands, including 'the warren of conies', hitherto belonging to 'the monastery of the Burg of Holy Peter', leased to John Lane in 1528 for the term of 80 years. Lane's successor, another John Lane, had died in 1578. Hatton did what he did for all his estates at that time, he employed a skilled surveyor, Ralph Treswell, to make him a map and inventory of his estate. This he did in 1587. It is our earliest map of the town.

In the event, Hatton died soon after, and in 1596 Sir William Hatton of Holdenby, his cousin and heir, for 4,000 marks sold to Edmund Sawyer the capital messuage and site of the Manor House, the demesne lands, the warren, two closes of land, one then lately in the occupation of Edmund Bacon and John Lane, the other called the Park, and all other the premises at Kettering granted by Queen Elizabeth to Sir Christopher Hatton ten years before. Exempted from this grant was the interest which William Tate of Delapre, and Francis Tate of the Middle Temple had in the premises, but this interest was apparently bought out by Sawyer at the time of the purchase. In 1602, presumably to strengthen his title, 'Edmund Sawyer, of Kettering, gentleman', upon payment of £180 obtained a grant from the Crown of the lands above-named, which he was to hold by the service of a hundredth part of a knight's fee. The *residue* of the Manor of Kettering, *i.e.* the court and other manorial rights, was exempted from the grant.

Edmund Sawyer came from a family of Kettering copyholders who had prospered in the 16th century. He was the second son of Henry Sawyer and his wife Elizabeth, the daughter of William Drury, himself a prosperous townsman. Henry lived at the *Swan*, then Kettering's foremost inn, which his wife had after his death in 1586. In a court action of 1603 she deposed that she had lived in Kettering all her life, and at the *Swan* for the space of 56 years. Further, she 'had bene a Customary Tenent of the Manor of Ketteringe of an estate by copie which Henery Sawier her husband late

12 *Brass showing Edmund Sawyer and his wife in the south aisle of the parish church. Drawn for Bull's* History of Kettering.

Edmund Sawyer Efquire late of this p iſh,
he married Anne the daughter of Laurance
Goodman of Blaſton in ẙ Countyof Leceſter
gent ℣ had iſſue by her 15 Children he liued
to ẙ Age of 69 yeares ℣ died ẙ 19th of Septemᵇʳ
Anō Dñi 1630 ℣ lyes interred in this chancell

R.J. Williamſ Delᵗ

deceſed did surrender to her use'. In 1604, Edmund Sawyer acquired the badge of status which made him a gentleman, a coat of arms and a crest from the College of Arms. He and his successors were to hold the Manor House and the former demesne lands for about a hundred and thirty years. If they had been in possession of the court and manorial rights they would have been true squires of Kettering, but they were not. Nor were they ever knighted. Needless to say, that did not stop them acting as if they were squires. From the time of Queen Elizabeth to that of George II the Sawyers were the town's foremost family.

Turning from the manorial lands and properties to the manorial court and manorial rights, when King James I came to the throne Sir Edward

Watson was appointed Steward of the court. Like all kings, James was strapped for money and was soon pressing Watson to squeeze more income from fines in the court. Sir Lewis Watson assisted his father in the management of Kettering manor and gradually took on the role of Steward.

Because of the way the manorial rights were divided and sold to eager investors, their history is bewilderingly complex, though Bull (a solicitor, learned in the Law) tells it with some relish. In the 22nd year of the reign of James I (1624-5) the manor was given to certain trustees for his son, Prince Charles, for the term of 99 years. However, in 1630, the Prince, now King Charles I, sanctioned the grant of the remainder of the term of 99 years to the City of London, who assigned the said remainder to William Child and Thomas Gardiner. In turn, these two, in November 1631, assigned it for the same rental to ten individuals from Kettering, including several Sawyers. Gradually, in the course of a century, by death and sale, the ten parts fall into fewer hands. By the 1720s, six parts were in the hands of the Watson family, two belonged to the Sawyers and two to John, Duke of Montagu. In 1728 the Duke acquired the two parts that had been sold by the Sawyers, and from that time the manor has been divided in those proportions between these two great local landowning families.

In these manorial rights were several elements. One was the fee farm rent, an annual payment, originally to the Crown, of £66 7s. 10½d., arising out of the rents from the free and customary tenants, from the cottages, and from market tolls. At the time of the Civil Wars the receipt of this fee farm rent passed into other hands: Sir Jeffery Palmer acquired it in 1652. Eventually, in 1728, it passed to trustees for John, Duke of Montagu and remained in his family until fee farm rent was finally extinguished in 1891. Another element was the profits from fairs and the market. In 1634 these were purchased from the other owners of the manorial rights by Sir Lewis Watson, and stayed in his family until the local authority bought them in the late 19th century. Other manorial rights included the ownership of the mills and the lord's monopoly on the grinding of corn and malt in them, and his ownership of the common bakehouse and the monopoly on the baking of bread therein.

The Manorial Courts

A run of court rolls for both manors for the Elizabethan and Stuart period survives in the records of the Watson family (albeit with serious gaps) and, as a valuable service to local historians, Charles Wise published substantial extracts from them in the *Kettering Guardian* in 1901 (reprinted in *Northamptonshire Notes & Queries*). Although their procedures followed the medieval form of a court (with a sworn jury of nine or ten prominent men), in some of their functions they were the main organ of local government of the time, dealing with matters we would expect a modern council to take on. In practice the courts had a number of different functions – probably the most important (certainly to the manorial lords) was sanctioning the transfer of copyhold property or leasing property to customary tenants. Over the years, hundreds of these changes in property were recorded. Wise provides a mass of such transactions, from which can be extracted a good deal of information on a range of subjects – individual properties (mostly small), the genealogy of families, inns, trades, misdemeanours and much else.

From time to time, there were cases arising from the alleged infringement of the monopoly on the grinding of corn, malt and grist in the lord's three mills. Wise published in full the depositions of witnesses in a case brought before the Court of Exchequer in 1629 by John Sawyer, who had acquired the manorial milling rights, against two bakers who had been having their corn ground elsewhere. Some witnesses recalled that in their long lives the royal monopoly extended to the Rectory manor; some said the opposite. Some bakers, such as William Abell in 1634, argued that they operated on such a large scale that the lord's mills could not grind all the corn they needed to supply their customers. Again, there were occasions when millers on neighbouring manors ground corn cheaper than it could be done in Kettering. No tenants dwelling in Kettering, the court decreed in 1604, 'shall use Kydding, loding or carrying of corn out of this lordship' with the intention to grind the same at any 'foreign mills', upon pain of a fine of ten shillings for every default. ('Kydding' was buying corn in one place and selling it in another.) The lord also had the monopoly of the common bakehouse. Tenants were obliged to bake their bread there, and nowhere else.

Manorial courts were also concerned with breaches of the peace and public safety. If people were involved in fights serious enough to lead to bloodshed they would be ordered to appear. In March 1608 it was presented that Thomas Cockes had assaulted and drawn blood from John Pack, for which he was fined 3s. 4d. And that John Pack had assaulted and drawn blood from the said Thomas Cockes, for which he was fined 3s. 4d. Periodically there was activity against those who were not keeping their chimneys in a safe condition, and people were required to scour their drains and not allow their dunghills to abut their neighbours' walls or otherwise cause nuisances.

Each meeting of the court heard reports from the parish officers, unpaid and compelled to serve their year in office, of transgressions against the bye-laws and customs of the manor. Some of these concerned the quality of the food sold in the market. In 1604 the two bread tasters presented the names of 13 common bakers of bread who had broken the assize of bread (probably for selling underweight). The two ale-tasters presented 19 common brewers of ale, 17 of whom were alewives, for breaking the assize of ale. The two provision tasters presented the names of 26 common butchers for 'taking excessive profits', eight common fishmongers likewise and six common chandlers likewise from the sale of candles. All were fined according to the tariff. The two leather searchers who kept their eye on the quality of leather and its tanning reported that, this half-year, 'all was well'.

The court gave much attention to agricultural matters. Effectively, the complex yet well-understood working of the open-field system, a mixture of individual and common farming, was overseen there. From time to time bye-laws relating to a range of matters involving open-field husbandry were laid down, or reiterated. When 'stoning-out' the boundaries between the lands of individuals was to be done (usually on Good Friday); what 'the stint' was relating to common grazing; encroaching on 'the lord's waste'; who had rights to cut furze on the common; who had gleaning rights; the duty to scour the water courses and a dozen or more other matters.

The manorial court was a medieval institution which, as we shall see, was to have a very long life. One word which occurs frequently in its vocabulary is 'common'. The medieval manor was a face-to-face community, and the manorial court laid great stress on working for the common good, punishing those who offended against it. The changes of the later medieval years and the effects of the Reformation tended to promote a growing economic and religious individualism. There are also glimpses of the way puritan morality was enforced, or was attempted to be enforced, in these court rolls. In 1585 eleven Kettering men were fined for playing 'globas' (bowls) under a statute of Henry VIII which restricted the sport, with others, to noblemen only, because it was the duty of the lower orders to work not play. That Kettering men would not be denied their bowls is shown by the fact that in 1610 there were similar fines. In that same court of 1585, Richard Holding had to pay 12 pence for receiving into his house 'a person of ill-fame and bad report' and John Askew paid the same for permitting gaming in his house. In 1610 Edward Dison was fined for permitting 'unlawful games' in his house and the same court made it a bye-law 'that no Inholder or Alehouse keeper within this town of Ketteringe shall permit any Labourer or any man's son or servant to continue tryflinge, playinge or spendinge their money in any of there howses after eight of the clock in the afternoone, neither upon any Sabbath or festyvall day in time of devine service' upon pain of a fine of 3s. 4d. No doubt if more manorial court rolls had survived after 1610 there would have been other examples.

Five

KETTERING IN THE
SEVENTEENTH CENTURY

Economic Developments

By about the time Queen Elizabeth came to the throne the population seems to have reached again the level it had been in the early 14th century. Agriculture was doing well, but much of the wealth of England was based on the profits of commerce, both international and home-based. London, always by far the biggest city in England, benefited from this and was growing more rapidly than ever. With the growth of internal trade, towns such as Kettering, on main roads to London, became part of an economic system supplying the massive capital. In the *Calendar of State Papers Domestic* for 1624 there is a letter noting that 'the Kettering carrier leaves London every Wednesday', and no doubt there had been a London carrier long before that.

In this period Kettering's markets began to flourish. In the mid-16th century Leland described it as 'a pratie Market Toune' standing on 'Hilling Ground'. About 1586 Camden said it was 'a Mercat town well frequented, niere unto which standeth Rouell much talked of for the horse faire there kept'. That writer makes no reference to Rothwell market and that may be because much of the business of that town's ancient market had been diverted to Kettering. Perhaps that was why Sir Thomas Tresham erected his market house a few years later – to try to make Rothwell market more attractive to buyers and sellers. The fact that he never completed the building may have had other causes, but it seems symbolic of the failure to revive the market. As in all market towns there was a number of inns. The following are mentioned in the manorial court rolls in the years before 1700 – the *Cock*, the *Lyon*, the *Red Lyon*, the *Kings Head*, the *Gray Hownde* and the *Swan*. So profitable was a flourishing inn that rich copyholders would acquire them, as in the case of Henry Sawyer and his wife with the *Swan*. Until the 18th century, this inn, located at the High Street corner of Parkstile Lane (now Market Street), where the modern bank now stands, was the greatest of the town's inns, the venue for important meetings and the manorial courts. The list of Kettering's hostelries was to expand in the first half of the 18th century.

In the first year of the reign of Charles I, the Earl of Westmoreland, whose house was at Apethorpe, in his capacity of Custos Rotulorum secured

13   *The early 17th-century Sessions House, which later became the Market House. This drawing was made shortly before it was demolished in 1805 as part of the improvement of the market place.*

royal approval for the holding of the winter meeting of the Court of Quarter Sessions in Kettering instead of Northampton. Travelling was so difficult that Justices from his area had to put up at inns for two nights, whereas if the Sessions were held in Kettering they could transact business and return home without an overnight stay. He was of course thinking about himself and his immediate neighbours rather than Justices fron the Western Division. The King, as lord of the manor of Kettering, was pleased to grant his wishes and, at his own expense, the Earl erected a Sessions House in the market place. In 1628 his widow wrote to the King praying that her son may have the Custos Rotulorum in his father's place and that, if it had already been disposed of to Lord Spencer (as it had), that the holding of the Quarter Sessions after Christmas in Kettering may be maintained. The episode was part of a tussle between the two families that went back to a recent election, and was noted by Lord Montagu in a letter of 1625 when he remarked, 'I am afraid we shall have some more scuffling shortly among the Justices; the Earl of Westmoreland carried such a high hand over his fellow Justices by virtue of his Custos Rotulorum-ship, that it cannot be borne'. Lord Spencer was presumably taking him down a peg. How long the winter Sessions continued to be held in Kettering is not certain. Probably not long. The Earl's Sessions House, however, remained in the market place, serving as a market house.

The population of England and Wales almost doubled between 1541 and 1656. In the absence of parish register evidence before 1637, it is impossible to say whether this growth was matched in Kettering, though it seems likely it was. In the two decades from 1640 there was an excess of baptisms over burials of 264 in the 1640s and 113 in the 1650s. However, in the first half of the 17th century there were four outbreaks of the plague in Northampton, and Kettering may not have escaped, but we lack local information. Other factors, such as migration, affect population statistics; in the absence of direct evidence it seems likely that people were moving into Kettering from the countryside because of the activity of enclosing landlords, as well as for more conventional reasons.

The enclosing of arable fields and diverting them to pastoral use (particularly sheep grazing) was highly profitable and was going forward in the district at this time. The loss of agricultural work and the frequent depopulation of settlements was resented by the common people, and when enclosure and depopulation coincided with harvest failure and epidemics, as they did in 1607, there was trouble – in this case destruction of enclosure hedges by 'levellers'. Across the Midlands from Warwickshire into Leicestershire and Northamptonshire there was an outbreak of levelling by large bands of peasants. The Northamptonshire one was led by one Captain Pouch, so named 'because of a great leather powch which he wore by his side, in which purse hee affirmed to his company, that there was sufficient matter to defend them against all comers, but afterward when hee was apprehended, his powch was searched and there was only a peece of greene cheese. Hee told them also, that hee had Authoritie from his majestie to throwe downe enclosures, and that he was sent of God to satisfie all degrees whatsoever, and that in his present worke, hee was directed by the lord of Heaven'. Pouch, whose real name was John Reynolds, was a characteristic figure thrown up by medieval and early modern peasant risings. Such men almost always claimed that they were not against the King, but against evil subjects or bad advisors, and that God was with them.The point about this particular outbreak, which was provoked by the enclosing of Newton and Pytchley, was that local landowners, finding they could not rely on the trained bands, took the initiative, suppressing the levellers using their own tenants and labourers in a brief but sharp engagement at Newton, near Geddington. The leaders were tried for treason, hung, drawn and quartered and their quarters were

displayed at Oundle, Thrapston and other places. Kettering men were
involved and the names of some of them are known. In the records of the
Montagu family a document of 1607 lists the names of 133 men who
confessed to having taken part in the levelling and humbly begged
forgiveness from the King (there being far too many to put on trial).The
largest contingent (44) came from Weldon, 27 were from Corby, 19 were
from Kettering. All are named and their trades given: five husbandmen
(farmers), six labourers, three butchers, two tailors, one baker, one weaver
and one smith. Their names included those of Meadows, Salmon, Wallis,
Cave and Eare. Smaller numbers owned up from places such as Thrapston,
Desborough, Harrowden, Cransley, Lowick and Naseby.

Enclosure and particularly depopulation were against official government policy, always sensitive to the threat to law and order arising from such
incidents as at Newton. A commission was appointed to look at what had
been happening in the Midlands; for a time it seemed as if some enclosures
would have to be thrown down, but in the end nothing was done. Enclosure
continued, but in a piecemeal sort of way: Barton Seagrave was enclosed in
1633, Loddington in the later 1650s. Where did those disposesssed by
enclosure go? They made for 'open' places such as Kettering and forest
villages such as Corby and Kings Cliffe. However, most parishes around
Kettering, including Kettering itself, remained open-field until the drive to
total enclosure came in the 18th and early 19th centuries.

The growing numbers of the poor in the later 16th century were perhaps
more a result of the general growth in the population than enclosure. The
traditional way of poor relief was through charitable bequests made in wills.
One hundred and sixty-eight surviving wills made by Kettering people from
1512 to 1700 were checked for such donations. They indicate that poor
were remembered more often in wills before than after the Reformation.
In 1512, Thomas Lyne left the value of five sheep to be distributed to the
poor. At that time it was customary to leave money to be distributed at the
funeral, or annually at an obit. The generous William Flecton in 1500
left 13s. 4d. to the poor of Kettering on the day of his burial and also left
(in reducing amounts) other sums to the poor of Rothwell, Thorpe Malsor,
Orlingbury, Pytchley, Barton and Warkton. Flecton also left 'to every poore
body in the almshouses' one penny out of the ten shillings to be spent at
his obit. In Richard Taylor's will of 1535 we have mention of 'the four
bedesmen of Kettering', who were each to receive four pence. Bedesmen,
sometimes inmates of almshouses, generally walked in the funeral carrying
their beads and were provided with mourning apparel. The last will to
mention an obit is that of John Lane, bailiff of Kettering, in 1546, when he
requests that the poor receive dole on that occasion annually and also at all
his requiem masses. Between then and 1565 there are no bequests at all to
the poor in surviving Kettering wills.

In the time of Queen Elizabeth, poverty was on the increase. In
particular, there was concern about the unemployed, the 'sturdy beggars'

and 'masterless men'. Possibly because of this, from the time of the will of John Billing in 1565, who bequeathed ten shillings to the poor people to pray for him, bequests to the poor begin to appear in wills again. The following year Agnes Ayre, widow, left six pence to the 'poor mens boxxe' in the church. In 1575 Henrie Chastland left five shillings to the poor of the parish at the discretion of the overseers. By then, legislation was clarifying community responsibility to the poor. An Act of 1563 stated that in each parish two or more able persons were to be appointed gatherers and collectors of the charitable alms of parishioners, an office which was combined with that of the overseers of the poor in 1597-8. By 1601 'the Old Poor Law' was in place, making it the duty of the parish to relieve the old, the infirm, the sick, the widowed and the orphaned out of a poor rate, and to set the unemployed to work. The organ of parish government was the Vestry meeting, which grew in importance from this time.

There are no surviving records for Kettering Vestry before the later 17th century, but individual charity carried on alongside parish involvement. Nineteen of the 90 wills surviving from 1605 to 1700 show that the poor were remembered. On the whole, the bequests are larger than in the previous century, no doubt reflecting the fact that the well-to-do were growing richer. The largest bequest was that of William Cave, yeoman in 1617, who gave to the poor of Kettering 'twenty poundes of lawfull English mony'. Another large sum, £11 10s., left by John Basely, clerke, was spread around: to the poor of All Saints Parish in Oxford 20s., and in Northamptonshire, to the poor of Everdon 20s., to the poor of Broughton 20s., to the poor of Cransley 20s., to the poor of Loddington 10s, to the poor of 'Rowell alias Rothwell' 40s., and 'to the Publique Stocke for the use of the poor in Kettering' £3. His widow, in her will of 1679, left a further £5 to the Kettering poor.

In contrast to the listings of apprentices, freemen and members of the corporation which exist for boroughs, information about the trades of Kettering and the wealth of the town in the 17th century is patchy. As in most towns the richest of the shopkeepers were mercers and a long and very detailed probate inventory of John Pettiver, a mercer who died in 1640, has survived. A vast list of the various cloths he held in his shops and warehouse is given: perpetuanas, hollands, taffeta, lawns, silks, cambrick, calico and a dozen others. Interestingly, he also stocked sugar, sugar candy, currants and tobacco. The total value of his possessions came to £435, including over £100 in debts owing, which must make him one of Kettering's richest shopkeepers of his time.

One of the most considerable of the copyholders was Richard Alderman, who died in 1608. Eleven sets of property, each of which had a rent payable to the lord of the manor, were transferred in the manorial court to his brother and heir, Edward Alderman. What happened to the Alderman family is unclear because of the lack of manorial records for much of that century, but they disappear from Kettering. The property may have passed to female heirs, though it is possible that they moved elsewhere. They had lived in the town for some considerable time, an Alderman being one of the two richest tax payers in 1524.

Puritan Kettering

When the 45-year-long reign of Queen Elizabeth ended in 1603, all three parties in the religious divide entertained hopes that the new King, James VI of Scotland, would look upon them with favour. Catholics were the most sanguine, hoping that the son of Mary Queen of Scots would grant them freedom to follow their religion unmolested. Puritans looked towards a monarch raised in the traditions of the Scottish Kirk to support their petitions for a further reform of the Church of England in the direction of presbyterianism. Churchmen and women, orthodox supporters of the 1559 Settlement, looked to James to uphold the episcopalian system. They did not look in vain; James found in the Church of England a church he had been looking for – deferential, hierarchical, and above all supportive of his idea of the Divine Right of Kings. The failure of the Hampton Court Conference to agree on its reform in 1604 spread dismay among the puritan clergy and laity, especially in Northamptonshire. The Act of Uniformity was to be enforced and the most lasting memorial to the Conference was to be the 'Authorized Version' of the English Bible. Authorised by King James, that is. That year, Sir Edward Montagu, one of the County Members of Parliament, delivered an address from his constitituents regretting 'the suppression of grave, learned and sober-minded ministers for not observing certain ceremonies, long since by many disused' – certainly in Kettering parish church, as we shall see. Catholics were even more dismayed. Tiring of the patience of their elders under the Elizabethan persecution, some of their young men hatched the Gunpowder Plot, a plan to wipe out the whole English establishment in one act of terrorism. Its failure brought terrible retribution on the perpetrators, among whom Francis Tresham was fortunate to die of natural causes in the Tower. But his death did not prevent the rapid slide into bankruptcy of his once rich and haughty family, who soon vanished from history, leaving only enigmatic buildings as their memorials. Catholics found themselves faced with the continuation of the Elizabethen recusancy laws and Jesuit and seminary priests were banned from England: to celebrate Mass remained treasonable. All Catholics could hope for was to shelter behind certain recusant landed families and put their faith in the next-in-line for the throne, who acquired a French Catholic wife. By 1647 a list of popish Recusants in Northamptonshire requested by the Commissioners for Managing Estates under Sequestration in the Civil Wars consisted of a mere 11 names; Thomas Aprice of Tansor, Jane Morgan, widow, of Heyford, Francis Plowden of Ashton in the Walls, George Pulton of Desborough, Ralph Sheldon of Barton, William Sanders of Welford, Dame Francis Tresham, widow, of Liveden, Edward, Lord Vaux of Harrowden, Piers Welsh of Glendon, Piers Herbert of Pipewell and Lord Brudenell of Deene.

The enforcement of 141 ecclesiastical canons aiming to secure uniformity threatened disobedient puritan clergy with suspension or deprivation. A petition from Northamptonshire against the suspension of non-conforming ministers, signed by 45 individuals, was presented to the King by Sir Edward Montagu and Sir Valentine Knightley. It was returned to them for amendment. On their refusal to do so both were put out of all commissions in the King's service and ordered to depart to the country. Sir Edward Montagu was reconciled to the King thanks to the influence of his brother, dean of the Chapel Royal. Although a devoted member of the Church, Montagu, like many others of the gentry, had puritan leanings and would have welcomed reforms. He was patron to the combination lecture instituted in Kettering about 1625. This was a characteristic puritan teaching device, a regular lecture or sermon given by one of a combination of ministers who preached in turn, often in one another's company. In a critical report on the state of Kettering church made in 1631 it was pointed out that 'The surplice is torn and is not beseeming to be worn at so great and publick assemblies as often are at this Church at the lecture and other times it being a market town'. The lecture continued until 1637, when it was suppressed by Bishop Dee of Peterborough who refused to let Lord Montagu (as he was by then) revive it.

By then Charles I was on the throne and, in William Laud, the King had an Archbishop of Canterbury resolute in his efforts to enforce uniformity. When the Archdeacon of Northampton visited Kettering parish church in 1631 under Laud's mandate he found the place badly maintained, scruffy and carrying unmistakable signs of disobedience. The words 'decent' and 'beseeming' (usually in the negative) recur in the report. Scruffiness was the result of puritan disdain for formality and ceremonial; their Christianity stressed the centrality of the individual's relationship with God and the setting for this mattered little. Not so for the Laudian church: 'The communion tablecloth is old, stained, torne and unbeseeming and insufficient for soe great a Congregation.' The Book of Common Prayer was old and battered, and required texts such as the *Book of Homilies* and Erasmus's *Paraphrases* were missing, as was 'a booke to register the names of strange [ie. visiting] preachers *which is as needful there as anie place of the Cuntrie*'. The register book of christenings, marriages and burials was 'undecent' (how 'undecent' we will never know, because it has not survived).

There was another visitation, in 1637. It found that the church fabric and fittings were still undecent and unbeseeming, but concentrated considerable attention on the continuing disobedience of Thomas Harris, the rector: 'the secrid service hath not as yet beene officiated at the table but the minister doth promise constantly to perform the same and to certifie thereof the next [archdeacon's] court after All Saints'. And he also promised not to neglect the prayer for the Catholic church, some of the collects appointed, and to use the phrase 'the peace of God' after the sermon, as laid down by the Book of Common Prayer. It was also reported that there was no silver plate for the Communion bread 'save only the cover of one of the Chalices which can scarce contain a tenth part of the bread which is to be consecrated at one tyme for the Communicants of so great a parish. There is but one flaggon which they estimate to hold above three quarts so that they are acustomed to bring wine potts to the Lords Table as if it were at a Taverne'. Clearly, the authorities were not having much success in Kettering.

The rector's conduct was not the only one to come under scrutiny in the visitation. The behaviour of John Seaton the schoolmaster was commented on. The churchwardens stated 'how the Schoolemaster behaves himself they cannot directly certifie for he hath beene at Pitchlie upon Sundays very neare this halfe yeare past'. They noted that Seaton was not licensed to serve the cure of Pytchley, though he had a licence of sorts. The church-wardens also noted that he taught his pupils catechisms from the writings of contemporary divines,'but not the catechisms appointed by the book of Common prayer, as appeared to us upon examinacion of the scollers and upon the scoolmasters own confesssion'. So, disobedience then in Kettering Free School as well as the parish church.

Kettering and the Civil Wars

Most prominent among the Kettering puritans were the Sawyers. Old Edmund Sawyer, whose brass lies in the family aisle in the parish church, and his sons were on the body of trustees who appointed John Seaton schoolmaster and were leading opponents of the King's methods of raising taxes during the years he ruled without Parliament. In 1638 Francis Sawyer got into trouble when he forcibly resisted bailiffs serving him with a distress warrant for non-payment of Ship Money. For this he was summoned before the Council in London, examined by the Attorney-General and forced to give bond for £100 that he would appear upon six days' notice. Ship Money was widely unpopular. In early 1640 the Grand Jury of the Sessions held in Kettering presented a petition to the Bench complaining of the 'great and unsupportable grievance lying uppon us and the Cuntrey, under the name of shipp money'. Two months later a summary of all the grievances against the King's policies was submitted in a Petition of the Freeholders of the County of Northampton to the House of Commons, when Parliament was recalled. It complained that

> of late we have been unusually and insupportably charged, troubled and grieved
> in our consciences, persons and estates by innovation in religion, exactions in
> spiritual courts, molestations of our most godly and learned ministers, ship
> money, monopolies, undue impositions, army money, waggon money, horse
> money, conduct money, and enlarging the forest beyond the ancient bounds,
> and the like; for not yielding to which things, or some of them, divers of us have
> been molested, distrained and imprisoned. We have entrusted John Crewe, Esq.,
> and Sir Gilbert Pickering, Knt. and Bart., chosen knights for this county to
> present these our grievances …

The King's attempt to rule without a parliament came to an end because of his and Laud's attempt to make the Scottish church come into line with the English. In Northamptonshire there was difficulty in raising men and money for the war. In August 1640 there was a meeting at the *Swan* in Kettering to consider the Etcetera Oath, which sought to bind clergy never to consent to the altering of church discipline. The ministers there resolved to lose their livings rather than conform. They also bitterly objected to the war with the Scots. Present at the meeting were both Francis Sawyer and Thomas Harris.

Northamptonshire returned strongly puritan M.P.'s to both Short and Long Parliaments. The enemies of Charles I were in no mood to co-operate; they insisted on the redress of grievances, the removal, trial and execution of the King's strong men, Laud and Strafford (a sacrifice for which the King never forgave himself), and the granting of the claims of Parliament. Parliament had clearly triumphed. Why then did civil war break out two years later? Because the extremists pushed the King too far, in particular with a Root and Branch Bill and a Bishops Exclusion Bill designed to make the Church of England into something like the Scottish Kirk. People began to rally round the Church and King. After his failure to arrest the five Parliamentary leaders in early 1642, Charles I abandoned London and raised an army. The first Civil War had begun.

In general terms, though there were plenty of exceptions, a significant number of squires took the parliamentary side, while the aristocracy lent personal and financial support to the King. Among local squires who actively supported the parliament were Sir John Norwich of Brampton Ash, Sir Gilbert Pickering of Titchmarsh, Sir Christopher Yelverton of Easton Maudit and Sir Richard Samwell of Upton. Within Kettering, the Sawyers were active in the attack on Wellingborough in 1642 in which Captain John Sawyer, 'a most godly and eminent man to the Puritan cause', was shot while entering the town. His brother Francis, enraged by his brother's death, murdered an innocent bystander, Mr Flint, curate of Harrowden, the sort of incidents which occur in any war, but seem particularly savage when neighbour kills neighbour. Not all the Sawyers were parliamentarians. An Edmund Sawyer was later in arms for the King, and in 1656 Joseph Sawyer 'son of John Sawyer, late of Kettering' was imprisoned in the Tower for joining an insurrection against the Protector's Government. Civil Wars split families.

They also brought suffering to aristocrats who supported the King. Old Sir Edward Montagu, now Baron Montagu of Boughton and 80 years of age, tried, as Lord Lieutenant of the county, to execute the King's Commission of Array calling out the trained bands. He was prevented by Sir Gilbert Pickering and others and escorted to London, where he was interned in the Tower. There he died in 1644, a sad end to a long and notable life. Thomas, Lord Brudenell, left Northamptonshire to serve the King as did most of the other Royalists. In 1643 Deene was plundered by Cromwell's troops. As a

Catholic, Brudenell was sequestered for both recusancy *and* delinquency, and had to pay heavily before being able to take possession of his estates again. When the war started, Sir Lewis Watson tried as far as possible to commit himself to neither side. When the Royalists seemed to be getting the upper hand and the local parliamentary leaders gathered for safety in Northampton he looked to support the King. He was doubly unlucky. Early in 1643, Lord Grey of Groby, the Leicestershire parliamentarian, scattered the royalists troops in the Harborough-Oundle area and took possession of Rockingham Castle. A short while after, Colonel Hastings, the Leicestershire Royalist commander, appeared and seized Sir Lewis and took him off to Belvoir Castle on the accusation that he had made no real attempt to hold Rockingham for the King. However, the castle was soon back in the hands of the parliamentarians, who defended it against all efforts to retake it. Sir Lewis successfully petitioned to be allowed to join the King in Oxford to try to convince him that he had not been remiss in his defence of his castle. He had a miserable war.

There is very little information on how the wars affected Kettering. No newsworthy incidents seem to have happened in the town, such as the pursuit and killing of Thompson, the Leveller, at Walgrave in 1649, or the occupation of the common by Diggers at Wellingborough a year later. No doubt Kettering was as vulnerable as other places to the depredations of armed sorties, particularly from the Royalists. What they were seeking were money, provisions and horses. Fairs and markets were held irregularly if at all and long distance trade was interfered with. Probably, as in other places, there was little enthusiasm among the common people for either side. On the religious front, puritanism won. All people in official positions had to swear to accept an English Solemn League and Covenant. In 1643 the episcopal system was abolished. The public use of the Book of Common Prayer was forbidden and was replaced by a *Directory for the Publique Worship of God*. Although presbyterianism was instituted by Parliament, there was to be no uniformity. The rise of Independency [Congregationalism] and a range of other protestant sects, and victory of the New Model Army, meant that presbyterianism, officially the new church, was deprived of the power to enforce uniformity. In Kettering, Thomas Harris remained rector until 1646. We do not know why he ceased to be rector. Possibly he could not accept presbyterianism or declined to take the Solemn League and Covenant or perhaps he simply died. After him there seems to have been no settled minister until 1649, when William Spauldon appears as a presbyterian 'intruder'. In 1651 John Maidwell became rector: he was to remain until 1662.

As in all revolutions, as events become more radical early supporters fall away and harder and more determined men come to the fore. A sticking point for many was the trial and execution of the King. Most parliamentarians among the gentry and aristocracy could not go along with regicide, and the Sawyers may have fallen into that category. One local squire who stayed the course was Sir Gilbert Pickering, who represented the County in both the

Short and the Long Parliaments and sat on the Parliamentarian County Committee. He was also a member of the County Committee for Sequestrations of Malignants' Estates which had instructions from Parliament to seize all the property of bishops and 'other persons opposed to the Parliamentary forces in any manner', and 'two parts' of the property 'of all and every Papist'. In religion he was described as 'first a Presbyterian, then an Independent, then a Brownist [separatist] and afterwards an Anabaptist; he was a most furious, fiery, implacable man; and was a principal agent in casting out most of the learned clergy'. Pickering was one of the King's judges at his trial, but attended only two sittings and did not sign the death warrant. He was a member of each of the five Councils of State of the Commonwealth, and sat for Northamptonshire in the 'Little Parliament' of 1653 and in the two Parliaments called by Cromwell as Lord Protector. In 1657 Pickering was summoned to Cromwell's House of Lords and was appointed Lord Chamberlain to the Protector, being 'so finical, spruce and like an old courtier'. He continued in that office under Richard Cromwell. After the restoration of Charles II he escaped punishment through the influence of his brother-in-law, Edward Montagu, Earl of Sandwich. His fate was perpetual incapacitation from office; others should have been so lucky. Two centuries later Cobden was still lamenting that the government of England was 'a matter of families'.

It was less a matter of families in Cromwell's decade – the 1650s – than before or after. Kettering's leading Cromwellian was John Browne, about whom almost nothing is known except that he was one of the Commissioners for Militia to Suppress Insurrections and Preserve the Peace for the Counties of Northampton and Rutland, set up in March 1655. This was one of the pillars of Cromwellian control and Browne must have been a man of some importance. The dominant figure of this committee of public safety was Major William Boteler (or Butler), Oundle born, one of 12 Major-Generals who controlled England when military rule was imposed. Boteler was responsible for Northamptonshire, Rutland, Bedfordshire and Huntingdonshire. Another committeeman was Robert Horsman from Rutland, Governor of Rockingham Castle at this time. These were new men, some drawn from ranks of society below the land-owners, which is perhaps why we hear so little of them after the Restoration.

Six

NONCONFORMITY AND THE CHURCH

The Early History of Nonconformity

The Restoration of the Monarchy was quickly followed by that of the Church of England to its position before the Civil Wars. After their bitter years in the wilderness its supporters in Parliament were in an unforgiving mood. Conformity was demanded. All clergy, teachers and college fellows were required to subscribe to a new Act of Uniformity and given until St Bartholomew's Day, 24 August 1662, to do so. Those who refused to take the oath, and there were many, were ejected from their livings. Amongst them was John Maidwell (or Maydwell), rector of Kettering. Much esteemed in the town and district, Maidwell was not about to desert his people. 'Here is constantly held a Conventicle [meeting] in a barn on Sundays about noon, and also on Thursday or Friday', reported the Archdeacon of Northampton in 1667. 'Half the town are thought to be there on Sundays and many from other towns so that they make 4 or 500, and among them are seen some few gentlewomen, the rest are yeomen, husbandmen, tradesmen, etc. and inferiour people. Most of them also go to church. Their teachers are Mr Maidwell late Rector there, Mr Alsop, Mr Willis. Here also a small minority of Quakers which doth not increase.'

The tradition in Kettering is that an Independent church was formed soon after Maidwell's ejection, and certainly before 1665. The first, undated, entry in the Church Book reads, 'An Account of the names of those who are in church fellowship att Kettering and have ingaged to walk together to the rules of the gospell under the ministry of Mr Maidwell pastour there'. Below are listed the names of 95 townspeople and another 91 from neighbouring places. As with other first generation Nonconformist ministers, Maidwell faced serious persecution. A series of Acts were passed which aimed to suppress Dissent. For various reasons, what they achieved was to marginalise Nonconformity rather than wipe it out. At the time of Charles II's Declaration of Indulgence of 1672, which licensed ministers to hold conventicles, provided they registered where they were held, Maidwell informed the government that his meeting was at 'Widow Cooper's new house, Kettering', and other local ministers were registered at houses in Cranford, Great Oakley, Thorpe Malsor (John Maunsell's house),

14 *The first Independent Meeting House, vacated in 1723 and pulled down in 1791. This drawing by R.J. Williams was made from an old model for Bull's* History of Kettering.

Titchmarsh, Geddington, Wellingborough and Rothwell. Clearly, there was a concentration of Nonconformity in the district, though Archdeacon Palmer was explicit that the greatest of their meetings was at Kettering. Another early source, the Compton Census (of religious allegiance) of 1676, records that there were 'no papists, 1350 Conformists and 300 Nonconformists in the town'. Maidwell was to establish a settled home for his congregation in a thatched building 'at the bottom of Mrs. Baker's premises near the Market Place' several years befor the Toleration Act of 1689, which marked the turning point for Nonconformity. The first leader of Kettering's Dissenting tradition died in 1692, and lies buried in the chancel of what was once his own parish church.

As Archdeacon Palmer noted, the other early set of Nonconformists were Quakers, who were there as early as 1661, as the first entry in their register, '1661, III, 8', makes clear. At this period the Society of Friends were perhaps the most bitterly persecuted of the Nonconformists, though there is little evidence of how this directly affected the Kettering Friends. When their meeting house was erected is not certain. Bull says the first mention of it is in the manorial court roll of 1735, when five Quakers were admitted as tenants to certain premises and a burial ground.

Maidwell was always going to be difficult to succeed as minister, and people who formulate their own religion as they go along are always prone to dissension and splits. In 1696 William Wallis, the minister, and six others left and formed a Baptist meeting. There followed a succession of pastors who came and went until Thomas Saunders from Coventry 'brought peace' in 1721. He built up the congregation so effectively that in 1723 they moved to the present site in Gold Street and built the 'Great Meeting'. There was another successful minister in the person of Benjamin Boyce from 1740 to 1770, then more dissension until the arrival of a young student fresh from Daventry Academy, Thomas Northcote Toller, in 1775. He was ordained in

1778 and remained until his death in 1821. He was to be succeeded by his son, Thomas. Between them they were to make the name of Toller famous in the annals of Kettering and Kettering in the annals of Congregationalism.

William Wallis and the others 'dismissed' from the Independents found a home in Bayley's Yard, Newland Street, but it was not long before another Independent minister, John Wills, formed a second Baptist cause in Goosepasture Lane in 1715. About fourteen years later, the people from Bayley's Yard united with those of Goosepasture Lane. However, in the next 20 years the cause went into decline with disputes over such issues as 'open communion' and baptism by total immersion. Eventually dissension was ended in 1768 with the drawing up of a new covenant. The following year the Baptists purchased the house, warehouse and garden of Mr Beeby Wallis in Gold Street and converted the warehouse and garden into a meeting house, soon known as the 'Little Meeting', with its own burial ground. Over the next two decades there were further splits and pastor-led defections. However, in 1782, a young minister from Soham in Cambridgeshire, the Rev. Andrew Fuller, was appointed. He was to make the name of Kettering notable in the history of the Baptists, and not only in this country.

In the century or so following the 'Great Ejection' of 1662, the achievement of the Nonconformists was to have survived, which they did more successfully in some parts of the country than others. Puritan North-amptonshire was one of these. Within the county, some towns were more Nonconformist than others. Behind Northampton, Kettering ranked second with Wellingborough. Within a generation or so after 1662, puritanism's connection with the godly squires (such as the Maunsells), its erstwhile supporters, was for the most part severed. From now on Nonconformists were in the main drawn from the ranks of the small farmers, tradesmen and artisans and their womenfolk. Cut off from the rest of society, which regarded them with some disdain (though not in Kettering) as an outcast minority to be tolerated, at best, icily, Nonconformists got on with their lives, intermarried and, over time, many prospered. Generally, they led a quiet inward-looking existence, but eventually created connectional networks wider than the confines of merely local society.

Amongst the Baptists, Kettering produced two men of some note. Dr John Gill, born in 1697, the son of a deacon in the church, rose to be an eminent minister and biblical scholar. In 1719 he was invited to become pastor of the Baptist congregation in Horsleydown, Southwark, London, and remained their minister for the rest of his life (51 years). He published many works and sermons, and entered into many a controversy. In 1748 the Marischal College and University of Aberdeen conferred on him the degree of Doctor of Divinity on account of his knowledge of the scriptures and of the oriental languages 'and his learned defence of the scriptures against deists and infidels'. About six years younger than Dr Gill, John Brine had a similar, and connected, career. After becoming a preacher in his native town, he was called to be minister to a Particular Baptist church in Coventry. A few years later he moved to London to be minister at Curriers' Hall, Eastcheap. There he came into contact with Dr Gill, with whom he formed a close friendship. In the three and a half decades of his life in London Brine played a very active part in the life of the Baptists there. He died in 1765 and was buried in the Dissenters Burial Ground at Bunhill Fields, where Gill was also laid to rest after his death in 1771. Both Gill and Brine were of the High (or Hyper) Calvinist school of theology. Believers in predestination, salvation was available only to the Elect, the chosen of God. Northamptonshire Nonconformity in their time was High Calvinist territory.

As the 18th century wore on, Independents and Baptists began to act together in what came to be called 'the Dissenting Interest'. On the political front they were zealous Whigs and Protestants, active whenever any threat to the settlement of 1689 arose, as it did with the Jacobites in 1715 and 1745. Local Whig grandees, such as the Spencers, found it useful to keep in touch with their leading ministers to see how Dissenters felt on current issues. By the 1780s, after a century on the defensive, they began a campaign to have their civil disabilities removed. As it happened, the timing was unlucky. The movement for a repeal of the Test Acts was frustrated by the start of the French Revolution. It became impolitic to attempt to reform England's 'matchless constitution': reforms were suspended for the duration. But the contributions from the Kettering congregations to the campaign fund raised in Northamptonshire were substantial.

The Church Restored

It cannot have been easy for Maidwell's successor, Thomas Williamson, as rector of Kettering. Maidwell stayed in the town and was esteemed, at least by some, as evidenced by several bequests to him in wills. A significant part of the rector's income was still top-sliced by the notorious deal between Burton and the Watsons of Rockingham, which is no doubt why incumbents who were able to do so became pluralists. And years of puritan occupation had neglected the church. An inventory of goods and utensils in the Churchwardens Book in 1725 records gifts of a silver plate and a silver salver, and two brass candlesticks. Compared with their Nonconformist rivals, upon whose pastorates their histories were centred, the lives and characters of the Anglican clergy often remain oddly elusive. Indeed, the annals of the Georgian Church in Kettering are difficult to reconstruct in anything but the barest outline. Little is known of Williamson, former Intruder at Weldon, who conformed and was instituted in December 1662. His origins, education and life as rector are unclear, save that he remained incumbent until his death in 1670.

Even less is known of his successor, William Fowler, rector for the duration of the 1670s. In 1680 Samuel Sherwin, born and educated in Leicester, a Cambridge graduate, succeeded. He stayed only four years, returning to his native town to become Vicar of St Margaret's and of Knighton. His successor was Francis Sawyer, thought to be the fourth son of John Sawyer of Kettering. When he became rector in 1684, he had been vicar of Upper Isham and of Thorpe Malsor for 12 years. He surrendered the latter in 1689, but remained in possession of Kettering and Upper Isham until the time of his death 20 years later. The living then passed to Robert Watkins, about whom almost the only thing known is that, as Bridges noted, there once stood a fine tomb in the churchyard recording the death of his wife in 1713, at the age of thirty-nine. Watkins left two years later.

Watkins' going ended the succession of relatively short incumbencies. Between then and 1814 Kettering was to have only three rectors. The first was Thomas Allen, born and educated in Oxford, who became a priest the year he graduated, and was instituted vicar of Irchester in 1705. Ten years later he moved to Kettering, where he remained until his death, 40 years later. A scholarly man, he was the author of several works of a devotional nature, including *The Practice of a Holy Life* and *The Christian's Sure Guide to Eternal Glory,* both of which were translated into Russian, for 'the use of all Muscovy'. We know rather less of his successor, Gilbert Bennet (or Benet), Rector 1755 to 1783, not even where he was born, bred, or educated. In his latter years his curate was the Rev Joseph Knight, who succeeded him in 1783. In all, Knight was to spend 40 years in Kettering, dying in 1814 at the age of sixty-seven. He enjoyed three livings, all handily close. In 1777 Knight was presented to the vicarages of Newton and of Geddington, which he retained for the rest of his life. Obviously well connected, he became chaplain to the Duke and the Dowager Duchess of Buccleuch and Queensberry. Happily for Knight (and his successors), in his time his Kettering stipend underwent a marked improvement.

Church Life in the 18th Century

In the absence of any memoirs relating to the duties of the living or of wider life of the church it is difficult to arrive at a picture of the 18th-century church. The rector baptised, married and buried his parishioners, wrote sermons and preached them on Sunday, and, if so requested, at funerals. Rectors of Kettering generally employed curates for the everyday chores, some of whom augmented their stipend as master of the Free Grammar School. Church life was formal, orthodox, unevangelical. For a long time after the Civil War era, enthusiasm was distrusted.

Physically, the parish church, as it always had, towered over Kettering, whose houses, as contemporary drawings show, were, with the exception of the manor house, little different from the farms and cottages of nearby villages, low-slung and roofed mainly with thatch. People told the time by the church clock, and as well as being called to church on Sundays, every day were summoned to work in the morning, to their mid-day meal and to their beds at night by its bell. Local events such as the assembling in Kettering of the magistrates of the Northern Division, or the passing through the town of some great person, were greeted by the ringing of the bells, as were national events such as the monarch's birthday, the defeat of the Jacobites at Culloden in 1745, and General Wolfe's capture of Quebec 14 years later. A re-casting and increase in the number of bells in 1714 made it easier to change-ring, and speed ringing became a competitive sport, as two surviving Georgian peal boards in the church record. Although neither mentions it, these record contests with St Margaret's, Leicester between 1730 and 1732, on which bets were placed and mocking notices inserted in the Stamford and Northampton newspapers over which team could ring the full peal of 5,040 changes in the fastest time.

Georgian Kettering told the time not only by the church clock but also by the sound of the church chimes. When they were first installed we do not know, but the parish records refer to a repair of them in 1671, and in 1733 Thomas Eayre II, the Kettering bellfounder and clockmaker, was given an order for a new set. With a repertoire of 11 tunes they were part of the everyday sound of the town. In the 1850s they fell out of repair and, possibly because of ratepayer opposition, were not restored until 1872. When, in 1890, the church was given a major restoration, they were dismantled by the church authorities and removed without any consultation. Their loss was a break with the pre-industrial past, and their tunes, to which local people put their own words, were recalled with nostalgia as long as there were people alive to remember them.

In other ways, the parish church was an integral part of the culture of the place. Its patronal festival, Kettering Feast, which always takes place in the first week of July, commencing on the Sunday nearest to 29 June (the feast day of Sts Peter and Paul) and continuing over the next two or three days, was the great annual summer holiday. On Feast Sunday there were always well-attended services in the church and in the chapels, and former residents came back to visit family and friends. On the Monday and Tuesday people took time off work to enjoy more secular entertainments – fun fairs, concerts, dancing and the like.

Another area of the life of the town in which the Church exercised influence was education. For much of the time between the Restoration of Charles II and the accession of Queen Victoria, it almost seems that the role of master of the Free Grammar School was not so much to provide sound schooling as to be a useful supplementary employment for local clergy. In this regard it was no different from scores of other grammar schools. The history of education in Kettering, particularly for the pre-Victorian period, remains to be written. It is not even possible to compile a complete list of the men who had the school in the period. We know that Robert Clipsham conformed in 1662 and was licensed as master, though how long he stayed is not clear. William Fowler was master (as well as rector) in the 1670s, and was succeeded in both positions by Samuel Sherwin. It was in Sherwin's time that a new start was made in the affairs of the School. In 1681 the Court of Chancery ordered an inquisition into the state of its administration, occasioned by the fact that all the guardians of the trust were dead. The following year, a Decree in Chancery set out who the new guardians and overseers of the school were to be, confirmed their powers to let the school properties and appoint and dismiss future masters. The schoolhouse was to continue to be used as the house of the master, where he would teach Latin and English to scholars born or living in Kettering. The diocesan records reveal that a Mr J. Penn succeeded Sherwin, though whether or not he was in holy orders is not clear. Thereafter the masters usually were, though after Sherwin none of them was the rector, the post usually being reserved for curates. What does seem apparent is that the school was small, probably fewer than thirty pupils, since there is no mention of an usher (assistant to the master) being employed. If this is so, before 1700 the Kettering Free School was smaller than neighbouring schools at Fotheringhay, Oakham, Oundle, Peterborough, Uppingham and Wellingborough.

Much remains to be found out about the school in this period. However, a return made by the rector, the Rev. B.W. Fletcher, in 1818, in response to a request for information from the Select Committee on the Education of the Poor, is revealing. He said that the master's salary was £88 18s. lod. per annum, a most useful supplement to any curate's pay, and that 34 boys were being taught at present, but that 'sixty or seventy years before' the school contained 75 pupils. It was not unusual for grammar schools to decline in the second half of the 18th century, and some fell into being elementary schools. In any case, if their masters were curates, it follows that their energies may well have been devoted to other activities offering better prospects of advancement. Bull tells us that a Mr Warner appears to have been schoolmaster towards the end of the century and was succeeded by his son, who had been a sergeant in the army. In 1801 the mastership passed to the Rev. James Hogg, a Yorkshireman, with the sort of bad habits which usually signify someone bored by teaching. Hogg occasionally did duty in Kettering church, and then became, in succession, rector of Glendon and then vicar of Geddington and Newton. However, he held on to the Free School until his death in 1844. Under him it declined: a Government Report of 1833 noted that 'great complaints are made against this school, in consequence of the master professing to teach only the Latin and Greek languages'. The decline was even more abysmal under his successor, the Rev. Richard Morton, who had been Hogg's curate at Geddington. When Morton was appointed curate at Burton Latimer, the number of boys dwindled to two or three, perhaps because those wanting to avail themselves of the master's teaching had to walk over to Burton for their lessons. Nonetheless, possessing a freehold until such time as he chose to relinquish it, Morton held on to the school until he became vicar of Rothwell and Orton in 1856.

The information contained in the returns to the Select Committee on Education in 1818 mentions a charity school in the town, set up under the will of Mrs Aldwinckle of 1792, in which 16 girls were taught to make lace. Possibly in the 18th century there were also 'private adventure' schools, dame schools and schools for the better-off, but no evidence remains of their existence. Since 1792, however, new schools had appeared. There was now a National (Church of England) elementary school (which caused Hogg to complain that it was taking away boys from his Free School) and there were four Sunday Schools, one each for the Church, the Independents, the Baptists and the Methodists. The Church school was attended by 177 boys and girls, the others by a total of 364 children. By then, Kettering, like everywhere else, was entering a new religious and moral era. These new schools were the results of the Evangelical Revival.

The Evangelical Revival

The Evangelical Revival, as its name indicates, was about spreading the Word, evangelising those outside the Church and Chapels, as well as those inside for whom religion had become mere observation. At first the message and methods of Evangelicals caused offence alike to conventional Christians and to those untouched by either Church or Chapel. Evangelicals not only aimed to reconstruct individuals, but to make society more godly, restrained and sober. The organisations through which they tried to do this included schools for the children of the poor, Bible Societies, societies for the prevention of cruelty to animals, for prison reform and for anti-slavery agitation. If their greatest efforts went into trying to evangelise the poor, their greatest successes were with the growing middle-classes. More remarkably, through such converts as Selina, Countess of Huntingdon, William Wilberforce and Lord Shaftesbury, they even made an impact on the religion and morals of the upper echelons of society. It has also to be said that the alarm created by the French Revolution's attack on religion was just as important as the Evangelical Revival in ushering in these changes. Be that as it may, by the time Queen Victoria came to the throne, Evangelicals had become a major influence, and in few places more strongly than in Kettering.

The origins of the Revival were diverse. Although its best remembered leaders are John and Charles Wesley, the founders of Methodism, from about 1730 the Revival was inspired by the teachings and writings of men from across the religious spectrum. Northamptonshire clergymen played a part. John Wesley always acknowledged his debt to the Rev. William Law's *Serious Call to a Devout and Holy Life* (1728). Another early influence was Philip Doddridge, Independent minister in Northampton from 1729 to 1751. In his *The Rise and Progress of Religion in the Soul* (1745) and *The Family Expositor* (1739-56), in his hymns, sermons and correspondence, and, not least, through his Dissenting Academy, which existed to train future Nonconformist ministers, he was of influence not only among Nonconformists, but with some Anglicans as well.

Within Kettering, Thomas Northcote Toller was one of the heirs of Doddridge. The son of a Somerset attorney, he received his education at the Dissenting Academy at Daventry, whence it had moved after Doddridge's death. In 1775 he came to Kettering. For over four and a half decades until

15 *Thomas Northcote Toller (1756-1821), minister at Great Meeting Independent chapel for over forty years.*

his death in 1821 he ministered to the Independents of the Great Meeting. Under his pastorate, their cause began to flourish.

His Baptist counterpart was the Rev. Andrew Fuller, who came from a family of farmers from Wicken, near Ely, in Huntingdonshire. Invited to Kettering in 1783, he remained at Little Meeting until his death in 1815. Possessed of great energy, he was a good preacher and the writer of a number of influential works, notable amongst which was *The Gospel Worthy of All Acceptation* (1785). Arguing that Christ died not only for the Elect but for all people, Fuller did much to direct the Particular Baptists towards a more evangelical form of Christianity. His ideas proved very influential, not least in North America. Fuller was also instrumental, with a group of like-minded ministers, in founding the Baptist Missionary Society, the inaugural meeting of which took place in Kettering in 1792. This was an important new step: at that time, with the possible exception of the Moravians, general missionary enterprise was unknown to Protestantism. Subsequently, a remarkable number of men and women from Kettering and other places in Northamptonshire left to work in the mission fields of the Empire. The most famous was William Carey, 'the Wycliffe of India', who, before studying for the ministry, began life as a shoe maker. After pastorates in Leicester and Moulton, he left for Bengal, where among other tasks he undertook the immense labour of translating the Bible into the native language, a process which involved turning Bengali, hitherto a spoken language, into a written one. The efforts of these, and others, made Kettering's name notable in Nonconformist circles. The formation of the Baptist Missionary Society was an important step in the Evangelical Revival. It was not long before the Independents and the Church of England had their own missionary societies.

Thomas Northcote Toller was succeeded by his son Thomas, who remained at Great Meeting until 1875, which meant that the two of them ministered in Kettering for a century, a remarkable record. More of a scholar and less of a preacher than his father, it was said that Thomas Toller's true vocation was a professor's chair. Be that as it may, his prestige was high amongst his followers and his church grew so much that, in 1849, the meeting house had to be enlarged and new Sunday schools erected. When Toller completed his jubilee in 1871, he was presented with an address and a cheque for 700 guineas, and crowds came for the service and the meeting afterwards. Four years later, on the centenary of his father coming to Kettering, he retired. The Tollers gave continuity to the Independents, who counted among their members a cross-section of the manufacturing and shopkeeping élite of the town, names such as Stockburn, Waddington, Goosey and Bird being prominent.

If the Tollers gave the Independents stability, the Baptist experience was more troubled. Baptists were always prone to dissension, and Fuller was always going to be hard to follow. He was succeeded by his assistant, John Keene Hall. Although supported by the majority of his hearers, Hall's style and views resulted in a secession in 1824, led by John Jenkinson. Although the charismatic Jenkinson had only 14 followers originally, they surprised the people at the Little Meeting by establishing a viable church. Eventually they raised funds to open Ebenezer Calvinistic Baptist Chapel. Jenkinson is a figure of some interest, being an early Temperance advocate, a parish politician and the author of the Kettering Chartist manifesto. In 1849, he left Kettering to become minister of Oakham Baptist chapel. Without him, Ebenezer soon collapsed, the building being sold for a shoe factory. After

16   *Engraving of 'The Rev. W. Carey and his Brahmin Pundit', 1836. Carey used Indian scholars to assist him in his translation of the Gospels into native languages, especially Bengali.*

17   *The Wesleyan Chapel, Silver Street, erected 1867. It was demolished in 1933 as part of a scheme to widen Silver Street and a new church was built in School Lane.*

retirement Jenkinson returned to Kettering, by which time most of those who found it hard to forgive him for his secession had died.

John Keene Hall died in 1829, relatively young. His successor was the Rev. William Robinson, fresh from Bristol Academy. Energetic and a good preacher, in his time 'open communion', first proposed by Hall, was eventually adopted. More numerous than the Independents, the adherents of Fuller (as the chapel later became known) were just as political. In this they were led from the front by Robinson, an ardent Reformer. His was an era when politics hinged very much on religious differences, nowhere more than in Kettering. Among Robinson's congregation were some of the town's leading figures, the most prominent of whom were the Gotches. Robinson stayed until 1852, when he moved to Cambridge.

The Evangelical Revival was not solely the work of Dissenters. Methodism took root in Kettering in 1811 but, as one of its ministers recollected, 'our society and our regular congregations were numerically insignificant as compared with the powerful "interests" of the Congregationalists and the Baptists'. Their first minister, the Rev. Joseph Fowler, a Bradford man, found that, if Bradford was, in his words, 'the most Wesleyan', Kettering was 'the most generally evangelical town in the kingdom'. In his time in Kettering, Fowler developed a profound respect for Toller and Fuller and was happy to sit at their feet. The first Wesleyan meeting was hidden away in a side street, but in the course of time Wesleyanism began to flourish for the simple reason that Wesleyans attracted people that neither Church nor Dissenters could reach.

Within the Church of England, evangelical curates played their part in the promotion of 'vital religion', often meeting with bitter opposition. The first in Kettering was Abraham Maddock, whose journal, recording his triumphs and frustrations, survives. A lawyer by training, ordained in his 40s, Maddock was curate from 1761 to 1770. Preaching was his forte; he was in demand for funeral sermons, sometimes drawing extraordinary crowds. His journal bemoans 'the Deadness of both Ministers and Professors of all Denominations', and the lowness of church attendance. Ploughing his lonely furrow, he received support from Evangelical friends from Olney, the Rev. John Newton and William Cowper, the poet and hymn writer. Finally, however, his local enemies made life intolerable and he left to become curate of Creaton. With unfashionable beliefs and without a patron, he was never given a living. Until his death in 1785, Maddock remained a miserably-paid curate.

Another Evangelical curate who left an account of his life was the Rev. George Bugg, curate in turn at Welby and Stoke in Leicestershire, Kettering and then Lutterworth. The summary of his sufferings in the cause of preaching vital religion is set out in the long-winded title of his pamphlet *Hard Measure; or Cruel Laws in Liberal Times: Illustrated in an Authentic Narrative of the Sufferings Endured and the Pecuniary Loss sustained by the Rev. George Bugg, A.B., in Three Dismissals from his Curacies, Under the Influence of the 'Curates' Act; Without a Fault Alleged* (1803). Bugg put his dismissals down to his vulnerability as a curate, a position which could be terminated at any time by the Bishop withdrawing his licence, which is what happened in these three places. Bugg never quite explains why, though it seems certain that his evangelical stance alienated influential parishioners in each place and led to complaints to the episcopal authority. Bugg came to Kettering in 1803 as curate to the elderly Rev. Joseph Knight. He worked hard, especially with the newly-formed Sunday School, and had few troubles until the accession of a new rector, the Rev. Brice William Fletcher, in 1814. At first, Fletcher intimated that he would take the duty upon himself and Bugg sought and found a new post. Then Fletcher changed his mind and asked Bugg to stay. Fourteen months later, Fletcher returned from Peterborough with the news that the new Bishop, Dr Parsons, wanted to terminate Bugg's employment, despite Fletcher's support of his curate. In the end, Fletcher discharged Bugg, and there followed an unseemly passage of events concerning eviction from his house and arguments over the lease and salary payment. Sad to say, he was no happier at Lutterworth.

Once rid of Bugg, Fletcher settled into the enjoyment of his living. He had the church repaved, galleries were erected and he spent over a thousand pounds on the rectory. But Fletcher's happy Kettering existence came to an end over a bitter dispute which needs a Trollope or a Jane Austen to do it justice. The struggle hinged on the arrangement made when Lord Sondes presented the living to Fletcher, who had been his tutor and had accompanied him on the Grand Tour. In order to safeguard the right to the living of any of Lord Sondes' younger brothers, the arrangement was that a bond for £12,000 was entered into that Fletcher would resign, after a month's notice, if one of the brothers took holy orders and wanted the living. In 1820, in order to make way for the Hon. and Rev. Henry Watson, Fletcher was given notice. He declined to go, and eventually Lord Sondes took legal action against him in the Court of King's Bench. Fletcher contended that the bond was void on the grounds of simony. The matter raised issues of great complexity in church law and was to drag on through the courts for eight years. In 1827 the House of Lords finally allowed Fletcher's appeal that the original agreement was simonaical and therefore illegal. Lord Sondes' lawyers then contended that Fletcher's presentation to the living was also illegal. And, as Lord Sondes' right to present to the living had lapsed, so also had that of the Bishop. A presentation to the living, still vacant in law, could only be made by the Crown. The King duly presented the Rev. Henry Watson. However, Fletcher physically prevented Watson taking possession and an action was brought at Northampton Assizes to obtain possession of the temporalities of the church. The jury found for Mr Watson, and he was shortly after (in May 1828) allowed to take peaceable possession. In the event, the Hon. and Rev. Henry Watson did not stay long in the rectory, resigning in 1830. In due course he inherited the Rockingham estate (together with the patronage of the living of Kettering).

By the time the Rev. Richard Vevers took over, the Evangelical Revival was in full flow. The town now had a range of bodies and institutions representative of this movement. The Baptist Missionary Society, the Church Sunday School and the arrival of the Methodists have already been noted. In 1810 the Independents had started their Sunday school, and in 1812 a branch Bible Society had been formed to ensure that religious literature was distributed to the poor. This was an inter-denominational initiative, but the following year a National School was opened to ensure that the children of the town received their elementary education under the aegis of the Church of England. Strong though the Dissenters were, their school – the Kettering British School – did not come into existence for another two decades. The year 1813 also saw inter-denominational meetings to petition Parliament for the toleration of Protestant missionaries in the territories of the East India Company, whose charter was up for renewal. The following year, Dissenters protested at the peace treaty with France allowing the French to renew their slave trade, a business the British had banned in 1808. The Anti-Slavery movement began in earnest in 1823, with petitions to Parliament to meliorate the condition of slaves in the West Indies, which became a major cause for Kettering evangelicals. Slavery in the colonies was to be abolished in 1833, but the treatment of blacks in Jamaica had already become a major issue for Kettering's Dis-

18 *The Rev. William Knibb (1803-45), an authentic, unbending Kettering Nonconformist. He gave his support to the abolition of slavery, and to the blacks of the island in their uprising.*

senters. In the slave revolt of 1831 the Kettering Baptist missionary, William Knibb, who had gone to Jamaica as a replacement for his dead brother in 1824, was accused of inciting the rebellion. 'Knibb the notorious' and others were put on trial, but acquitted. White mobs destroyed Baptist and Methodist churches. Soon after the rebellion, Knibb came back to England, denouncing the treatment of slaves and arguing the case for emancipation at public meetings. He continued to work for the blacks under the system which replaced slavery, dying there in 1845, at the age of 42. In Jamaica his name is still remembered. In Kettering he was, and still is, celebrated as a hero.

In his farewell sermon in 1875, the Rev. Thomas Toller recollected that, in the early years of the century, Kettering was known as 'the Holy Land', 'because of the closeness with which the Lord's day was honoured' and because almost everyone in the town attended some place of worship. Some

19 *The North End National School of 1859. The Church was aware that the town was about to grow northwards, and the school helped to create a congregation for St Andrew's church which followed a decade later.*

verification of this is to be found in a local religious census, taken in 1828, which also clearly indicated the numerical strength of the Dissenters:

Churchpeople	1150
Independents	1196
Baptists	640
Calvinistic Baptists	240
Wesleyans	550
Quakers	27
'Of no sect'	40
Total	3843

As the population of the town in the Census of 1831 was given as 4,099, it seems clear that pretty well every baby born in Kettering was either a little Anglican, Dissenter or Methodist. The Religious Census taken in 1851, though tricky to interpret, seems to confirm this pattern of religious allegiance:

	'Best attended service'	Sunday scholars
Parish church	407	238
Independents	528	194
Baptists	451	193
Calvinistic Baptists (Ebenezer)	80	42
Calvinistic Baptists (Workhouse Yard)	'No meeting that day'	
Friends (Quakers)	29	—
Wesleyans	270	100
Primitive Methodists	64	—
Totals	1,829	767

If these remarkable statistics are perhaps untypical of country towns generally, Kettering resembled such old puritan Midland towns as Leicester, Bedford, Northampton and nearby Wellingborough.

Another indication of the rise of evangelicalism is that for most of the 19th century Kettering's Anglican clergy were invariably Low Churchmen. Perhaps in such a Protestant town it could not have been otherwise. Not much is known of the views of the Rev. Richard Vevers, rector 1830 to 1838, but more is of the Rev. Henry Corrie, who succeeded him. Corrie qualified as a doctor but, finding vital religion, took holy orders. He served first as Watson's, and then Vevers' curate, moving in 1837 to the living of Blatherwicke. But after a numerously-signed petition to the patron from church people in Kettering, he was offered the living. An appreciation of Corrie after his death in 1846 was contributed to *The Citizen* by William Robinson: 'By the blandness of of his manners, his familiarity with all ranks and sorts of the inhabitants, and his kindness, he won favour with all classes.' Robinson paid tribute to Corrie's earnestness and evangelical sentiments, but added waspishly, 'certainly he was not distinguished by mental vigour, or by any glow of imagination. He was the worst reasoner we remember to have met with.' Kettering's Baptists did not reckon much to poor reasoners. Corrie's successor was his curate, the Rev. Thomas Hellier Madge, remembered as 'strictly evangelical'. Madge died in harness in 1862, his most lasting monument being the North End National School.

PART TWO
The Rise of Industrial Kettering

Seven

LATE STUART AND GEORGIAN KETTERING

Landowning and the Land: The Passing of the Sawyers

Possibly because they took their records with them when they quit their estate, we do not know as much as we would like about Kettering's leading family, the Sawyers. Three detailed memoranda in the Churchwardens' Book record disputes in the late 17th century between the townspeople and Edmund Sawyer, who had succeeded his father in 1645. Two concern a row over the sharing of the costs of maintenance of the aisle in the parish church which the Sawyers used. The first was a typical dispute between a litigious squire and undeferential churchwardens, and agreement was only arrived at after the matter had gone to the consistory court of the Archdeacon of Northampton. It provided that so long as Edmund Sawyer and his family occupied the seats they had used for some generations past, and so long as other parishioners who wanted room were permitted by Sawyer to sit in the 'aisle or chancel anciently belonging to his house', the churchwardens were to repair the same 'except only ye pavement of ye said lower chancel, which shall be maintained and reapaired by ye said Edmund Sawyer because it is ye buriall place of his family'. The other matter, which went before an independent arbitrator, concerned the rights of Kettering farmers to common their animals after Lammas in the Hall Meadows and Sawyer's part of Kidsholm, to which Sawyer had denied them access. The arbitrator confirmed the farmers' rights and, for the other side, the right of Sawyer to fold sheep from his pasture grounds on his arable land in the common fields after harvest, hitherto obstructed by the farmers, was also confirmed.

This Edmund Sawyer died in 1680, leaving his estate to his two sons, also bequeathing five pounds to John Maidwell, the nonconformist minister. The elder son, Edmund, was a London merchant engaged in the Levant trade from his base at Aleppo. In his will of 1687, made on board the ship *Asia*, of which he was part owner, he left his share of the Kettering estate to his brother, Henry. Another bequest was to his sister, Joyce Sawyer, of £600 for a hospital for six poor women, which she duly established. This almshouse still exists.

In 1720, the Sawyer connection with Kettering ended when Henry Sawyer and his son, another Edmund, sold the manor house and estate, some

20   *Sawyer's Hospital.*

700 acres or so, to Francis Hawes, probably because of their involvement in
the South Sea Bubble. Hawes, who was also connected with the Company,
took possession, but there was to be no Hawes dynasty, because a year later
the estates of the Directors of the Company were confiscated and sold for
the benefit of investors who lost when the Bubble burst. In 1724 the Sawyer
estate was purchased by John, Duke of Montagu, with a confirmatory bar-
gain, sale and release in 1727. His estate lying immediately adjacent in
Weekley and Warkton, the Duke must have been pleased to snap it up. At
the same time, in 1728, John Duke of Montagu, together with Edmund and
Charles Montagu, acquired the feefarm of Kettering and four-tenths of the
lordship of the manor. From that time forward, the Montagus of Boughton
were an influence in the affairs of Kettering.

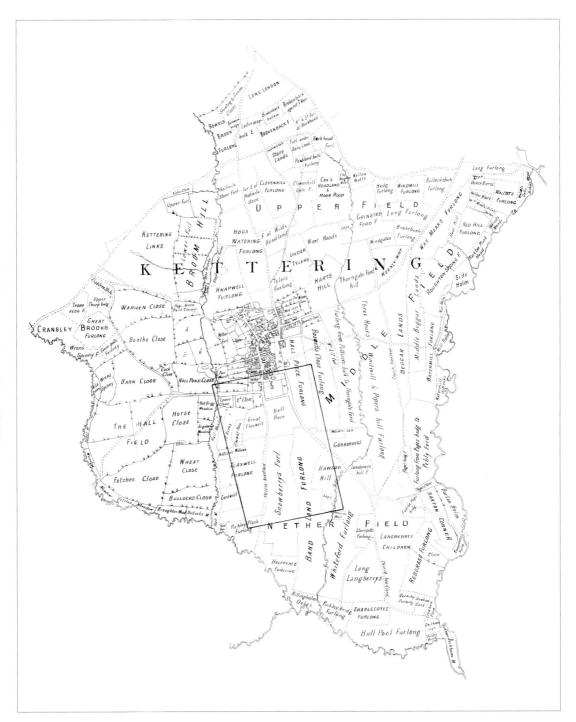

21 *A copy of Brasier's immensely detailed map of Kettering in the 1720s made for John, Duke of Montagu, showing the furlongs, the main divisions of the open field. For a detailed mapping of the lands within the furlongs in the rectangle marked south of the parish church, see pages 70-1.*

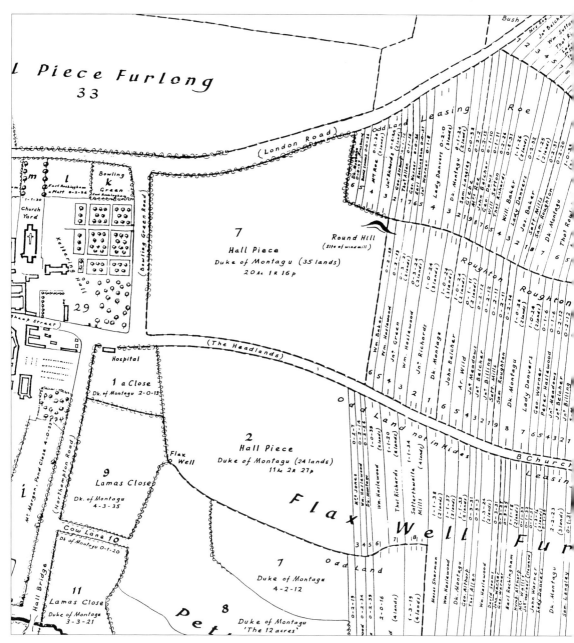

As he did with other parishes in which he owned property, the Duke commissioned a surveyor to produce an accurate map of Kettering, showing who held what. This minutely detailed piece of work, made by William Brasier in 1727, must be one of the finest maps of any open-field parish in existence, and can be seen in Kettering Museum. What it shows is the layout of a classic open-field system. Kettering Field is divided for the purposes of cultivation into three, the arable land is divided into furlongs, each furlong

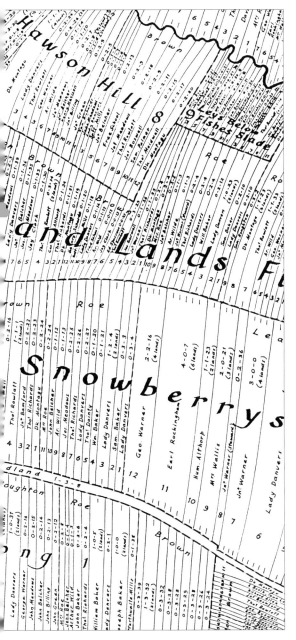

22 *Closes, furlongs and lands (strips) south of the parish church, drawn from Brasier's map by Peter Taylor.*

further subdivided into 'lands' in the possession of different owners, who let the land to tenant farmers. Even as late as the 1720s, the planned regularity of the distribution of these lands, originally laid out in medieval times, can still be seen. The Hall Closes, the anciently enclosed manorial demesne, the core of the Duke's newly acquired estate, are shown lying west of the town, south of the common called the Links, though the Duke also had lands in the arable furlongs as well. The low-lying damp land by Cransley, Slade and the Ise Brooks was set aside as meadows. So large, elaborately coloured and minutely detailed is Brasier's map that it is virtually impossible to reproduce, though Mr Taylor's painstaking redrawing of it enables part to be shown here.

As the schedule of proprietors attached to the map indicates, his purchase left the Duke, with 783 acres, the largest landowner in Kettering. The next largest, with 216 acres, was the Lady Danvers, followed by the rector, with his glebe of 111 acres. But the Duke was not in a position to dominate. The pattern of ownership was, in fact, one of great fragmentation. The three largest landowners mentioned were the only ones to have 100 acres or more. The rest was owned by 87 people or charities, 45 of whom had less than ten acres. One effect of this was that the enclosure of Kettering by Act of Parliament, requiring the assent of the owners of two-thirds of the land, was to be delayed until the early 19th century.

Surprisingly little is known about 18th-century farming and farmers, except that Kettering Field was chiefly given over to the production of corn. The land was fertile and produced abundant crops. There being few old enclosures within the parish, except those belonging to the former Sawyer estate, there was little commercial farming for the London market, or concentration on sheep or cattle production, though there was in parishes adjacent. The main function of the sheep and cattle kept by the farmers was to manure the land and provide milk and meat for local consumption.

Market Town

In 1676, Kettering was the sixth largest town in Northamptonshire; by 1801 it had overtaken Peterborough, Oundle and Daventry and was then third, behind Northampton and Wellingborough. However, Northamptonshire is scarcely the place to look for examples of marked urban growth in the 18th century. In 1676 the Compton Census (made for religious purposes) gives a figure of 1,650 persons 'young and old' for the town. About fifty years later, Bridges states confidently that the town contained 2,645 inhabitants. If these figures are correct, then, despite such setbacks as the Plague visitation of 1665-66, in which 80 persons died, between the Restoration of Charles II and the accession of George I the town seems to have experienced a population growth of about a thousand. Thereafter, for the rest of the 18th century, population expansion seems to have been negligible. In the first national census in 1801 Kettering is listed as having 3,011 inhabitants. Figures calculated from the parish registers suggest why, though, of course, they tell us nothing about net migration, and have serious gaps:

Statistics of Baptisms and Burials from the parish registers, 1660 to 1769

Decade	Baptisms	Burials	Net growth
1660-69	433	438	-5
1670-79	374	322	52
1680-89		statistics not available	
1690-99		ditto	
1700-10		ditto	
1710-19	678	581	97
1720-29	659	622	37
1730-39	503	711	-214
1740-49	663	758	-213
1750-59	584	866	-272
1760-69	677	1022	-405
1770-1800		statistics not available	

Clearly, Kettering was a desperately unhealthy place in the 18th century, especially from 1730. The reason is not hard to find; as far as can be known, it seems many of the epidemics which produced such high numbers of deaths were smallpox, the disease most feared in that century. How Kettering responded to the smallpox will be examined below.

Despite its vulnerablilty to infection, all observers of Kettering at this time testify to the prosperity of its market. Blome in his *Britannia* (1673) noted that the Friday market was well frequented, and served with corn, cattle, sheep, hoggs and provisions. Morton in his *Natural History and Antiquities of the County of Northampton* (1712) refers to the fact that Kettering's market rose at the expense of Rothwell's, which seems to have become extinct after the plague caused it to be held in Kettering in 1655. Rothwell market never revived, though its June horse fair long remained important. One indication of the expansion of trade and business in Kettering is that, in 1662, Lord Rockingham received the royal grant to hold a horse fair in addition to Kettering's ancient fair on the Thursday before Easter, and, in addition, two new fairs were granted, one on the Thursday before Michaelmas Day, the other on the Thursday before St Thomas's Day in December. The charter also gave the Earl the rights to the tolls of these fairs and to hold courts of piepowder (to settle disputes and other matters on the day of the fair). In 1748, a fourth fair was effectively added to the list, on Thursday before Whitsuntide. By the next decade this had been moved to the Friday. There were, in addition, Statute Fairs every September and October for the hiring of farm and domestic servants. These were the annual holiday for rural workers. Freed from their contract with one employer, young men and women came into town to meet, enjoy the fun of the fair, and eventually engage for the next year with another (or the same) master or mistress.

About 1721 Thomas Eayre made a map of the town for John Bridges' projected county history. Whilst the layout was still essentially the same as shown on Treswell's map, some growth had taken place in the north end of the town around Lower Street and Northall. Architecturally, Kettering was unremarkable: much of the housing was of one or two storeys, made of local stone or timber, wattle and daub, most roofs being of thatch. 'The Sessions House, Church, and a small Hospital (Sawyer's) are the Chief Things of Note in it', declared the author of *Magna Brittanica*, about 1724, though he remarked, 'Tis seated upon an Ascent of a small Hill on a dry and sandy Ground, in a free and pure air'. Bridges, whose home was Barton Seagrave Hall, must have known Kettering well, and provides more detail:

> To the north west of the church is the mercate place, a row of houses in the middle dividing the sheep market from the Butcher row. At the end of the Butcher row is the Sessions house, a good stone building supported by pillars. Eastward from the mercate place is Newland, which breaks into four streets shooting towards the four points of the compass. In the centre Newland pond where the four streets meet. In one of the pond walls is the stump of a cross,

presumably all that was left of the medieval cross there on the Elizabethan map. It seems odd that Bridges fails to mention High Street or Gold Street, unless for him they were all part of the market.

The Thomas Eayre who made the map of Kettering for John Bridges was the most remarkable of a family, of whom there were three men of that name in the 18th century, grandfather, father and son. He was the second. His father, who died in 1716 was a Quaker blacksmith, and his son followed him in that trade, though not in the Quaker faith, having been baptised. Thomas II (1691 to 1758) was a man of many talents. For some years he followed the business of clockmaker, making and repairing timepieces for landowners and being employed by the authorities of several parishes, including Kettering, in the maintenance of their town clocks. Being a skilled draughtsman and surveyor, he came to the attention of Bridges, who employed him to make plans of towns and drawings of buildings, which were to be engraved for Bridges' *History*. The death of his patron in 1724 terminated that line of work, although he did produce the first large-scale map of the county. When he did this is not certain, though clearly it must have been before 1758. However, it was not engraved (by Jefferys) until 1779, with a second edition in 1780 and a third in 1791 (*see front endpaper*).

Eayre was best remembered for his skill in bellfounding. He and his brother John were casting bells in their foundry in Wadcroft Lane from at least 1717. Over 200 examples of their bells are known, and can be found in a number of places in the counties abutting Northamptonshire, though the greatest number are in Leicestershire and Northamptonshire. On Thomas II's death, the business passed to his son, but Thomas III eventually went bankrupt. The last known bell from Kettering is dated 1762, and Eayre died in or before 1770. He was not, however, the last Eayre to be in bellfounding. His uncle Joseph started a foundry at St Neots, which was carried on after his death by Edward Arnold, until he moved to Leicester. The St Neots foundry then passed to Robert Taylor, whose son started the famous bellfoundry in Loughborough which still exists. Descendants of the Eayre family through the female line lived on in Kettering for several generations.

One of the abiding hazards to property and sometimes life itself in towns was the danger of fire. There was a serious one in 1679, inevitably blamed (as most things were at that time) on the Catholics, and there were fires in twenty of the ninety years between 1722 and 1811. In some years there were more than one; in 1722 a second fire in the month of June caused losses of £909. The worst was in 1766; it was started on 5 November when a squib was thrown into a barn. Sixteen houses were destroyed and £2,300 paid out by the insurance companies.

After a fire, wherever possible, properties were rebuilt in stone with solid roofs. Some good houses were erected in Georgian Kettering, the Mission House, Chesham House and Beech House, all in the Lower Street/Northall area. However, Kettering did not become another Stamford. Although on a main road to London, it was not one of the same importance as the Great North Road, and Kettering never developed the wealth of that particular town. Nonetheless, moves for improvement which affected most market towns from about 1780 were felt in Kettering. In the main, this took the form of improving the market place, getting rid of 'Rotten Row', the line of small shops which had evolved out of the infilling in the market place over several centuries. A sketch map drawn up in 1785, which Bull published in his second volume, shows the occupants and the businesses of these shops, revealing a concentration around the market place typical of most market towns.

Before the appearance of the trade directories it is difficult to find much about the overall pattern of shopkeeping and trades in Kettering in the 18th century. The earliest survey is Robert Smith's *A Brief Account of the Streets & Lanes of Kettering; With the Names of the Owners and principal Occupiers of Every Estate*, which he published in 1826 to accompany his new plan of the town. In it he lists every house, its owner and the occupiers and their businesses.

Trades, occupations and businesses in Kettering in 1826

Food & Drink: Bakers 8, butchers 7, grocers 8, poulterers 2, shopkeepers (unspecified) 3, public houses 12, inns 3, maltsters 2, spirit dealers 1.

Clothing & Footwear: Boot & shoemakers 7, drapers 5, dressmakers 1, glovers 1, hosiers & haberdashers 1, milliners 1, tailors 1.

Woodworking: Cabinet makers 2, chair turners 1, coopers 2, patten makers 1

Ironworkers: Blacksmiths 3, braziers & tinsmiths 1, cutlers 1, shear & sickle makers 1

Building Trades: Builders & surveyors 3, plumbers & glaziers 1, slaters & plasterers 2, stonemasons 4.

Leather (other than footware): Saddlers 3

General stores: Chandlers 1, ironmongers 2, pot merchants 1.

Agriculture: Corn factors 1, farmers 13, (market) gardeners 6, woolstaplers 1

Others: Basket makers 1, booksellers 1, brushmakers 1, clockmakers 1, clerk & office agent 1, flax dressers 1, merchant (unspecified) 1, post office 1, watchmakers 2.

Manufacturing: Brushmakers 1, boots and shoes 1 (Gotch & Sons), silk 1 (Samuel Gibbon), worsted 1 (Richard Waddington).

Professional: Attornies 2 (Henry Lamb, Thomas Marshall), apothecaries 1, bankers 1 (J.C.Gotch), chemists & druggists 1, clergymen 4, surgeons & apothecaries 2 (William Gibbon, William Roughton), veterinary surgeons 1 (John Hawthorn).

N.B. Some tradesmen, particularly grocers, are listed with more than one business, e.g. Grocer & Farmer, Grocer & Lace dealer, Grocer & Chandler, Grocer & Druggist. These have not been double counted.

This pattern was typical of a country town and had probably changed little in the preceding century. Smith says little of the industries of Kettering. He does, however, notice the presence of a worsted manufacturer, two woolstaplers and a silk manufacturer, of whom more later. Before Smith (who was a market gardener) all we have to rely on are notices in the *Northampton Mercury* and what visitors to the town have to tell us about the place.

Kettering supplied all the services the district needed. As well as the butchers, bakers and other shopkeepers, the 1785 plan of the market

23   *A late 17th-century farmhouse in Walker's Lane (once Pudding-bag Lane) photographed just before demolition in 1911. It had been in the possession of James Jaquest, farmer.*

place shows that there was a bookshop and stationers owned by Nathaniel Collis, a visit to which afforded that zealous traveller, Lord Torrington, some pleasure, recorded in his diary for 1793. Entering a stationer's shop he was surprised to come across 'a most excellent catalogue of books: The master, Mr Collis, thinking me a bit of a conoisseur, beg'd to shew me his collection of curiosities, kept in an upper small room, and is, indeed, curious and diverting, consisting of petrefactions, fossills, eggs, armour, stuff'd birds &c; and tho' not the rarest, and most expensive articles, yet it proved the owner to be a man of research, and honourably inquisitive'. Such characters, noted Lord Torrington, 'I live to find'. Catalogues of the books Nathaniel Collis had for sale in 1770, 1771, 1783 and 1793 survive in Northampton Central Library. Much of his trade came from the purchase of clergymen's libraries, and his list for 1783 has 7,750 volumes. Collis died in 1813 at the ripe old age of 84, having lived in Kettering about seventy years. Between 1783 and 1793 he took Thomas Dash into partnership, and, after Collis's death, Dash carried on the business, and was also a printer. Their antiquarian interests involved them in the publication of Bridges' *History and Antiquities of Northamptonshire* in 1791, and Dash possessed a unique copy of that work, with many extra illustrations, which is now in the British Library. In due course, the business passed to his son William, who carried on as a bookseller, stationer and printer for many years. Before his death in 1883, William Dash presented his father's pamphlet collection to the Northampton Library, presumably because one did not then exist in Kettering.

Wayfaring and Inns

From about the time of the Restoration, inland and coastal trade in this country expanded in parallel with the growth of overseas commerce. Market towns situated on main roads to London found that both their local and long distance business began to flourish. Kettering was one such. Situated where two roads from London converge, Kettering's inns did good business until the coming of the railways. Going north from Kettering, travellers had the choice of taking the road to Market Harborough and (following the route of the modern A6) proceed via Leicester, Derby and Manchester, or journeying via Uppingham and Melton Mowbray to Leeds. When the *George* hotel was offered for sale in 1825 it was described as being 'situate on the great Road from London to Glasgow' and that the Glasgow Mail 'runs from the House, and is worked by the Tenant'. In addition to the London roads, two other lines of communication passed through the town. One was the route linking Leicester with East Anglia via Market Harborough. The other was the cross country route from Oxford to Stamford, via Northampton and Wellingborough. Travellers from Leicester to Peterborough by way of Thrapston might also pass through Kettering.

Because of the growth of wayfaring, from the later 17th century there was need to improve the nation's roads and the method used was to place stretches of them under the management of a turnpike trust, set up by a local Act of Parliament. The first to affect Kettering was the one passed in 1751-2 for turnpiking the road from Market Harborough to Brampton in Huntingdonshire. Two years later, the London route from Rockingham to Olney was turnpiked, as was the Kettering to Knotting road (via Higham Ferrers). However, it was not until as late as 1819 that a completely new turnpike road between Northampton and Kettering, avoiding Wellingborough, was made.

At various places on these roads were tollgates, and near each gate stood the 'pike keeper's' cottage or toll house. Typical of these were the toll house and gate erected in 1810 at the junction of the roads to Thrapston and Wellingborough, near to what is now the entrance to Wicksteed Park. As well as collecting tolls it was the duty of the gate keeper to operate the weighing machine. Parliament had authorised their use in 1741 to make loads over a certain weight pay extra toll. These machines were unpopular with carters and carriers, who were liable for toll surcharges.

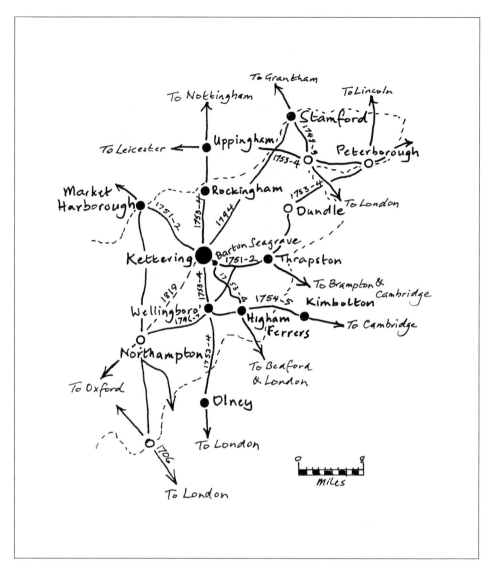

24   *Sketch-map of the turnpike roads through Kettering from 1751.*

Carters and carriers had been familiar figures on the roads long before the advent of turnpikes and weighing machines. Before the availability of 19th-century trade directories it is difficult to find much information about them, but there are indications that local and longer distance carriers operated throughout the 18th century. The worsted industry, Kettering's most important trade, must have employed the former to bring in wool from the surrounding areas, and the latter to transport the cloth to the London market. Local carriers were also engaged in the transport of coal. In the 18th century it was cheaper to buy sea-coal from Newcastle than pit-coal from Leicestershire and Warwickshire. However, this only became possible

25 *Advertisement in the*
Northampton Mercury,
25 October 1762.

> **{ 123 }**
>
> THESE *are to inform all* Noblemen, Gentlemen, Tradesmen,
> *and Others,*
>
> THAT the KETTERING and UPPINGHAM Old Stage Broad-
> wheel'd FLYING WAGGON for carrying all Sorts of
> Perishable Goods, which always Inn'd at the Horshoe in Goswell-
> Street, London, and set out from thence every Saturday, is now
> removed to William Black's at the Cross-Keys in St. John's-Street,
> and sets out from the said Inn every Saturday at Twelve o'Clock,
> and will be at the George in Kettering every Tuesday by Four
> o'Clock, and at the Swan in Uppingham every Wednesday
> Morning by Ten o'Clock; and returns from the said Inn at One
> o'Clock the same Day, and sets out from the George-Inn in Ket-
> tering every Thursday Morning at Six o'Clock as usual, and will
> be at the said Cross-Keys Inn every Saturday Morning by Three
> o'Clock. All Customers Favours will be gratefully acknowledged.
> Proper Care will be taken for taking in Goods and Passengers at
> the said Cross-Keys Inn, and delivering out the same.
> Performed (if G O D permit)
> By your humble Servant,
> **THOMAS WRIGHT.**
> N. B.   Plate, Money, Writings, Jewels, Watches, will not
> be acounted for, unless entered and paid for as such.

when the River Nene was made navigable above Peterborough. An Act of 1724 provided for the river to be improved for commercial use as far as Thrapston, and another in 1756 ushered in its navigation as far as North-ampton. The Kettering Overseers' Accounts list payments for the carriage of coal at the beginning of the century from Yaxley, on the 'old course' of the Nene, then later from Oundle, and, after 1724, from Thrapston.

The vehicle used by long-distance carriers was usually a 'stage waggon', a cumbersome, broad-wheeled vehicle, covered with a canvas top and pulled by six or eight horses. By 1750 the so-called 'Flying Stage Waggon' had made an appearance, and, by changing horses, progressed more speedily. Certain goods required even faster transport. A notice in the *Northampton Mercury* that year advertised the Kettering New Flying Machine to carry venison to London. Advertised to run 'all the venison season', it also car-ried passengers. The service was still running a decade later, and probably longer.

In the second half of the 18th century, the Wright family were Kettering's main proprietors of stage waggons. Joseph and Thomas Wright advertised their 'Flying Stage Waggon' in the newspapers. By 1791 the *Universal British Directory of Trade and Commerce* informs us that the business was in the hands of Thomas Wright & Son, 'Coach and Waggon Masters'. Their stage wag-gons then ran twice weekly to the *Cross Keys,* St John's Street, in the City of London, one via Thrapston and Kimbolton on a Tuesday, the other on a Thursday, via Higham Ferrers, Bedford and Hitchin. Both took two days to London, and the same to return. In 1799 Thomas Wright informed the public that he was retiring and by the 1820s the Kettering stage waggons were run by Knighton & Co. By 1830 the London journey was being done three times a week.

Before about 1830, when they begin to appear in the trade directories, it is difficult to identify local carriers. In 1765 John Bland, 'book keeper to Mr Thomas Wright', advertised in the *Northampton Mercury* that he was running his waggons from Kettering to Northampton and to Bedford. By 1830, and no doubt much earlier, there were carriers to Leicester, Market Harborough, Stamford, Wellingborough, Thrapston and Weldon as well, and they picked up parcels in villages on the way. The place most visited was Harborough. One reason for its importance was that the Grand Union Canal opened an arm into the town in 1809. This brought Kettering within reach of a new set of national communications. From their Harborough office, Pickfords had daily services to London, Manchester and Liverpool, and fly-boats to 17 counties. For Kettering, their most important commodity was pit-coal; by the mid-19th century the town was using more pit-coal from the Midlands than sea-coal from Newcastle *via* the River Nene navigation.

By 1850, there were 25 local carriers. Nearly all operated from public houses, which furnished all their requirements – accommodation for their carts, feed for the horses, a place to pick up parcels and passengers and gather news. Most frequently used by carriers were the *Sun*, the *Old White Horse*, the *New White Horse*, the *Duke's Arms*, the *New Inn*, the *Nag's Head* and the *Three Cocks*. In the 1840s two carriers were women – Elizabeth Warner, working between Kettering, Rothwell and Wellingborough, and Sarah Penn, between Kettering and Old. With the coming of the railway, the era of long-distance road transport was soon over, but the carrier's cart remained an essential link in the rural economy until country buses appeared in the 20th century.

There is no record that Kettering had any stage-coach service before the coming of the turnpikes. In 1753, the year the Act was passed for the turnpiking of the Kettering to Newport Pagnell road, a coach was advertised to run along that route to London. The proprietors, Thomas Collis and Benjamin Payne, informed travellers that the coach would leave from the *George* every Monday and Friday morning. At the same hour another coach would leave the *Old Cross Keys* in St John's Street, London and travel *via* St Albans to Selsoe in Bedfordshire, where it would meet the Kettering coach, and exchange passengers. After an overnight stop at the *George* in Selsoe, Kettering passengers would go on to London and the London passengers to Kettering by way of Bedford and Wellingborough. The journey, including the overnight stop, took two days. The following year Collis had a new partner, John Kirby. Their handbill announced 'the Kettering and Bedford coaches are joined in partnership'. By 1755 the Kettering Flying Stage Coach was announcing that it was doing the journey to London in a day and a half, which still required an overnight stay, but it was only a few years before the time to London was reduced.

26 *Advertisement in the* Northampton Mercury *of 14 April 1755 for Thomas Collis' 'Flying Stage-Coach' to and from London, via Bedford.*

Kettering Flying STAGE-COACH, *In one Day and a Half from* Kettering *to* London, BEGINS on Monday the 28th of this Inſtant April, 1755; ſets out from the George Inn in Kettering every Monday and Wedneſday at Twelve o'Clock in the Day, and, for the Conveniency of Paſſengers, will go every Monday through Wellingborough to Olney, lye at the Swan Inn in Olney every Monday Night; ſets out from thence on Tueſday Morning preciſely at Five o'Clock, and be at London that Night; likewiſe, for the Conveniency of Paſſengers on the Bedford Road, will go every Wedneſday through Higham to Bedford, lye at the White-Hart Inn in Bedford on Wedneſday Night, and ſet out from thence every Thurſday Morning at Five o'Clock, and be at London that Night. Alſo the above-mention'd Stage-Coach ſets out from the Old Croſs-Keys Inn in St. John's Street, London, every Wedneſday and Friday Morning preciſely at Five o'Clock, and, for the Conveniency of Paſſengers on both Roads, goes every Wedneſday from London to Bedford, lyes at Bedford that Night, and will be at Kettering on Thurſday by Twelve o'Clock; and on Friday goes from London to Olney, lyes at Olney that Night, and will be at Kettering on Saturday by Twelve o'Clock.

Perform'd (if God permit) by
THOMAS COLLIS.

Each Paſſenger is allowed to carry twelve Pounds Weight, all above to pay one Penny per Pound; Children in Lap Half Price.

Paſſengers and Parcels are taken in at the Swan at Wellingborough, Swan at Olney, Green-Dragon at Higham, Knotting-Fox, White-Hart at Bedford, and all other Places as uſual.

Prices to and from London		
Kettering	0 14 0
Wellingborough	0 12 0
Olney and Newport	0 10 0
Higham-Ferrers	0 12 0
Knotting-Fox	0 10 0
Bedford and Silſoe as uſual.	

No Money, Plate, Jewels, Rings, Watches, or Writings, to be accounted for, unleſs enter'd and paid for as ſuch.

To be lett, at Kettering, by the Owner of the above Stage-Coach, A very handſome Hearſe and Mourning-Coach, with able Horſes, alſo Poſt-Chaiſe, or One-Horſe Chaiſe, to any Part of England.

Paſſengers may be fetch'd ten or twenty to the Stage the ſame Day it goes out, likewiſe may be carried ten or twenty Miles the ſame Days it comes in, by applying to

Their humble Servant,
T. COLLIS, of Kettering.

In the short run, the turnpike system did not necessarily lead to great road improvement. In his *Observations on a Tour In England* (1801), Charles Dibden commented, 'Kettering is famous for nothing I know of but its execrable roads'. They had such prodigious ruts in them that he and his family and servants had to get out and walk 'over a road the caricature of ploughed ground'. Bad roads led to accidents such as broken axles, but the greatest hazard was winter weather. There was also the danger of highway robbery. In the *Northampton Mercury* of 15 October 1750, readers were informed, 'Last evening at about seven o'clock Mr Mattock, a Dealer in the Woollen Manufacture, Mr Palmer, a Glover and Breeches Maker, and another Tradesman, all of Kettering, having been at Harborough Fair, were on their return home stopped by two Highwaymen'. Mattock was relieved of £30, Palmer of £7 and his watch and greatcoat, and the other tradesman of what money he had. However, the robbers were gentlemanly enough to return four guineas to a distressed Mattock.

The names of the proprietors of these early stage coaches change frequently. Collis was replaced by a James Ellot, who was soon replaced by John Cleaver whose 'Kettering Flying Coach or Berlin' set out from the *George* for London on a Monday and returned on Wednesdays, taking a day and a half each way. In 1765 the coach service advertised in the *Mercury* was now 'The Uppingham, Kettering and Wellingborough Flying Stage Coach'. Uppingham passengers stayed overnight in Kettering and set off every Tuesday at 3 a.m., arriving in London late the same night. In 1777 travellers were informed that, from April, 'The Oundle, Thrapston, Kettering, Kimbolton, St Neots, and Biggleswade Fly' would make a thrice-weekly journey to London, and this service continued into the next decade. By the 1780s a series of changes ushered in 'the golden age of stage-coach transport' and for more than fifty years Kettering's inns and the people who serviced the users of the road, the vehicles and the horses did very well out of the business.

Georgian Kettering as a Social Centre

As a well-traded market town, Kettering attracted people for social as well as commercial reasons. In the provision of sport and entertainment the inns and other licensed houses played a central role. In the years since 1700 the names of more licensed premises appear in the manorial court records (though not all were necessarily new; some may have changed their sign). But, in order of appearance in the records, we find the *Crown*, the *Katherine Wheel*, the *White Hart* (now the *Royal Hotel*), the *King's Arms*, the *White Horse*, the *Black Bull*, the *Peacock*, the *Chequer* and the *Wheat Sheaf*. The *George* first appears in 1712, though there is a strong possibility that it may once have been the ancient *Cock* inn (there being the Cock Yard adjoining it) and it might have changed its name in anticipation of the accession of King George I. The *George* took over from the *Swan* as the town's chief inn and posting house.

In the early 18th century a popular annual event for a short time was the Kettering races, which began about 1727. A newspaper advertisement of 26 August 1728 reveals their form. There were to be two races for Galloways (a horse popular at that time) on separate days over 'Kettering's new course'. As usual in local race meetings, a stipulation was that any horse entered must be kept at such public houses 'as had paid five shillings or upward towards the plates'. The Kettering race meetings lasted only a few years, until 1737. Why they came to an end is not clear, but it seems likely that people putting money into them were not getting sufficient return on their outlay. However, they did attract people into the town: inns provided refreshment before the races began at 3p.m. Soon, other attractions came to be provided. In 1733 a 'Ball for the Ladies' was announced to be held held at the *George* on the night of the second day of the races. In September 1736 the *Gentleman's Magazine*, in a vignette of such occasions, printed amusingly unkind verses from some anonymous satirist about a local figure who had made a fool of himself at the Ball.

KETTERING BALL.

Of female prowess let Alexis tell,
Who in a late encounter vanquish'd fell.
By company allur'd, on pleasure bent,
He, the last moon, to Kettering races went,
Where lords and louts, and belles and beaus resort,
Grave priests and country squires to see ye sports:
Farmers and fox hunters to custom yield,
And humbler thistle-beaters take the field.
This pastime o'er, to diff'rent sports they fall,
Some game, some drink, and some frequent ye
ball;
This last Alexis chose (unhappy choice),
And leads up bright Belinda in the dance,
When swift the buxom damsel whirls him round,
And lays her partner fainting on the ground.
Asham'd and vex'd th' inglorious foil to bear,
Afresh he leads up the too vigorous fair,
Till thrice (so oft the fates his shame repeat),
The doughty hero swoons beneath her feet,
She, not concerned a whit, the victim leaves,
And brisker Damon in his stead receives.

27 *A poem from the* Gentleman's Magazine *of September 1736, which captures the rustic nature of Kettering Ball. We may never know who Alexis, Belinda and Damon were – but contemporaries undoubtedly did.*

Another event of the time was the Flower Show. In July or August the Friendly Society of Gardeners and Florists held their competition for the six best blossoms of 'wholeblowing carnations', with a first prize of 15 shillings and a second of six shillings. In April 1737 'a Florists' Feast' was held, when six shillings was offered as a prize for the best Auricula, the same for the best Polianthus and nine shillings for 'the greatest rarity from the kitchen garden'. On all these occasions, 'ordinaries', fixed price meals, were offered in the inn where the show was held. On St Cecilia's Day (22 November) concerts were held, usually with a ball or Assembly to follow. In 1754 prospective patrons were informed that 'the greatest care will be taken to keep the room warm', and the following year 'a great band is bespoke to play country dances'. In 1758 the date of the concert was moved so that those attending 'would have the advantage of a full moon when travelling home'. The following year it was advertised that 'On Monday, Dec. 3, the Feast of St Cecilia, Old Style', a concert would be held, and 'after the Concert a Ball'.

By the later 18th century Kettering, in common with other flourishing market towns, developed a winter 'season' for the regular provision of balls, assemblies and concerts for the local gentry and professional families. These were usually held in the assembly rooms of the *George* and the *White Hart*, which were also the venues for plays put on by visiting companies of actors, and benefit concerts. Towards the close of the century, concerts of sacred music became popular. Most were held in one or other of the assembly rooms, but the 'Grand Selection of Sacred Music from Handel' in June 1792 was held in the parish church, with profits going towards the fund for a new organ.

The inns hosted a miscellany of other events, public and private. In January 1747, 'A grand Entertainment was lately given to many of the Gentlemen belonging to his Grace the Duke of Montagu's late Carabineers, at the *Duke's Arms* in Kettering, by Quarter Master Collis, who was at the Taking of Carlisle from the Rebels; when every one expresse'd his Zeal for the Government, by many loyal Healths, &c. &c. [the Rebels being the Jacobites with the Young Pretender].' The *George* had a bowling green, used for other events as well as bowling. Kettering's first hot air balloon was launched from it in 1784: 'The Effect was majestic and beautiful, as the Balloon carried up its own Fire, and rose through the Clouds in about five Minutes'. Montgolfier balloons were only invented in 1782-3, which indicates how fast new forms of entertainment spread, even in those days.

Woolcombing and Weaving

In the late 17th century Kettering's economy was diversified by the introduction of the trades of woolcombing and worsted weaving. The author of *Magna Britannia*, published in 1724, notes that the woollen manufacture was 'introduced and settled there about fifty years ago by one Mr Jordan, whose Posterity still manage a considerable part of it. Their loom work, as they call it, consists chiefly of Shaloons, Serges, and Tammies.' Shalloon, named after Chalons in France, was a closely woven material chiefly used for linings; serge was a durable twilled cloth of worsted, and tammy a fine worsted cloth of good quality, with a glazed finish. A pamphlet of 1741, quoted in James' *History of the Worsted Manufacture in England* (1857), recalled the rise of some towns, and the fall of others in that line of manufacturing: 'Sudbury … Farnham … Newbury … then Kettering, a little market town in Northamptonshire, from manufacturing twenty or thirty pieces of dyed serges weekly, fell into making shalloons, rivalled the towns above mentioned, and sent into London market upwards of one thousand pieces per week.' It seems apparent that what drew Jordan and others to the town was the availability of local wool and cheap labour. A similar initiative to introduce weaving into Oundle at this time failed. Not so in Kettering: the woollen trade became the town's staple for a century, and spread to Rothwell, Desborough, Corby and certain other villages. In fact, by 1777, there were twice as many weavers as shoemakers in Northamptonshire. Probably because it was a domestic trade, where the wool combers and weavers worked in their own homes, once it had finally gone, it left few physical traces of its existence behind. It is Kettering's forgotten industry. Little is known of Jordan, except that he was that relative rarity in late 17th-century Kettering, a Catholic. We may safely assume that it was the establishment of the worsted business that was one reason Kettering's population grew between the 1660s and the 1720s, as people moved in seeking work.

The earliest documentary reference to weaving is in the Churchwardens' Book, which records the letting of a common close to Edward Dyson 'for to sett tenters in it', the frames on which the woven cloth was stretched on tenterhooks, to be shrunk and bleached in the open air. On his map of 1721, Thomas Eayre drew four rows of tenters in the Dam Meadow. The best description of the organisation of the business is in Donaldson's *General View of the Agriculture of the County of Northampton* (1794):

> The wool in the first instance, is bought by the manufacturers of the growers or farmers in the neighbourhood; it then undergoes a very minute assortment, and the different kinds of wool which are found in every fleece are appropriated to supply the proper markets in the different parts of the kingdom, where they are respectively manufactured. Thus, for instance, the finest is sent into Yorkshire for clothing, or to Leicester for the hosiers; and some of the longest staple wool is worked at home into moreens [a cloth used for curtains], tammies, calimancoes, and everlastings [a durable kind of cloth]. After the wool is sorted, and the different kinds are assigned to the respective purposes for which they are best adapted, that which is intended to be manufactured at home is combed, and then delivered out, in small quantities, to the lower class of people in the neighbourhood, to be spun and reeled, for which they are paid so much per pound, according to the fineness of the thread into which it is converted; it is then returned home to the manufacturer, who has it wove into such kind of stuff as the quality of the thread will best answer.

The work of spinning and reeling was done by females and boys of from ten to fourteen years of age. The sorters, combers and weavers were all men. Donaldson records that the trade 'was in the highest perfection it has ever attained at the beginning of the present war' (against Revolutionary France). His estimate is that, at its peak, from 5,000 to 6,000 people were involved in the business in the whole county. Of these, perhaps about ten per cent were in Kettering.

By the 1740s, the trade was well established, and the *Northampton Mercury* of 24 April 1749 carried the following notice: 'The Gentlemen of the Woollen Manufacture design to walk in Procession on the next Shew Day [of cattle], being Thursday the 11th of May; in which will be exhibited, as an emblem of Trade and Commerce, Jason with his Golden Fleece, Bishop Blase [the patron saint of woolcombing] in the ancient Episcopal Habit on Horseback, attended with Pages, and a Vast Number of the Fraternity with Flags, Caps, and Sashes, most curiously wrought. The Procession will begin about Twelve o'clock'. Over the next four decades this became a regular event in Kettering. In the 1740s and 1750s so many weavers came into Kettering that accommodation had to be found for them in barns and outhouses.

For many years, the market for the sale of local tammies and the other worsted products was the *Duke's Head*. It is clear that the industry in Northamptonshire was part of a wider network with manufacturing centres in the counties of Huntingdon, Cambridge and the Isle of Ely, Essex, Hertfordshire, Bedford, Leicester and Rutland, because, when persistent friction arose between employers and workers over such matters as 'false

28   *Chesham House, Lower Street, the home of the Gotch family until their bankruptcy.*

reeling' in the 1770s, it was the manufacturers of these counties who combined to secure legislation to prevent abuses and provide for inspection of the 'putting out' system. Presumably for convenience of access, their general meeting each year was held in the *White Hart* in Kettering, where a committee of 15 was appointed to carry the Act into operation. The dominance of woolcombing and worsted weaving is shown most clearly in an analysis of the occupations of the men listed for the militia in 1777. Of the 376 men between the ages of 18 and 45 (a very large sample of the total workforce) no fewer than 193 (51per cent) were engaged in these trades in Kettering. No other occupations came anywhere near this. The next largest occupation was food and drink, with 27, the building trades with 19, and the same number in the clothing trades. Perhaps surprisingly (in view of what was to happen in the Victorian era) leather and footwear provided work for only 16 men.

The Universal British Directory of Trade and Commerce of 1791 states, 'The manufacture of the town is sorting, combing, spinning and weaving of tammys and lastings, of different sorts, all of which are sold white as they come off the looms. About five hundred weavers [in the Kettering area] are employed'. There is no intimation that this trade would soon be in crisis. More ominously than was realised at that time, the *Directory* notes 'this trade hath brought many poor into the town' and that the poor rates were rising.

The Arrival of Footwear

The year after the Militia listing of 1777, Kettering's boot and shoe industry was established by Thomas Gotch, the son of a prosperous freeholder in the parish of Glendon. By 1770 Gotch and his wife were living in 'a fair-sized stone house' in Kettering, though what his occupation was before he ventured into the wholesale manufacture of footwear is not clear. What drew him into the business were the opportunities offered by government contracts for footwear for the armed forces, in Gotch's case the navy, arising out of the frequent wars waged by the British state at that time. It was this development which spread out the production of footwear from its original location in Northampton to Wellingborough, Kettering and the other towns and villages where it eventually became the staple trade. The massive and prolonged wars against the French between that time and 1815 continued to expand the requirements of the government and opportunities for the firm of Gotch to flourish. In order to bring in new capital Gotch took James Cobb, a local ironmonger, into parnership in 1786. Soon after the war against Revolutionary France began, Thomas Gotch purchased Chesham House and converted adjoining barns into a 'factory' and warehouses. He took his son, John Cooper Gotch, into the partnership and the three of them became proprietors of the Kettering Bank as well as the footwear business. With their enlarged financial resources, the firm opened a tannery near Chesham House to integrate the manufacture of leather with the supervised production of boots, the making of which was put out to workers in Kettering and district, who made the boots in their own homes. As manufacturers, bankers, leading Baptists and political liberals through four generations, the Gotch family played a major role in the history of the town. However, they stood alone as footwear manufacturers, unchallenged by any competitors until as late as the 1850s. Indeed, it was only the shock of their bankruptcy (from which they recovered) that caused others to set up in the business, which in turn led to footwear manufacturing becoming the staple trade of Kettering. But that was some time in the future. For contemporaries in the late 18th and the early 19th centuries, Kettering's main industry was textiles.

Local Government in the 18th century

Not being a borough, Kettering was governed by the same institutions as a village. In this there were three separate but complementary elements: the

manorial court, the parish vestry and the Justices of the Peace. As we have
seen, the twice-yearly court of the lords of the manor was chiefly concerned
with the maintenance and regulation of copyhold tenure, 'encroachments
on the lords' waste' and the management of the open-field system. There
was also the matter of the regulation of the market. To enforce the customs
and regulations a number of officers were appointed by the court: two
constables, two headboroughs (deputy constables), two flesh searchers,
two leather searchers, two chimney searchers (to try to prevent fires), two
ale tasters and two bread and butter weighers. Specifically to oversee the
working of the open fields were the fieldman, neatherds to keep the common
herd of beasts (or neats) grazing only where allowed, shepherds to do the
same for their common flock, and there was the pindar who locked up stray
animals in the pound until owners redeemed them by paying a fine.

The manorial court had no powers to levy taxes and most of these
manorial officials were unpaid (though neatherds and shepherds were paid
by the farmers, and the fieldman had the income from the letting of certain
town lands in the open fields). The court's income came from its power to
fine and the profits went to the lords of the manor. However, because they
had to pay a lawyer to act as their steward and rent a room in one of the
inns to hold the court, income was modest. To the lords of the manor the
most valuable part was the market tolls.

Until the middle of the 19th century the main organ of Kettering's local
government was the parish vestry, the meeting of the town ratepayers.
Because it had the power to raise money through the parish rate, and because
all (paid-up) ratepayers were eligible to attend meetings, the vestry was a
more representative and dynamic body than the manorial court. The parish
officers appointed by and responsible to the vestry were the churchwardens,
the constables, the overseers of the highways and the overseers of the poor.
The main sources of the churchwardens' income were from the letting of
the church headlands (small parcels of land in the open fields), fees for
burials in church, and church-rate when repairs to the church were needed.
In the 18th century all parishioners paid church-rate, with the exception of
the Quakers, who refused for conscience sake. It was not until the 1830s
that they were joined by other Dissenters, who by that time were becoming
more aggressive towards the Church. The churchwardens were also
responsible for the costs of services in the church (communion wine, the
church plate and so on), cleaning the church, maintaining the bells and
paying the bellmen and maintaining the equipment for fire-fighting – leather
buckets, long ladders and 'fire draggs', which were kept in the church. The
fire engine was kept in an Engine House on Bakehouse Hill. Churchwardens
were also required to attend the visitations of the archdeacon, pay for the
ringing of the bells on public occasions, which in 1761 consisted of ringing
for the King's birthday, the occasion when 'Prince Ferdinand defeated the
French in Germany', the Prince of Wales' birthday, the coronation of George
III, the taking of Havana in the Seven Years' War, the King's accession, and

on 'Ringing King William' (commemorating the accession of William III) on 4 November and 'Powder Plot' the following day.

Churchwardens had a variety of other responsibilities. They paid head money on birds and animals considered at that time to be agricultural pests. Sparrow heads were worth two pence a dozen. A shilling was paid for fox heads. Hedgehogs, or 'urchins', were worth four pence, and polecats, or 'fulmers', not uncommon in the early 18th century, carried the same tariff. Although the overseers of the poor were responsible for relieving the parish poor, churchwardens were responsible for people passing through. In 1671 'a gentleman that came out of the woods in great distress' was given ten pence, and a poor woman with a 'letter of request' received six pence. The collection of church 'briefs' was also another of the churchwardens' duties. A brief was a royal mandate for a collection towards some worthy cause sent to clergy and churchwardens and read from the pulpit. At the close of service the clerk took the collection and at some later date the funds raised were handed over to a travelling collector. Commonest among briefs were appeals for help with fire damage, few towns escaping that particular danger, as we have seen in the case of Kettering.

The two parish constables responsible for law and order (and certain other matters) were not the same as modern policemen. Like the other parish officers they were ordinary ratepayers nominated to serve, unpaid, for a year. They had the right to refuse and pay a fine, but could be, and were, nominated again another time. In practice, most of the ratepayers of substance served the main parish offices. Their expenses were paid and their accounts were scrutinised by the vestry and had to be approved by the magistrates. Constables were responsible for the apprehension and secure keeping of prisoners and their delivery before the magistrates, or to gaol.

They had other duties. They collected the county rate and other taxes and delivered the monies to the head constable of the Hundred when ordered to do so. The records have a few (though not many) references to the constables overseeing the bellmen and the watch, and they were responsible for the 'home guard', the men of the trained band in the 17th, and the Militia in the 18th centuries. In 1757 the raising of the latter was made a parish responsibility. All men between the ages of 18 and 40 were liable to serve, and the constables were periodically required to draw up lists.

Another parish officer was the overseer of the highways, sometimes referred to as the 'waywarden' or 'way overseer'. His duty was to supervise 'statute labour' on the parish roads. As we have seen, from the mid-century, responsibility for main roads passed to Turnpike Trusts, but minor roads remained under the overseers of the highways until the middle of the next century.

From Tudor times the biggest item of expenditure in local government was the relief of the parish poor. Those responsible for this were the overseers of the poor, and their duties were perhaps the most onerous of all parish offices. Overseers probably originated as collectors of parochial alms

COUNTY of NORTHAMPTON.
Division of Kettering.

THE ASSIZE of BREAD, to be made of Wheat, set the 12th Day of June, 1820, by us, Two of His Majesty's Justices of the Peace in and for the said County, acting for the said Division, to take Place on Monday the 19th Day of June instant, and to be in force fourteen Days.

Description of Loaf.	Avoirdu-pois Weight.	To be sold for	
		Wheat-en.	House-hold.
	lb. oz. dr.	s. d	s. d.
The Peck Loaf	17 6 0	3 4	3 0
The Half-peck Ditto	8 11 0	1 8	1 6
The Quartern Loaf	4 5 8	0 10	0 9
The Half-quartern Ditto	2 2 12	0 5	0 $4\frac{1}{2}$

W. V. ROBINSON,
J. HOGG.

29　*Notice in the* Northampton Mercury *about the Assize of Bread with prices fixed by the magistrates for two weeks, June 1820.*

and supervisors of the 'rogues and vagabonds' (the unemployed and itinerants). Under the laws passed in 1597 and 1601 (the famous 'Forty third of Elizabeth') the parish was made totally responsible for the relief and management of their own poor, and the raising and payment of the money needed to do so. Few records survive for before 1712, but the re-markable series of account and minute books which commence in that year provide a clear picture of the poor of Kettering and their relief in the 18th century. Until the 1760s the expenditure on the poor was remarkably steady. From then on it began to increase. The trade directory of 1791, quoted above, notes ominously 'the parish rate is about ten shillings in the pound. The workhouse has generally one hundred and fifty or more in it; and many poor persons are relieved out of the house'. Worse was soon to come.

Perhaps one reason for the stable nature of poor relief in the first two-thirds of the century was the employment offered by woolcombing and worsted weaving. The principal recipients of parish relief were the vulnerable, old people (mainly widows), orphans and the sick. Other factors could also throw people 'on the parish'. Poverty always increased in winter, particularly in times of exceptionally very bad weather around Christmas and the New Year, as in 1739-40, February 1766 and in 1776-7 when the cold was so intense that the Thames froze. Another cause was a rise in the cost of bread, the staple food of the people. This was usually the result of poor harvests forcing up the price of grain and flour. The poor were prepared to put up with a lot, but not with the dear bread, which they roundly blamed on profiteering by farmers, millers and bakers. In the 18th century there was little use informing the hungry poor that it was all because of supply and demand: in times of dearth they rioted. Bread and flour were seized and distributed or sold by the rioters at the old prices.

30 *Old Workhouse Lane, drawn by Hugh Wallis for Bull's* History of Kettering.

At the time of the Kettering fire of November 1766 it was noted in the *Annual Register*:

> The damage amounts to upwards of £4000. Much grain and corn were burnt, which the Farmers had been backward in selling; & the poor, who are indeed half starved, & very wretched through the high provisions, would not assist to extinguish the flames, but rather stood rejoicing at the farmers' misfortunes, & tauntingly asked one of them, while his wheat hovels and barns full of grain were burning 'Will you take seven shillings a strike (bushel) now for your wheat?'

Such events alarmed those in authority. Yet, though riot was feared (and punished) by the government, there was also a conviction that 'provision' needed to be expedited by those in authority. Under a law passed in the first year of the reign of George I, magistrates had the power to execute the Assize of Bread. In August 1757 the Justices, acting on information made by the constables of Kettering, handed out stiff fines for every ounce deficient in the weight of their bread to six bakers from the district, and ordered the constables to search the market for loaves deficient in weight.

Their decisions were printed in the *Northampton Mercury*. Some 'Scores of Loaves' were brought in, which were condemned and 'given to the Poor of Kettering'. Moreover, under the Assize of Bread, magistrates had the power to fix the price of bread for the next 14 days and have their decisions printed in the newspapers. The Assize of Bread remained in force into the first two decades of the next century, but fell victim to government thinking influenced more by the new 'science' of economics than fear of bread riots. Nineteenth-century governments were more sympathetic to business and trade than to the poor.

Another matter which concerned the overseers of the poor in the Georgian era was outbreaks of the smallpox, which, as well as causing the same sort of fear and panic that the plague had done down to the later years of the 17th century, affected the general economy of the town. In 1730 an outbreak led to the almost total desertion of the market, and the outbreaks in 1752, 1778, and 1782 resulted in considerable sums having to be paid to doctors and apothecaries for inoculation. Paying the medical bills of the poor was part of the remit of the overseers.

For the relief (and control) of the able-bodied poor, as early as 1718 the vestry spent £180 on a house, a malting and two tenements and equipped them as a workhouse (which gave its name to Workhouse Lane), anticipating the Act of 1722 authorising such developments. This empowered parish authorities to adopt a private/public partnership initiative solution, and contract out the running of the workhouse and relief of the poor, rather than face doing this for themselves. Sometimes the scale of distress became so large and obvious that help arrived from outside, as in the 1782 smallpox crisis, when the Duke of Montagu and several other local gentlemen made a generous charitable contribution to relief funds. Eighteenth-century Kettering, in common with most other places, had its own charities for the relief of several kinds of poor, though none of them was on a large scale.

As we have seen, the Justices of the Peace were an integral part of the local government of Kettering, yet, once the Sawyers had departed, none was drawn from within the town. Had Kettering been a borough it would have had its own magistrates, but the men who sat on the Kettering bench were invariably local gentry or clergy from neighbouring parishes. Whether this bothered Kettering in the 18th century seems unlikely. Their main function, then as now, was to dispense justice in matters of petty crime. Governing Kettering, and indeed living in Kettering, in the 18th century had its problems, as we have seen. They were, however, to be much increased by new ones which came along in the 1790s.

Eight

KETTERING IN CRISIS

The Collapse of the Cloth Industry

In the parish records of Kettering there is a large collection of trade indentures which record the apprenticing of almost 500 poor boys (and some girls) to give them a start in life. An analysis of the trades to which they were put between 1690 and the end of the 18th century reveals that 60 per cent of them went into woolcombing and weaving, the majority with masters within the town. After 1791, the number apprenticed to these trades falls away markedly. The collapse of the woollen industry came with dramatic swiftness. It reduced the workers and their families to poverty and the parish authorities to distraction in their efforts to relieve the poor. Kettering's economic crisis was prolonged. It was not until the later 1850s that things began to improve.

Writing in 1794, Donaldson noted that, since the beginning of the war a year or so previously, employment had declined by more than a half. More than half a century later John James observed: 'In casting the eye backward, and reviewing the condition of the worsted manufacture during the last fifty years one is forcibly struck with its rapid development in the West Riding … Yorkshire, especially Halifax, Bradford and Wakefield, have drawn from Devonshire, Warwickshire, Northamptonshire and Norwich a considerable portion of their manufactures: serges from the west of England; shalloons from Kettering; camblets and many other articles from Norwich.' Yorkshire was able to do this by using new technology, producing more cloth cheaply and in greater quantities than their southern rivals.

In a report on the State of the Poor in Kettering in 1795, the writer paints a graphic picture of conditions in the town. He notes that since the start of the war business has considerably declined: 'for 1s. work a spinner is now only paid 8d. A man who could earn in the woollen business 14s. a week three years ago, cannot now get more than 7s.' Prophetically, he notes that 'The poor in this town are very numerous: the rates very high, and expected to increase'. Which they did. About 100 men, women and children were maintained in the workhouse, and a further 145 families received relief at home. In addition, 64 militia men's wives received weekly allowances from the parish. About 400 men from Kettering had entered the militia 'and nearly as many have enlisted in the Army'.

From local and government sources it is possible to produce figures showing the way the poor rates grew inexorably in the later 18th and early 19th centuries.

Yearly average cost of poor rate in Kettering, 1712 to 1834

1712-26	£307
1748-53	£452
1775-84	£1,244
1785-94	£1,298
1792-1800	£2,000
1801-12	£3,160
1813-22	£4,873
1823-34	£4,253

The war years saw appalling privation, with economic dislocation and high taxation, great increases in the price of bread caused by bad harvests in 1795 and 1812, and the terrible winter of early 1814, the worst weather 'known in the memory of man'. Between 1813 and 1815 country banks in Stamford, Oundle, Market Harborough and Northampton collapsed under the strain of the times.

In the wars Kettering proved as patriotic as the next place. As already noted, Kettering men served in the regular army and the militia, and a troop of volunteers was raised locally. This volunteer Home Guard was commanded by John Cooper Gotch, the banker and boot manufacturer. A Kettering troop of Yeomanry cavalry was also formed in 1794, drawn from the ranks of the tenant farmers and their sons in the surrounding district. Commanded by Captain the Hon. George Watson, in January 1808 they presented him with an elegant silver vase 'appropriately ornamented, of antique shape, and capable of holding one gallon'. In July the Volunteers presented J.C. Gotch with a ceremonial sword as a token of their esteem. The two events were surely not unrelated. When it came to rituals, Kettering's shopocracy was not about to be outdone by County tenantry. As for Kettering plebs, they served in the Militia, the only element in these home forces to be, as soldiers, other than largely ornamental. Kettering men were numbered among the 1,400 Northamptonshire and Rutland Militia who spent 11 years away from home as garrison troops in Ireland (twice), Plymouth, Dover and Deal, Portsmouth and Norman Cross prisoner-of-war camp. The end of the war saw them in Edinburgh Castle, whence they returned to be disembodied in July 1814. The Volunteers were also disembodied at the end of the war, but the Yeomanry were not. Interestingly, when all the other troops of Yeomanry in Northamptonshire were stood down, the Kettering troop were not. Presumably Radical Kettering made the government, or maybe the local justices and landowners, nervous. Becoming the Royal Kettering Yeomanry in 1844, the troop survived. Every year they had six days' cavalry training in Boughton Park, and the Duke never neglected to send them a buck for their dinner.

The war ended in June 1814. A surviving handbill shows how it was celebrated in Kettering – with an open-air feast on the market place, in which proceedings were organised with military precision. In the event, celebration was premature. Napoleon made his escape from Elba in February 1815, returned to France and raised another army. As every English schoolboy used to know, he was finally defeated on the battlefield of Waterloo and deported to remote St Helena, from which there was no escape.

The ending of the wars brought relief, but not prosperity. Quite the reverse: it was followed by an increase in the privations of the poor, nationally and locally. Demands on the ratepayers peaked in the appalling depression of 1818-22, which hit agriculture as hard as industry, now shorn of government contracts. Thousands of ex-soldiers and sailors, some crippled, many with wives and families, wandered the land, seeking relief from parish officers as they passed through. After 1822 poor rates remained at war-time levels for the rest of the decade, and rose again in the depression of the early 1830s. These were very agitated times. Demands for political reform were suppressed by Tory governments until late in the 1820s.

31 *John Cooper Gotch (1772-1852), wholesale footwear manufacturer, banker, Baptist and political liberal, Kettering's leading figure in the first half of the 19th century.*

In Kettering, life was dominated by the plight of the poor and of the sometimes despairing efforts made by the local authorities to relieve them. The story is told in *Kettering Vestry Minutes A.D. 1797-1853*, published by the Northamptonshire Record Society in 1933. In the immediate aftermath of the war, from a third to a half of Kettering was on relief. The cost fell on very few people, and, as the burden went up, the number of ratepayers able to pay declined. In 1800, 265 people paid; in 1817, 196; by 1830 the list had fallen to 179. Not only did ratepayers have to pay for the poor, they had to levy the rates on themselves and administer the relief as well.

The Vestry minutes show the range of methods employed. The parish paid weekly allowances, as it always had, to poor widows, orphans, the old and impotent. The workhouse existed for the friendless, homeless and helpless. In 1790 it was able to hold 200, but was expensive to run and it was hard to check irregularities in its administration. Between 1793 and

KETTERING FESTIVAL

FOR CELEBRATING THE

PEACE,

WEDNESDAY, JUNE 22, 1814.

REGULATIONS & SIGNALS.

Regulations.

1. That a Dinner be provided, consisting of Beef, Plum Pudding, and Ale.
2. That the Tables be placed in the Market Place.
3. That a President be appointed.
4. That the Dinner be set on the Table at One o'Clock precisely.
5. That every Person appear clean and neat; and bring a Plate, Knife and Fork, and Half-pint Mug; and conduct themselves in Good Order.

Signals.

The 1st Bugle to sound at Twelve o'Clock, for assembling at the respective Stations, according to the Directions on the Tickets.

The 2d Bugle to sound a Quarter before One, for the Carvers to take their Stations, and for the different Parties to advance to their Tables.

The 3d Bugle to sound for placing the Dinners on the Tables.

The 4th Bugle to sound for all Persons to rise uncovered, for Grace before Dinner.

The 5th Bugle to sound for Grace after Dinner—all uncovered as before.

Toasts.

Each Toast will be announced by Sounding a Bugle.

1st Toast. Our good old King.—With *God save the King*, in Full Chorus, uncovered.
2d———— The Prince Regent.—With *Rule Britannia*, in Full Chorus.
3d———— The Queen and Royal Family.
4th———— The Allied Sovereigns.
5th———— The Duke of Wellington.
6th———— Blucher, Platoff, &c.
7th———— May Peace produce Plenty, and Plenty Gratitude.
8th———— Prosperity and Unanimity to the Town of Kettering.

The Remains of the Dinner will be distributed the next Day, by a Special Committee; but no Portion will be given to any Person who may have been disorderly or intoxicated.

FULLER, PRINTER, KETTERING.

32 *The celebration of Peace in 1814: Beef, Plum pudding, and Ale for all. Done to the sound of bugles. The hope was 'May Peace produce Plenty, and Plenty Gratitude'. Some hopes.*

1800 a series of poor harvests pushed up the price of bread and Kettering had a serious bread riot in 1795. The overseers tried to deal with the situation by purchasing flour in bulk, which they rationed out to the poor at a subsidised price. In 1817 a group of individuals laid in a stock of seed potatoes, and leased some land out to 72 men, the first appearance of allotments. Another device was what we would call unemployment allowances. Before 1793, a usual method of assisting those temporarily seeking help was to pay their rent and this continued when the really bad times came along. There was also the practice of topping-up low wages, sometimes called the Speenhamland system, which was applied widely in the 1790s.

With unemployed weavers forming a substantial part of the poor, the Vestry and overseers tried various 'make-work' schemes. In 1802 they ordered a stock of yarn and borrowed £700 to finance the weaving of tammies, but the initiative made a big loss. They tried again in 1805, with the same result. In 1817 the Vestry went in for the manufacture of linen and carried this on for some years, finding buyers for their 'Kettering Strong Linens'. But as a business it never managed to break even and they gave it up in 1824. The Vestry also went in for public works and occasionally set the unemployed to work on street sweeping or filling holes in the roads. The 'round system' was also used, whereby the unemployed were sent in rotation to ratepayers who had to find work for them, their wages being paid wholly or in part from the poor rates.

In the years after the Napoleonic Wars the plight of Kettering was not unique. Nationally, both industrial districts and rural areas suffered in what was one of the three worst depressions in the whole 19th century. But because of the early collapse of its staple trade Kettering suffered worse than most places, certainly in Northamptonshire. The minutes of the Vestry, as well as illustrating the scale of poverty and the work relieving it, also record the patience and desire to be just to the poor on the part of the Kettering parish officers. At some points they were at their wits' end and addressed petitions for help to the justices of the peace and the House of Commons. Occasionally, there were charitable efforts to help, such as when, in 1823, Lord Sondes had 2,800 yards of cloth distributed amongst 560 Kettering families at his own expense.

However, the national experience of the effects of the wars and the post-war depressions eventually led to the Whig Poor Law Amendment Act in 1834. This brought the workhouse system into being. Parishes were grouped into Unions, relief was taken out of the hands of parish officers and given to elected boards of poor law guardians, workhouses were built in a central place in each union, and relief made harder to obtain. A new era began. In 1838 the Kettering workhouse (now St Mary's Hospital) was opened to receive the poor of the 30 parishes in the Union. But if parish overseers no longer had to relieve the poor, passing them on to the relieving officer employed by the guardians, they still had to levy and collect the parish poor rates.

By the later 1820s, linen manufacture had gone, and the weaving of tammies and serges was all but dead. In 1826, Smith records one worsted manufacturer in the person of Robert Waddington, but he must have been the last. There was one final, long-remembered Bishop Blaise procession in 1829, organised by Mr J.M. Cole of Rothwell. The first since 1788, it was a ritual farewell to the old staple trade of the district. From about 1811 worsteds were replaced in Kettering, Rothwell and Desborough by the silk industry. A number of firms, with connections in the silk centres of Coventry and Spitalfields in London, set up in Kettering. The earliest was that of Samuel Gibbon, who had a small factory in Silver Street in 1826. A firm of Gibbon,

33   *Kettering Union workhouse, opened in 1838.*

Muddiman & Henwell, ribbon manufacturers, occurs in 1841. Another silk
enterprise was that of a Mr Bury in Pasture Lane in 1830. The main firms,
however, were those of Taylor, Walters and Riley. Francis Taylor is mentioned
as a silk manufacturer in 1841, though how long he lasted is not certain.
Stephen Walters (possibly of Sudbury in Suffolk) was in Kettering from
about 1837. He occupied a factory in School Lane, said to have been built
by Gibbon. Later, he had one in Horsemarket, where, by 1860, he was
employing 190 hands. Their work won a prize at the Great Exhibition of
1851. Walters was still there in 1869, but gone by 1870. Benjamin Riley,
said in 1855 to be 'of London', a manufacturer of velvets and silk plush, was
the largest of the local manufacturers, with factories in Rothwell and
Desborough as well as the one in Newland, where he employed about 300
workers. Riley gave up in Kettering in 1855, but carried on in Rothwell and
Desborough. Four other later ventures are mentioned. Elisha Loasby occurs
as a silk weaver of Swan Street in 1850, Arthur Wright started in 1858, when
he built a small factory in Market Street to house 40 looms. Thomas Kemp
& Sons were in Market Street in 1860 and 1864, but were gone by 1869.
A Thomas Brooks was in Market Street that year.

Silk is another of Kettering's forgotten industries. Always vulnerable to economic fluctuations, foreign imports and changes in fashions, it lasted for about half a century in Kettering and district. What brought about its demise was a Free Trade treaty with France in 1860, which led to cheaper French silk products flooding the home market. Silk was in a bad way all through that decade and was extinct locally by 1870. Luckily, by then footwear was taking off in Kettering under the stimulus of one of the greatest booms of the 19th century.

Although Gotch did well in the wars, there was a falling-off in government contracts for footwear after 1815. Kettering did not benefit in the transfer of London business out to Northampton and Stafford. It was not until the 1850s that the trade received its next stimuli, in the form of the Australian Gold Rush and the Crimean War, both of which generated huge demands for boots. Until then, the Gotches used the bank and the footwear firm to support each other, a strategy which in due course was to backfire, as we shall see. They got a fright late in 1825, when there was a run on the banks, and nearly went under. As for the footwear side, in retrospect it seems surprising that for around seventy years the Gotches faced so little competition. Their only rivals seem to have been William Dorr and his father. It may be doubted if they put up much of a challenge: the Gotches enjoyed a virtual monopoly. The essential point about footwear and silk-weaving in the first half of the 19th century is that, taken separately or together, they could not compensate Kettering for the loss of worsted.

The Enclosure of Kettering, 1804-5

In these years there were other developments on the economic front. In 1802 moves to replan the landscape and farming by the complete enclosure of the open fields began. This required a local Act of Parliament for every parish. The reporter on the State of the Poor in Kettering in 1795 observed, 'The people of the town seem averse to enclosures, which they think will raise the price of provisions, from these lands being all turned to pasture when enclosed'. Whatever the people thought, enclosure was entirely a matter for property owners. It took place for three reasons: to increase the value of land; to reorganise land holdings in order to create compact farms and thereby make farming more efficient (and raise the value of land); and to extinguish the system of tithe payments.With regard to the second point, the Bill was worded in the standard way, declaring that 'the several lands lie intermixed and are inconveniently situated, and are, in their present state, incapable of any considerable improvement; … it would be advantagous … if the same were divided and inclosed'. The third reason had little to do with the other two. Parliamentary enclosure was used to get rid of the age-old resentments associated with having to pay tithe to the Church of England (or to other possessors of tithe rights). With the object of establishing good feelings between farmers and the Church, enclosure was to prove a huge bonus for the clergy, especially the rector of Kettering.

Enclosure could not proceed unless the owners of two-thirds of the land gave assent. This was achieved at a series of meetings which started in the summer of 1802. In November the following year a Bill for enclosure was presented to Parliament. It was signed by the joint lords and lady of the manor (Lord Sondes, who had three-fifths, and the Duke and Duchess of Buccleuch, with two-fifths), the rector, Joseph Knight, 45 proprietors of land, and the trustees of the Church and Town Land, the Poor's Estates and the Free Grammar School. The Bill duly passed through the parliamentary process and became law in 1804.

Once an Act had been obtained, commissioners named in the Act had the task of collecting all the claims of those who who had property and common rights, and re-allocating land so that the new holdings should no longer be scattered in the open fields, but brought together in blocks, in order to create, as far as possible, ring-fence farms. Farmers could now cultivate the land 'in several' (*i.e.* individually) and never have to see their land become 'common' after harvest, as in the past. The process was designed to make land and farming more profitable, but, in order to achieve this, capital was needed to pay the heavy costs of an Act of Parliament and all the expenses of surveying, the construction of new roads and the planting of scores of miles of hawthorn saplings, which would grow into the hedges by which the fields would be divided, one from another. On top of this, the larger land proprietors would have to build new farms to be located in their ring fences away from the town, though (because of the sheer cost) this did not always happen: after many enclosures old farms in the town continued to be used. The payback was that land values, on average, doubled.

In all 2,262 acres were enclosed, 82 per cent of the land, the remainder being 402 acres of old enclosures excluded from the process. The details of who got what are as follows:

Details of the Kettering Enclosure Award 1805, in acres, rods and perches

The Rector, in lieu of his Tythes etc.	364	3	35
The Rector, in lieu of his Glebe	80	1	12
Duke & Duchess of Buccleuch	257	1	33
Grammmar School Trustees	32	1	12
Church & Town Estate	16	3	37
Lord Sondes	12	0	15
Kettering Poor (the trustees of)		9	1
75 others (plus 58.5 acres for roads etc.)	1487	1	4
Stone pits		3	28
	2261	2	3

The most noticeable feature was the size of the estate which passed into the hands of the rector. In 1802 the scandalous leases made by Burton to the Watsons in the 16th century finally fell in. The rector was now able to recover the great tithes, which had the immediate effect of raising his income from £30 to £120 a year. Reasons as to why moves to enclose were started in that year, and not earlier, suggest themselves. With the end of the last lease a complicated obstacle to enclosure was gone, and it seems likely that the legal representatives of the lords of the manor and rector got together to initiate the enclosure process. To compensate for the loss of his newly regained tithes, the rector was awarded a generous land settlement in lieu, together with a further award for glebe land the church formerly held in the fields of Kettering. Now, with an estate of 444 acres, the rector was the second largest landowner. Moreover, under the standard arrangements in parliamentary Enclosure Acts, he alone of all the proprietors was exempted from any payments towards the costs: his expenses were paid by all the others.

By 1830, according to figures he gave to the Royal Commission on Ecclesiastical Revenues of England and Wales, the average net income of the rector of Kettering had risen to a healthy £786, one of the highest in the diocese. Naturally, the Watson family, who had the right of presentation, wanted it for one of their own, but, as no one was yet of age, when the Rev. Joseph Knight died in 1814, Lord Sondes presented the living to the Rev. Brice William Fletcher, on the agreement that he would vacate it when a suitable Watson came along. Fletcher, however, enjoyed the rectory of Kettering so much, that, when the time came for the agreement to be activated, was ungentlemanly enough to refuse to resign. It took quite an effort to get him out, as we have seen.

The Duke and Duchess of Buccleuch were the next most substantial beneficiaries. However, as they were also possessed of upwards of 200 acres of land of old enclosures, the former Sawyer estate, they were slightly larger landowners than the rector, though not by much. The other lord of the manor, Lord Sondes, being a minor proprietor of land, received only a small allotment. However, he possessed the market tolls and the right of advowson. After enclosure, the ancient manorial court was shorn of its role of regulating the working of the common fields, farming now being a private enterprise rather than a manorial matter. However, the court continued to have an important part in the economic life of Kettering because tenure remained copyhold and all changes in ownership were subject to confirmation in the court and the payment of entry fines.

The remaining land enclosed was apportioned among 78 other claimants, ranging from individuals such as Thomas Gotch and George Wallis, with just over 100 acres each, down to others with quite modest holdings, the smallest of which were John Yarrall with 33 perches, and the Quaker Meeting with a single perch. In the list are a few corporate bodies, such as the Trustees of the Grammar School, the rents from whose property funded the School, and the Church and Town Estate, lands left for charitable purposes. Interestingly (given that most enclosure Acts before that time had ignored the interests of the poor) submission for compensation for the poor, who would lose old customary rights to gather brakes, furze and ling for fuel on the Links, was successfully made on their behalf by Thomas Gotch. The Poor received a nine-and-a-half-acre plot, from which rent was received and

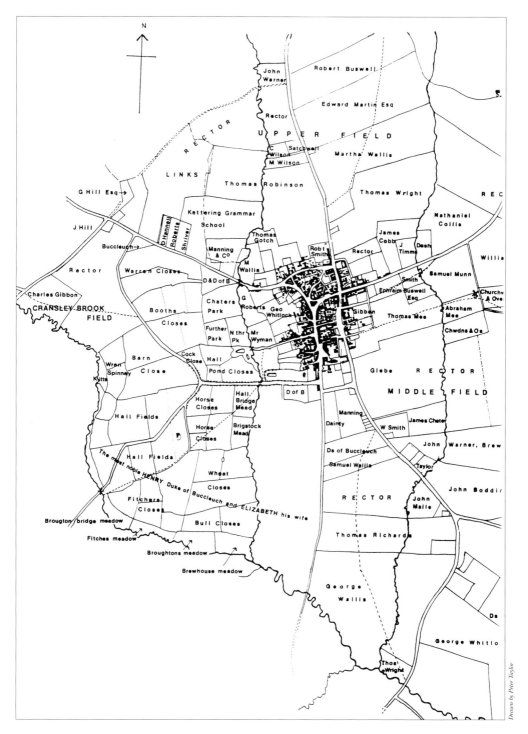

34 *Map of Kettering after enclosure. The open-field landscape had been replaced by the straight-hedged fields of the modern Midland landscape.*

distributed amongst them. How the people of the town reacted to enclosure is not known. There is no record of opposition or protest. Maybe the Poor's allotment helped to defuse misgivings. More likely it was because pretty well everybody, from the comfortable to the poor, had other things to worry about in 1805.

Wayfaring 1790 to 1850

By 1790 a series of changes in road transport had ushered in the golden age of stage coach transport. With the rise of manufacturing in the Midlands and North the national economy was growing rapidly; transferring the royal mail to stage coaches (instead of being carried by mounted post boys) set new standards of speed and punctuality; and improvements to road building and coach design all combined to make the British system of road transport the most advanced of its era.

In the early years of the new mail coach service, Kettering letters were taken three days a week to Northampton (via Wellingborough) and transferred to the mail coach for London. A return service was also in operation. By the beginning of the 19th century Kettering was on the direct London to Leeds route, and mail coaches made a daily stop to change horses at the *George* and to deliver and collect the mail. Occasionally, but not often, the Royal Mail was robbed. One local instance was on 26 October 1812. After changing horses and collecting letters the Leeds Mail left Kettering at 5.40p.m. for London. At 7.10p.m., it stopped at the *Green Dragon* in Higham Ferrers for the next change of horses. There the mail box was found to be empty, its lock broken. Between Burton Latimer and Higham the guard had left his seat to sit with the driver, which was strictly forbidden. It was assumed that this was when the robbery occurred. Officers were sent from Bow Street to investigate and in due course two men were arrested, tried and found guilty. They were hanged for their crime on Northampton racecourse on 13 August 1813.

The efficiency of the mails and the fact that they carried passengers presented stage coach proprietors with serious competition. To survive, they had to become quicker and more strict in their timetabling. Bull tells us that in 1787 'T. Wright's coach performed the journey between London and Kettering in 13 hours'. T. Wright was Thomas Wright, whose family had been long-distance carters since the 1750s and had now gone into coaching. By 1791 Wright was running a thrice-weekly service to London from the *White Hart*, leaving at 5a.m. and arriving in London at 7p.m. There was always a limit to how much could be cut from travelling times, the main way being to give passengers the briefest of stops for meals and refreshment.

The greatest strides in road making were made between 1810 and 1830 as a result of the work of Telford, Macadam and others. Mail coach timetables demonstrate what these improvements meant in terms of speed. The mails left London at 8 o'clock in the evening. In 1811 the Leeds mail arrived in Kettering at 7.25 a.m.; in 1837 it arrived at 3.56 a.m., the

Kettering & Uppingham
COACHES.

W. LEA AND Co.

Beg respectfully to inform the Nobility, Gentry, and Public in general,
that for their better accommodation, during the Summer,

THE KETTERING COACH

Will leave the GEORGE INN on

Monday, Wednesday, & Friday Mornings,

at 7 o'Clock, and arrive in London at half-past 4 ; it will not stop
to Dine on the Road.

☞ A Coach will leave the George and Blue Boar, Holborn, and Cross
Keys, St. John Street, for Kettering, on the same Mornings, at 9.

THE UPPINGHAM COACH

will leave KETTERING on

Tuesday, Thursday, & Saturday Mornings,

at 10 o'Clock, and arrive in London at 8 as before.

☞ A Coach will leave the above Offices in London, for Kettering and
Uppingham, on the same Mornings at 8,

₊ The above Alteration to take place on Monday, May 2d, 1831.

DASH, PRINTER, KETTERING.

35 *Coaching at its peak.
Notice of the Kettering and
Uppingham coaches in 1831.*

average speed thus having been improved from 6.56 to 9.45 miles per
hour in 26 years. By 1831, as the poster shows, Kettering had coaches to
London every day except Sunday. On Monday, Wednesday and Friday, the
Kettering Coach left the *George* at seven in the morning, arriving in the
capital nine-and-a-half hours later, with very tired and hungry passengers,
there having been no stop for food. On alternate days, the Uppingham
coach made a stop in Kettering to pick up passengers at the *George*,
arriving in London at eight in the evening. Each day, coaches left London on the reverse journey. By that time there was also a network of
cross-country stage coaches; the daily coach from Oxford to Lincoln called
at the *George* on its journey both ways.

To facilitate such cross-country journeys, proposals were made in 1818
to build a new turnpike road from Kettering to Northampton, the road
travellers use today. Before this, they had to go via Wellingborough. The
reasons given for the new road were to cut the journey for travellers between
Oxford and Stamford by five miles, to avoid 'the dangerous hilly route'

between Northampton and Wellingborough, and to give the villages in the district between Maidwell, Kettering, Wellingborough and Northampton access to a through route. The users of the existing route to Stamford, which went via Thrapston and Oundle, put up opposition, but Parliament was persuaded to approve the new road, and it opened in 1819. It was an improvement for travellers, but was never very profitable.

From about 1820, coaching became 'big business', and the smaller undertakers, except on cross routes of minor importance, were squeezed out by a handful of major operators. Improved road surfaces, better coach design and intense competition produced crack coaches which travelled long distances at great speeds. One of these was 'Peveril of the Peak', daily from London to Manchester, through St Albans, Luton, Bedford, Kettering, Market Harborough, Derby, Buxton and Stockport, taking 21 hours to do the run. It stopped, briefly, in Kettering both 'up' and 'down'. In 1831, the proprietor announced that the 'Peveril' would extend to Edinburgh, and do this in an unprecedented 44 hours.

The railway era arrived in Northamptonshire with the opening of the London & Birmingham line in 1838. Its effect on road communications was devastating. At its pinnacle, coaching was destroyed almost overnight. The roads of England emptied of long-distance traffic. Wayfaring had benefited Kettering's economy by providing good business for horse-dealers, fodder suppliers, innkeepers and publicans, coach proprietors, smiths and farriers, and leatherworkers such as harness and whip makers. The curtailing of road business was a significant loss to a town in economic difficulties. Moreover, with the cessation of the mails and stage coaches, Kettering's communications were severely disrupted. In 1840 there was a hope that a proposed railway from London to Manchester to rival the London & Birmingham would pass through, but it proved a chimera. A few years later, the *Citizen*, a local journal, declared that Kettering 'resembles in truth one of its celebrated streets called "Pudding-Bag" so-called because there is no way out of it but that by which you get into it'. The only public conveyances the town now had were a coach from Uppingham to Wellingborough station and back, and an omnibus to and from Wellingborough. If a traveller wanted to go to Leicester he had to go to Wellingborough, take the train to Bisworth, then to Rugby, and thence to Leicester. By this circuitous route his journey was more than doubled, took half a day, and could only be done by the most careful perusal of *Bradshawe's Railway Guide*.

Kettering's hopes of having a main line through the town were raised and dashed between 1843 and 1847, with two companies – the 'South Midland' and the 'Leicester & Bedford' – competing to raise the capital and secure the favour of Parliament. The battle was won by the South Midland, which threw in its lot with Hudson, 'the Railway King', and his Midland Railway Company. Acts were secured in 1847 and 1848, but when the Midland's profits and dividends fell sharply in 1849, nothing was done

and the powers lapsed. Kettering's economic future hinged on the coming
of the railway. To everyone's frustration, it would be another eight years
before it was possible to board a main-line train at Kettering or
Wellingborough.

Kettering Politics

In the 19th century politics in Kettering were lively to the point of rancour.
This was not unusual; the politics of many Victorian towns were like this.
However, Kettering's political scene was livelier than most. In the first place,
before the Reform Act of 1832 nearly everyone in the town was excluded
from the vote because the county franchise then belonged exclusively to the
40-shilling freeholders, and there were no more than one or two in Kettering,
where tenure was almost exclusively copyhold. Secondly, there being so
many Dissenters, barred from holding parliamentary and other offices by
the Test and Corporation Acts, there was a powerful disposition in favour
of a thorough reform of the political system. By the mid-1820s, Dissenters
were ready to re-activate the campaign to have their civil disabilities lifted.
Nonconformists were to be the backbone of liberalism, always prepared to
challenge the Church and the party which supported it. Thirdly, being on
a small urban island in a sea of rurality, dominated by Tory landlords, gave
Kettering's Radicals and Dissenters another reason to be ardent for Reform.

Things began to move their way in the later 1820s. Reform began with
the repeal of the Test and Corporation Acts in 1828. Kettering's Whigs and
Dissenters, led by John Cooper Gotch, petitioned for Parliamentary Reform
and played their part in ensuring the election of two Whigs, Lords Althorp
and Milton, for the County in the 'Reform Election' of 1831, a victory
which sent shock-waves through Toryism. When the Reform Act was passed
the following year, Kettering celebrated uninhibitedly. However, these gains
had limits. The Reform Act divided the county into two, doubling rural
representation. Kettering became the place of nomination for elections for
North Northamptonshire, which guaranteed excitement whenever there
was a contested election. Between then and 1872, when open voting was
replaced by the secret ballot, Kettering saw many a struggle for street
supremacy at election times. In general, the supporters of Reform usually
won; rough-housing the Tories became part of nearly every contested
election. On occasions, election day was more than boisterous. The most
violent was a bye-election in 1835, reported by a horrified Charles Dickens
in the *Morning Chronicle*. When Tory supporters rode into Kettering they
were so intent on taking over the proceedings that one of them, an excited
farmer from Bythorn, produced a loaded pistol and might well have
committed murder had he not been restrained by his friends. In fact, that
day things went their way; the Tory, T.P. Maunsell, won. The Whigs did not
have another success in North Northamptonshire until 1880, which was
very frustrating for Kettering's Liberal Dissenters. Their day would come,
but they were to have a long wait.

But what about the 'non-electors', the mass of the population deliberately excluded from the franchise by Whig Reform? Politically literate and incensed by their exclusion, by the suppression of trades unionism (especially the Tolpuddle Martyrs) and by the New Poor Law, it is not surprising to find that some of Kettering's working-class and small-shopkeeper Radicals turned to Chartism. In 1836 a Kettering Radical Association was established. Its first president was a brushmaker called Brownless (or Brownlees), its secretary was John Leatherland, a silk-weaver, and its treasurer was his cousin, the Rev. John Jenkinson. Economic conditions were deteriorating, the years 1838 to 1842 seeing one of the most serious economic depressions of the century. Unemployed silk-weavers and labourers were facing desperate privation, and the opening of a workhouse in Kettering infuriated the poor and their sympathisers. The Radical Association soon claimed a membership of over a hundred.

Chartists held meetings, petitioned sympathetic Members of Parliament and disseminated democratic ideas. Their 'extreme' political rhetoric brought hostility from Tories, and respectable people were shocked when two incendiary fires were started in February 1839: a wheat hovel and a barley rick went up in flames. A reward was offered, but no one was apprehended. In fact, Leatherland knew the perpetrator, but was sworn to secrecy. The Radical Association was rounded on by the curate of Kettering. When one of their meetings passed a motion abhorring the fires but pointed out that these things would tend to happen until the 'just claims of the working classses' were met, the curate acidly inquired what these 'just claims' were. The Chartists replied in a pamphlet, entitled *Our rights; or, the Just Claims of the Working Classes, stated, in a Letter to the Rev. T.H.Madge, Curate of Kettering; By the Kettering Radical Association*. Although the title page carried the names of 'G.T. Green, Brushmaker, Chairman and J.A. Leatherland, Secretary', the author was in fact John Jenkinson, which perhaps explains why the *Letter* had ten, rather than the usual six points of the People's Charter.

The difficulty facing Chartists was how to persuade or force Parliament to agree to these demands. There were some who argued that it could only be done by revolutionary means. This was debated by delegates to the National Convention, which met in London from February 1839. Delegates were unable to agree on the matter, though in the end 'physical force' arguments were rejected. In May, the Chartists presented a monster national petition begging Parliament to enact the People's Charter. It was ignored. The democrats' problem was that it was never possible to make Chartism into a national political movement. It remained localised and fragmented. In 1841, as elsewhere, at least four forms of Chartism were canvassed in Kettering. The main one was the National Charter Association, Feargus O'Connor's attempt to create a National Union of the Working Classes. In November, it was reported that the old Kettering Radical Association had dissolved itself and that its members joined the new body. In March 1841 the Chartist *Northern Star* newspaper reported that 'The spirited women of

Kettering' had got up a petition against the Poor Law, which was signed by 'about 600'. A second initiative of the time was William Lovett's 'New Move', which aimed to promote the People's Charter through a programme of political education, which attracted some support. Yet another approach was that of the Complete Suffrage Union, which argued for an alliance of middle- and working-class Radicals, with some agreed modification of the six points. This received the support of the Rev. William Robinson and other Nonconformist Radicals, such as the Rev. John Jenkinson. There was also a Kettering Chartist Total Abstinence Association, which aimed to persuade Chartists that an essential first step to getting the vote was to become Temperance men. Jenkinson, a recent convert to Teetotalism, was the leading light.

Opposed to Chartism was the Manchester-led Anti-Corn Law League, whose basic argument was that the economic problems of the time would be better dealt with by fiscal changes rather than an extension of the franchise. The League appealed to Nonconformist businessmen and other middle-class Radicals who persuaded themselves that promoting Free Trade was doing God's Work. Prominent locally were John Cooper Gotch and the Rev. William Robinson. In the end, the League triumphed, whilst Chartism, at least in the short-run, failed.

Chartism peaked a second time in May 1842, with the assembling of another Convention in London and the presentation of a second Petition to Parliament for the adoption of the People's Charter, which was again rejected. Chartism revived a third time in 1843. An attempt was made to create a more effective organisation around O'Connor's National Charter Association, which encouraged the formation of county Chartist Councils. In fact, the National Charter Asociation failed and the movement was kept alive by the familiar pattern of visiting lecturers and protest meetings over the ill-treatment of imprisoned Chartists. The next years, 1844, saw the arrest of Thomas Katterns, the Kettering weaver responsible for the arson incidents of 1839. The matter had weighed on his conscience and on that of John Leatherland, sworn to secrecy. Accompanied by Leatherland, Katterns gave himself up and was duly sent for trial. He was given 12 months' hard labour at the Lent Assizes, a lighter sentence than he would have received in 1839, when he would have been very lucky to have avoided transportation.

Chartism peaked one last time in 1848. A gigantic demonstration in London threatened the authorities, but ended tamely with the presentation to Parliament of a third and final Petition for the People's Charter. Once more it was ignored by the legislators. Once again a wave of arrests, trials and prison sentences followed. Thereafter, attempts were made to restart Chartism, but the popular Radical movement, ever more fragmented, went into decline.

Chartism was the politics of the poor, led, in the main, by the self-educated. The most important thing about it was its tenacity and its legacy. The movement had lasted upwards of two decades. After its demise, it was ignored for a generation. But, years later, when Radicalism revived in Kettering, so did memories of Chartism. When strong working-class organisations were formed, they were led by men who had been influenced by Chartists. When 'One of the Trade' wrote to the *Kettering Observer* in 1885, advocating the formation of a branch of the Rivetters and Finishers Union, he said, 'I take my stand under the old Kettering Radical banner of "Justice to All"' and the old banner was taken out and paraded.

Local Government

In the two decades after the Reform Act, local government in Kettering did not necessarily reflect party or religious tensions, though on one contentious issue it did – church-rate. From 1836, wherever Dissenters were thick on the ground, church-rate was resisted. Before the 1830s only Quakers refused to pay. However, as Dissent became stronger, Independents and Baptists also began to refuse. Their tactic was, on certain occasions,

CHURCH RATES!!

NOTICE.

Kettering to Wit. "The Rate-payers are requested to take notice that a Vestry Meeting will be held on Thursday next, the 12th instant, at Two o'Clock in the Afternoon, in the Parish Church, for the purpose of making a Rate or assessment for the Repairs of the Parish Church for the present year, and for such other expences as are by LAW chargeable on the Church Rate.

"Geo. Eldred.)
"W. Hircock.) *Churchwardens.*"

CENSUS 1851!!

NOTICE!!!

Kettering to Wit. The following are the numbers attending Public Worship on the Morning of the 30th of March.

Established Church.	Dissenting Places of Worship.
250	**1003**

The revenue to support the Creed of the above 250, is one eighth of the Net Rental of the whole land of the Parish, amounting to four pounds per head per annum. Not satisfied with this, they persist in demanding of these 1003 dissenters, a tax to aid a Political Establishment, and to perpetuate a system which they conceive to be based on principles of injustice and error.

1003 Dissenters of Kettering! attend the Vestry 10 minutes before Two o'Clock, on Thursday next to vindicate your principles.

T. WADDINGTON, PRINTER, KETTERING.

36 *Handbill calling on Nonconformists to reject an application for a church rate in 1851. The results of the recent Religious Census showing their majority in Kettering clearly got the Dissenters excited. The statistics deserve to be treated with caution.*

dents and Baptists also began to refuse. Their tactic was, on certain occasions, to try to persuade the ratepayers assembled in the Vestry to refuse to sanction a church-rate. Sometimes this was successful, sometimes not. The invariable practice in Kettering was that, after such a contest, the victorious party would parade the town with a band, and play loudest outside the houses of their most prominent opponents. If the Dissenters failed to block the rate, those who refused to pay were summonsed by the magistrates, and, if convicted, faced distraint warrants and the seizure of property. Those distrained enjoyed the bliss of martyrdom and the esteem of friends. On occasions, moderate Dissenters (usually led by J.C. Gotch) would offer the Church party a compromise. If funds were appealed for by *voluntary subscription* instead of by a church-rate they would subscribe, but if a rate was insisted on, they would oppose. Their basic argument was that if Dissenters, Wesleyans and Catholics had to build and repair their chapels out of their own funds (as they had), why should the church have the right to force non-church people to contribute to church repairs? This was a religious liberty argument which would ultimately triumph, but it needed a strong Liberal government to change the law. They had to wait until Gladstone did so in 1868. Thereafter, church-rate battles became the stuff of history.

In 1835 the Whigs brought in an important reform of borough government, but it did not apply to Kettering. Not being a borough before that date, and being too small to petition for a municipal charter after it, Kettering was left to carry on with its essentially rural organs of local government for some time to come. Local government in Kettering was a mixture of what was left of parish government, private enterprise and *ad hoc* boards set up under various Acts of Parliament. As already noted, enclosure had removed many of the powers of the manorial court, and the New Poor Law had largely taken over the parish's responsibilities for poor relief. What was left were such matters as highway maintenance, lighting, watching and paving. In 1834, a Gas Company was founded by local investors and the parish entered into arrangements for the lighting of the town and appointed gas inspectors. In 1839 Kettering came under the County Police Act, but still appointed a parish constable for some time to come.

As well as an antiquated and patched-up local government system, another problem which beset Kettering was its narrow tax base. Not only was Kettering industrially weak, these years, as already noted, saw the country hit by two of the worst depressions in the whole 19th century. The question was, how much exemption were the small ratepayers to have in paying for local government? In 1848, the parish leaders secured the Kettering Small Tenements Rating Act, which ended the exemptions hitherto enjoyed by many small ratepayers. This started a war between Kettering's parish Improvers, who wanted to upgrade local government services in the town, and parish Economisers, small ratepayers who fought tooth and nail to resist increases in local taxation. This had nothing to do with party politics. Indeed, some of the small ratepayer leaders (such as Jenkinson) were Radical Reformers. The same year, reflecting an increasing concern of the times, Parliament passed the first Public Health Act. The parish élite attempted to bring Kettering under the Act but were soundly defeated. It was the first of a series of similar defeats.

By mid-century, the big issue facing Kettering was not so much upgrading local government as whether or not Kettering was going to be able to revive industrially. For this, it seemed obvious that much depended on the coming of the railway. And come it did, in 1857. But not before the town suffered what seemed a devastating blow.

Nine

THE RISE OF INDUSTRIAL KETTERING

The Gotch Bankruptcy

John Cooper Gotch died in 1852. One of Nature's chairmen and hon.treasurers, for most of his adult life he had been Kettering's foremost citizen and served his town well. In addition to his business and religious life there was scarcely any parish or philanthropic activity in which he had not been intimately involved. The businesses passed to his sons, Thomas Henry managing the bank and John Davis the boot and shoe enterprise. Five years later the bank suspended payments and was forced into bankruptcy, and, because the two enterprises were run as a family partnership, the footwear firm was brought down as well as the bank. It was Kettering's shock of the century.

Elsewhere, 1857 was a year of bank crises, but the collapse of the Kettering bank had no connection with these. Its troubles were caused by a series of unsecured loans made to two clients who ultimately defaulted. The first was a farmer and shoe manufacturer of Little Harrowden, but, in the court of bankruptcy, it was the second, the Rev. A. Macpherson of Rothwell, an Anglican clergyman, who took centre stage. Macpherson had raised a series of loans from the bank, without sufficient collateral, on the strength of 'expectations of a legacy' and 'high hopes of a series of patents'. An amateur sanitary engineer, he was in thrall to that quintessential Victorian dream of turning nightsoil into gold, and took out a series of patents with which he hoped to make his fortune. As his debts mounted, Macpherson took up residence in Belgium and addressed a series of stalling letters to the increasingly anxious Gotches. Extracts from them outlining his fanciful projects were read out in court (and reported in the newspapers), causing the judge at one point to declare that the recklessness of Macpherson 'was of so grossly infatuated a character that it seemed like a romance'.

Whether the blame for this misjudgement is to be put down to John Cooper Gotch losing his grip in old age, or his son Thomas finding himself caught up in a process he could not extricate himself from, is hard to say; a combination of the two seems likely. Whatever the cause, the consequences were wide-reaching. About nine hundred creditors were affected. Most who lost their savings were individuals, but Friendly Societies and clubs in

38 *John Davis Gotch (1802-70). The brother of T.H. Gotch, he was in charge of the footwear side of the business at the time of the bankruptcy. Later he and his brother became partners in a new footwear business, which lasted until 1888.*

37 *Thomas Henry Gotch (1804-91), J.C. Gotch's son, who soon found himself in the Bankruptcy Court.*

Kettering and 19 villages around fell victim as well. Immediately after the bankruptcy proceedings, properties belonging to the Gotch family were sold – three farms, the bank premises in the market place, Chesham House in Lower Street, the nearby currier's shop and tanyard, and a range of other properties, including 11 cottages.

The Rise of Industrial Kettering

Severe though the Gotch bankruptcy was, it was not, as it turned out, an unmitigated disaster. Paradoxically, it seems to have had a liberating economic effect on the town. The collapse of the footwear business meant the end of a virtual monopoly and created an opportunity for new men to move into the vacated space. The first to do so was William Hanger, closely followed by Charles East. Important changes in footwear production were coming along at that time. The first was the introduction of the sewing-machine. An American invention for making clothing, a heavier-duty model was applied to the footwear closing process (the stitching together of the pieces of the upper part of a boot), and East is credited with being the person who introduced it into Kettering. Resisted in Northampton and Stafford, East, whose firm was launched in 1854 originally to manufacture machine-closed uppers, bore the brunt of the opposition to it in Kettering, and also reaped

39 *The stay factory of J. T. Stockburn, erected in 1875, Northall Street. It was demolished in 2000.*

the rewards. By 1858 opposition collapsed and the machine was duly introduced. However, no male shoemaker would sit behind a sewing-machine: closing became women's work. The trade came to be supplied by specialist firms of closers producing uppers in workshops and small factories. For the next three decades or so, the sewing-machine remained virtually the only machine in the trade. Makers and finishers carried on in the traditional way, collecting their leather and closed uppers from the 'factory', taking them back home, returning with the finished pairs of shoes at the end of the week. As they said in Kettering, 'the work comes down the street'.

There were other developments in that decade. The Crimean War, the first major conflict since 1815, and the Australian Gold Rush brought in huge orders for footwear. In Leicester, Thomas Crick invented a new way of making heavy work-boots. Instead of sewing the uppers to the welt, inner sole and the sole, sewing was replaced by the driving of rivets through the layers of leather, after which the rivets were flattened. This was a process which could be done with a simple machine, or by hand, and quickened and cheapened production. Rivetting became as widely used as stitching, and the trade got a whole new category of workers.

One perhaps surprising development was the fact that the Gotches were able to re-start as manufacturers (though not as bankers), in 1863. Often bankruptcy broke the morale as well as the reputation of businessmen. It failed to do either to the Gotches. Five years later, they built a factory in Newland Street and soon once more became the largest employers in the town. Quite how they were able to raise the capital to restart so quickly is not entirely clear. It might have been through the trust the Baptist business network had for them. And it seems likely that people were able to distinguish their worth as manufacturers from their shortcomings as bankers. It could also have been because they behaved honourably to their creditors; over the next twenty years they paid their debts in full. It might also have been that the view expressed by their friends – that they had been stampeded by 'an unscrupulous group of their creditors' insisting on bankruptcy proceedings, even though the shoe firm was profitable – was widely accepted in the town. The Gotch concern remained a major player until it ceased trading in 1888. After that, another generation of the family, the sons of Thomas Henry Gotch, was to figure prominently in Kettering's public life.

The introduction of the sewing-machine promoted a revival of textiles, in the form of clothing and stay-making. The first into wholesale production was Robert Wallis and his brother-in-law John Turner Stockburn, who started as drapers. In 1856 they set up as stay and corset manufacturers. Wallis died the following year, but Stockburn built up a prosperous business, opening a purpose-built factory in Northall Street in 1875. An ardent member at Toller chapel and an equally ardent politician, Stockburn became 'the Grand Old Man of North Northamptonshire Liberalism'. If J.C. Gotch was Kettering's foremost citizen in the first half of the 19th century, J.T. Stockburn was surely his counterpart in the second. In that same year of 1856, another Wallis, Frederick, set up a clothing business in the empty silk mill of Walters & Sons in School Lane. Two years later, he took John Linnell as a partner, and the firm of Wallis & Linnell, which was destined to be the longest-lasting of all the firms started in the 1850s, commenced. By 1906, the firm had six outlying factories and employed upwards of a thousand workers. In addition to Stockburn and Wallis & Linnell, in 1862 there were two other early stay-making factories, Messrs Wilmot & Co. and one belonging to a Mr Cocker. The enterprising Wallis clan had yet another business, that of J. and T. Wallis, mustard manufacturers.

The sewing-machine was also responsible for the rise of engineering, the pioneer firm being that of Owen Robinson. Born in Desborough in 1833, at the age of six he started work for a Desborough farmer. After that he worked alternately as farm worker and silkweaver for Riley's. Persuaded when he was 20 to come to Kettering by the minister of Fuller chapel, he began work for Walters & Sons. For a time he tried shoemaking and carpentry, but found his true vocation with machinery, starting as a repairer of clocks. The turning point in his life was when he was asked by Wallis & Linnell to repair some of their sewing-machines. Robinson built up his

40   *The clothing factory of Wallis & Linnell, one of the earliest enterprises in industrial Kettering, started in 1856 in the old silk mill of Walters. It was also one of the longest-lasting of Kettering's firms, going out of business in 1975.*

own machine-making business, graduating from a small factory in 1872 to a larger works in Victoria Street. Later, he branched out into the manufacture of printing machinery. Robinson was also a public figure, committed to Nonconformity, Liberal politics and Temperance. By 1870 there were three more engineering firms in the town.

Two other factors played a part in the rise of industrial Kettering, the enfranchising of copyhold tenure and the coming of the railway. In the Early Victorian period most business people would probably have agreed that one of the things that held the town back was that property was almost entirely copyhold. Whatever the advantages of that form of tenure in the past, in the 19th century it was its drawbacks which were felt. In 1834 there was an effort to persuade the joint lords of the manor to agree to a system of enfranchising copyhold, that is, upon payment of suitable fees, turning

NOTICE

It is decided that there shall be

A PUBLIC DINNER,

On Thursday next, the 14th instant,
AT FIVE O'CLOCK,
AT

THE ROYAL HOTEL,

TO CELEBRATE
THE

OPENING OF THE RAILWAY.

All Gentlemen who wish to participate in the festivity, will be kind enough to send in their names to the ROYAL HOTEL, not later than Monday Night.

ROYAL HOTEL, KETTERING, MAY 9th, 1857.

TOLLER, PRINTER, KETTERING.

41   *Handbill celebrating the opening of the railway – at long last.*

them into freehold. It failed. However, in 1852, the Copyhold Act was passed. It was applied to Kettering chiefly through the work of the solicitor, William Garrard, who was to act for many of the developers of the building estates which came on to the market when the town's expansion began. However, copyhold was not finally abolished as a form of tenure until the 1920s.

Undoubtedly the greatest stimulus to the turn-around of the economic prospects of Kettering was the opening of the railway, which took place in 1857. The project for a line from Leicester to Hitchin had been revived five years earlier, when a deputation of businessmen and property owners approached the Midland Railway Company. The Company itself had a powerful interest in seeing the line built. In 1852 its track stopped at Rugby and thence a third of a million tons of Midland coal was carried to London by a rival concern. An added incentive was the re-discovery of ironstone deposits in Northamptonshire and the re-birth of ironmaking in the county. An Act was duly obtained from Parliament in 1853 but the project was frustrated because of the prospect of war with Russia. In 1854 progress depended on enough capital being raised locally, and whether landowners could be persuaded to release land at reasonable prices. Both these objectives were achieved and a contractor was engaged to build the line. It took three years to complete. The opening in May 1857 was celebrated as a great event in Kettering's history. And a great event it was: coal and raw materials could be brought in more cheaply and in far greater quantities than hitherto and the town was soon in direct communication with the markets of London, Leicester, Nottingham, Derby, Sheffield, Leeds and Bradford. In 1867 the Midland's line into London was completed with the extension from Hitchin to St Pancras Station.

As a result of these developments Kettering's prospects were transformed. In the second half of the century it evolved into a thriving industrial town. This did not happen overnight. Footwear made slow progress in the '60s, there being a serious shortage of work in 1861 and 1862. Unemployment was worsened by the demise of silk weaving, which by 1869 was as good as dead. What carried Kettering (and the other footwear towns) forward

42 *The factory of Abbott & Bird in Green Lane. The partnership lasted from 1864 until 1890; the factory was erected in 1873.*

was the Franco-Prussian War and a great boom in the home market. Orders placed by the French government for army boots brought a tremendous amount of business to Northamptonshire. Between 1869 and 1871 the number of manufacturers in Kettering rose from eight to 24, though none were yet operating on a large scale. In 1871 only six employed 100 or more workers, the biggest being Gotch. Kettering had not yet overtaken Wellingborough as the second footwear town in Northamptonshire, though it was to do so in the following decade. The '70s saw the erection of the first 'factories', which might more accurately be described as warehouses, where leather was received and stored, and where clicking and perhaps some closing were done. The lasting, riveting and finishing processes were put out to men who found their own grindery and did the work at home, returning the finished articles and collecting their wages at the week's end.

The boom of the early '70s ushered in a period of industrial expansion which went on virtually unchecked for 20 years. The severe slump at the end of the decade was milder in Kettering than in other centres, nor was the town badly affected by the great industrial depression of 1885-7. It was not until the difficulties of 1891-6 that the great expansion slackened. In

43 *Walker Lasts, photographed in 1972. This was the factory of Charles East & Sons, the firm which introduced the sewing-machine into boot- and shoe-making in Kettering. The building has gone, replaced by a neat housing development.*

these years exports remained high, whilst at home rising working-class living-standards generated an increasing demand for footwear, clothing and other consumer goods. The career of William Timpson, perhaps Kettering's most successful businessman of the century, illustrates the opportunities these developments brought. Born in 1849, the son of a poor Rothwell silk-weaver, at the age of 11 he went to Manchester to join his brother, who had opened a shoe shop. After a spell back home learning shoemaking, William returned and went into partnership with his brother. Five years later, in 1870, he started up on his own. In the boom which followed, he opened another four shops in Manchester and Salford; by 1902 he had 37 shops. Forced by ill-health to return to Northamptonshire, having married a Kettering wife he settled in the town. For 40 years every other Tuesday he left by train to Manchester to do business, returning home at the end of the week to stay for the next 10 days. Eventually, he decided to start manufacturing. By 1922, when they opened a large new factory in Bath Road, Timpson's were producing 7,000 pairs a week, though the firm was still chiefly a retailing organisation.

An obvious reason for Kettering's expansion was that in and around the town was a large pool of cheap labour – shoemakers, former weavers and agricultural labourers and their families. As already noted, the expansion of footwear and clothing coincided with the demise of silk-weaving. A decade later came the great agricultural depression; from about 1880 the countryside emptied as labourers and their families found work in the industrial towns. For a small premium, men and boys could learn riveting, and girls could find work in the clothing trade. There being few other industries to compete for their labour, wages were lower in Kettering than in other footwear centres. A further advantage to employers was that, because the great majority of its workers worked outside factories, trades unionism long remained absent, a branch of the union not being formed until 1885.

Not only were labour costs low, the restricted use of machinery meant that fixed capital costs were low as well. For some years, it remained relatively easy to start up without substantial capital. Firms were small and numerous, competition was keen without being cut-throat. Most of these entrepreneurs were sons of Kettering shopkeepers and tradesmen and therefore used to business, others migrated into Kettering, a few 'rose from the seat' to be upheld as exemplars of the industrial spirit. Some ended in bankruptcy, tempted into the trade with insufficient capital or business acumen. Those who survived could make good profits. All this gave Victorian Kettering its particular industrial character. By 1876 there were some 26 manufacturers. Eight years later their number had grown to 44, additional to which there were 54 closers, riveters, finishers and blockers serving the trade. In 1890 it was estimated that Kettering's 45 manufacturers were turning out 50-60,000 pairs of boots a week, the largest producer then being East, for whom a large extension to his factory in Northall Street was currently being built.

Although predominately a footwear town, Kettering's ancillary trades also expanded. We have seen how the clothing trades developed, and by 1884 the four engineering firms of 1870 had grown to 11, producing agricultural machinery, sewing machines and, increasingly by then, footwear machinery. One of the most notable entrants was Charles Wicksteed, the son of a Leeds Unitarian minister. After serving an apprenticeship in a locomotive engineering works, he started up in the steam-ploughing business, which brought him to Kettering, where he opened a small works in the Stamford Road. A passionate and opinionated politician, Wicksteed was to play a prominent part in the life of the town, one of his projects keeping his name fresh to the present day. Another firm to have an important future was Mobbs & Lewis, who opened a foundry in Carrington Street in 1885 to manufacture its patent 'Easy Exit' iron lasts for the footwear trade. Alongside engineering, iron production started. In 1878 the Kettering Coal & Iron Company came into existence, putting two furnaces into blast near an ironstone quarry on the north-west edge of the town; a third was added in 1889.

44   *Workmen and boys in the factory of Henry Hanger, Junior, in St Andrew's Street, about 1885. Looking at the photograph, you can almost smell the leather.*

Industrial Kettering, 1890 to 1914

In economic history, the years from about 1874 to 1896 are known as 'the Great Depression'. This was an era of deflation, falling profits, increased competition and the rise of a unionised labour force. It also began to impact on Great Britain that it was no longer 'the workshop of the world'. Foreigners were beginning to demonstrate that they could produce more efficiently. In the case of footwear, the Americans led the way in introducing new machinery and started to become manufacturing competitors.

Kettering did well in the great boom of the early 1870s, and in that of the early and the late 1880s, which culminated in the great year of 1890. At this time, the town made a more basic kind of footwear than Northampton or Stafford – 'boots and shoes for the workshop and factory, boots and shoes for the million'. Things became tougher in the '90s. With the fall in demand at home resulting from the general slump of those years, competition became fiercer. Changes in public taste forced Kettering's manufacturers to produce a lighter, better-quality product, which increased competition with the older centres of the trade. (Women's shoes were not made in the town until the First World War.) From 1885, machinery started to come into the production process. The use of finishing and lasting machines, which began in 1893, was ultimately to force the work inside the factories.

By 1890, trades unionism had become established. Although the Rivetters & Finishers Union (soon to be the National Union of Boot & Shoe Operatives) started in 1874, they were unable to persuade the men in Kettering to organise until 1885. The person who did most to bring this about was Leonard Bradley, who came from Nottingham. Bradley rapidly emerged as Kettering's leading Labour man. The following year, a local Arbitration Board was set up, and the great footwear dispute of 1887 was followed the next year by the first Kettering Wages Statement. In 1890 an Employers' Association was organised, and on the union side the Clickers and Rough Stuff men were organised as No. 2 branch. By the following year (1891) it was said that two-thirds of the workforce were in the union, the only ununionised workers being the (male) pressmen and fitters, and the (female) machinists. With its workers now part of a national union and most of its employers joining the Employers Federation, Kettering became much more like other footwear centres than hitherto.

Between 1890 and 1914 the economic history of Kettering falls into distinct phases. The period 1891 to 1896 was a time of prolonged depression. The town suffered severe unemployment: the Kettering Relief Committee, set up in 1893, had much work to do. It was against this background (together with other difficulties already noted) that the great transition in footwear production was made. It had become apparent to manufacturers that an increasing use of machinery to ensure a standardisation of product was the only way forward. By 1890, it had also become union policy to promote 'indoor working'. The problem was that the old ways of working at home or in informal workshops was popular with the men, who were not enamoured of the prospect of working factory hours under factory discipline. This was a deep-seated prejudice which went back to the opposition to machine-closing in the 1850s. In these years, labour relations nationally were soured by very complex issues concerning wages, the employment of boys and the payment of older operatives using new machinery, though not as badly in Kettering as in other footwear centres. Nonetheless, battle lines for a showdown between employers and workers were being drawn up.

It took the 'Boot War' of 1895 to settle future working conditions in the trade. As with the 1887 dispute, there was a feeling on both sides in Kettering that they were being dragged into a conflict by outside forces, the arbitration system having worked generally satisfactorily over the past seven years. This was not the case in other major footwear centres. Strikes and disputes, which had necessitated the calling in of independent umpires, had increasingly exasperated the Employers' Federation, whose members were under other industrial pressures. In late 1894, the Federation withdrew from the National Conference, originally formed to prevent lock-outs and strikes in the trade. The failure to reach any settlement precipitated the lock-out of 1895. In Kettering both sides took their place in this national struggle. The Federated employers (39 of the 65 firms in the town) closed their businesses. At a mass meeting in Stamford Road Schools, the operatives backed the Union executive. Some six thousand workers were locked out, of whom about a thousand were union members.

The great Boot War was a watershed in the history of footwear. The factory system triumphed; by 1897 finishing machinery was said to be very nearly universal. Finishers now had to go 'indoors', or face redundancy. As with all industrial changes, many could not learn new ways and swelled the ranks of the unemployed. The dispute had cost the union dear, financially and in membership. In 1896 NUBSO was much weaker than it had been in 1890. Militancy was defeated, the men had been forced back to work on the masters' terms. The arbitration system was re-established: thereafter the trade experienced generally peaceful industrial relations.

The long slump of the '90s finally ended in 1897. Several years of good trade followed. Despite the Boer War affecting one of Kettering's overseas markets, the war (like every war) brought government contracts. Business remained good until 1903, described by one observer as the worst year in the history of the trade since 1855. The post-Boer War depression was prolonged. The Relief Committee, called into being once again in 1903, had to remain active until May 1909. However, the 'Long Nineteenth Century' closed with a boom from 1910 to the outbreak of the Great War. In retrospect, this (together with the sufferings brought by the war) cast a golden-glow over the pre-War years, giving a false impression of the sweetness of life in late Victorian and Edwardian England.

Since 1890, Kettering had been industrially transformed. By 1914, few now had the satisfaction of working in their own back-yards, in control of their own time. Inside the factories they worked under the direct control of the employer and his foreman. The division of labour ensured that no one now worked on one task for more than a few minutes. By 1914, Kettering's footwear industry had been reduced to 39 firms, of whom 24 were manufacturers and 10 were in the leather business; the era of entrepreneurs rising from small beginnings was largely over. Kettering no longer concentrated on cheap heavy boots for the million, but produced a range of lighter, better-quality footwear. However, the trade had reached its peak as an employer of labour, though greater productivity ensured that output would continue to increase until after the Second World War. But as early as 1905, anxieties were voiced that Kettering was over-reliant on one industry.

Ten

THE EXPANSION OF URBAN KETTERING

In the first half of the 19th century Kettering's population growth was modest. By 1851 it stood at 5,198, an increase of just over 2,000 in half a century. Thereafter, with the coming of industrialisation, expansion became more spectacular. By the time the Great War started, Kettering had around 30,000 people, a sixfold increase in a little over six decades. However, by then, the growth phase was over. Between 1901 and 1911 its population grew by a mere five per cent, a tiny increase compared with the 1860s, when the percentage was 23, the '70s, when it was 55, and the '80s, when it was 75. Growth in the '90s remained impressively high, but, with an increase of 47 per cent, was clearly slowing. Early 20th-century Kettering was a very different place from Early Victorian Kettering. Unlike the experience of the greater industrial towns, Kettering's expansion was not accomplished by the arrival of thousands of strangers, though of course there were some. What happened was that the country cousins came to town, turning their backs on the land *en masse.* This was perhaps why the place still retained the atmosphere of a large village, and why Kettering was, and perhaps still is, remarkably comfortable with its history.

At first, new accommodation was confined to the old town centre, but from 1857 development began on what had hitherto been agricultural land. A new Kettering began to emerge. Because of the meadows and the railway, there was little building to the west until quite late. To the south, development on the Duke of Buccleuch's land was largely middle-class villas and terraces, one of the first being Southview Terrace in 1870. Thereafter, the development of the Headlands, Broadway and Station Road district took place. The largely working-class districts of new Kettering were built to the north, on both sides of Rockingham Road, and on land immediately to the east of the old town centre, on both sides of Montagu Street and Stamford Road.

Development had to start with the enfranchising of copyhold, before streets and individual freehold plots on new building estates could be laid out and sold. The first of these was a tiny estate laid out by the Kettering branch of the Northampton Town & County Freehold Land Society some distance along Rockingham Road. Here, running east from the main road,

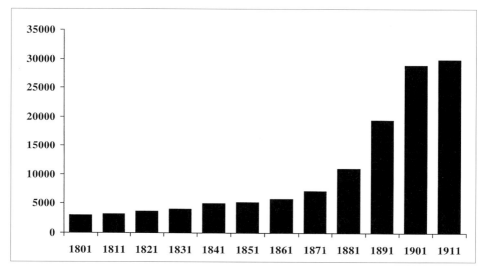

45   *The population growth of Kettering, 1801 to 1911.*

appeared the upper parts of Wood Street and Havelock Street on which were built the first terraced cottages of new Kettering.

Unlike Northampton, very little of new Kettering was developed by Land and Building Societies. Much of it was done by the town's leading business-men. Rather than bank or invest their profits they put much of them into urban real estate, purchasing blocks of land as they came on to the market, having them enfranchised, then employing surveyors to plan the streets and building plots and then selling these to speculative builders, businesses or individuals to build on. The first developer was J.T. Stockburn, who bought land east of the old town centre in 1865, on which Mill Road, Albert Street and Alexandra Street were laid out. Another was Thomas Bird, who, with a partner, developed several estates in the 1890s. But the most considerable of the manufacturer-developers were William Meadows and John Bryan. In 1876 they acquired almost 70 acres east of Rockingham Road. Because of the economic situation, they did not try to develop the estate all at once, laying out 14 acres at the start. They extended Wood and Havelock Streets eastwards and laid out the upper parts of King Street and Princes Street. On Havelock Street they built themselves a new factory, Nelson Works, into which they moved from their premises in Jenkinson's old chapel in Ebenezer Place.

46   *Town growth: a date stone, Southlands Terrace.*

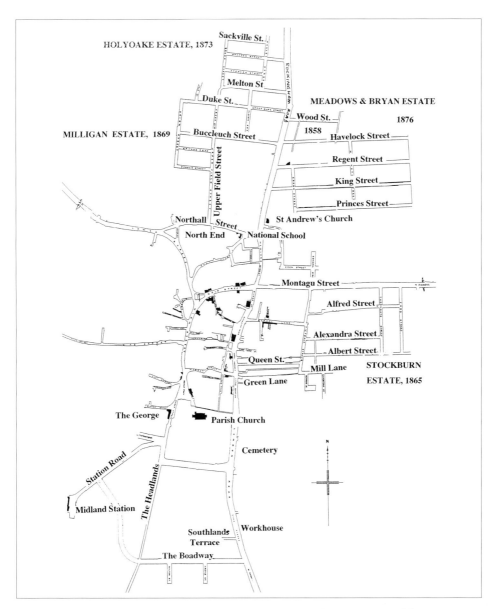

47 *Bursting out of the old town centre: Kettering's expansion to 1883.*

The rest of the estate was developed and sold off after 1883, when their partnership was dissolved. On the hundreds of plots on those long straight streets running from Rockingham Road to Bath Road were built terraced houses, shops, and factories, but (the developers being chapel-going Temperance men) few licensed premises. They took the view that, if the occupants wanted a drink, there were more than enough pubs in the town centre. After his partnership with Meadows ended, Bryan successfully carried on in manufacturing, and in 1895 bought and laid out 'Bryan's West End

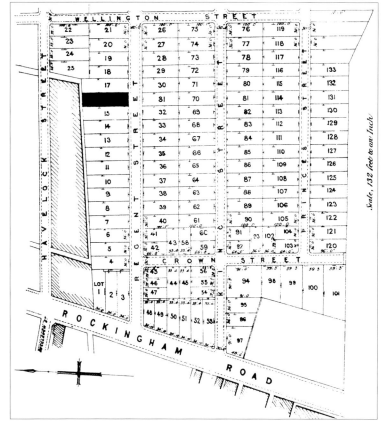

48 *Estate development off the Rockingham Road. Meadows & Bryan's 'First Allotment', 1876.*

Eatate', the principal development on the west side of the town. The Trafalgar Road, Commercial Road and Cromwell Road district was built up, Bryan removing Nelson Works from Havelock Street to larger and more modern premises in Trafalgar Road.

Even before they went into land-development, Meadows & Bryan had become involved in building the new Kettering. In 1872, such was the rate of expansion in the great boom, the town's builders ran into a brick shortage. The two existing companies could not produce enough to satisfy demand; millions of bricks from outside were having to be imported. So, using their profits from French army contracts, Meadows & Bryan started a brick-making business. However, that same year the Kettering Brick & Tile Company commenced, and, faced with its competition, Meadows & Bryan stayed in the brick-making business only a short while before putting their money into estate development with the purchase of the Rockingham Road land in 1876.

In 1885, it was claimed that a very high proportion of the house-owners on the Rockingham Road estate were working men. As well as wishing to make money by investing in land, employers such as Stockburn, Meadows and Bryan were keen to create freeholders for political reasons. The

49 *Ordnance Survey map of Kettering in 1901, published on a scale of six inches to the mile.*

'Particulars of Sale' of property in Kettering, as in other places, always carried the slogan 'Votes for the County'. Being keen Liberals, they assumed that house-owners enfranchised by acquiring a freehold would vote Liberal. Election results from 1885 show that they were largely correct in that assumption.

Not all developers were Kettering men, or Liberals. William Milligan, who in 1869 bought the land west of Rockingham Road he was to develop as Kettering's fourth building estate, was a Tory manufacturer from Dunstable. 'Milligan's estate', 100 plots of 'eligible freehold building land', soon became the Upper and Lower Duke Street, Buccleuch Street, Union Street and Grange Lane district. In 1871, ten acres immediately to the north of Milligan's estate were bought by Messrs Holyoake Bros. of Leicester, footwear manufacturers. Enfranchised by the previous owner, Robert Chettle, this development was surveyed and laid out by a Leicester surveyor, but was not offered for auction until 1875, when one of the partners died. Much of it was disposed of to Leicester speculators, who expected to sell at a profit, but their plans were thwarted by a downturn in the trade cycle; as late as 1884 much lay unsold. Eventually, the Holyoake Estate consisted of Melton, Spencer, Grafton, Sackville, Brooke and Oakley Streets.

By the 1880s, other bodies were looking for property in which to invest their profits. Following the dictum that no investment was 'as safe as houses', the Kettering Industrial Co-operative Society began to build houses to be let for rent. There is a nice terrace of eight of their houses in Princes Street, with a carved stone proclaiming 'Union is Strength' on one of the gables. In 1899, the Society went into estate development, purchasing land on the northern edge of the town, which was eventually built-up as Kingsley, Neale and Blandford Avenues. In the process, workmen uncovered part of the site of the Romano-British predecessor of Kettering. A few years later, on another edge of the expanding town, Anglo-Saxon burials were uncovered along Stamford Road.

Thus, in a piecemeal sort of way, as land became available for development, new Kettering grew up around and beyond the old town centre. Put together like a jigsaw puzzle, by 1914 these individual developments had coalesced into an almost solid urban mass. As in most other industrial towns, created with little else in mind than meeting a demand and making a profit, little thought was given to the need for open spaces and playgrounds. There was a scheme for a park on the west side of the town to mark the Queen's Jubilee in 1887, but it came to nothing. But in 1891 the Local Government Board applied for a loan to purchase land for a park for Kettering's North-End, and Rockingham Road Park was opened for use three years later. Soon, two other developments nearby followed with the opening of the North End Recreation Ground and Kettering Town Football Club's ground. New Kettering was largely unplanned; like Topsy, 'it just growed'. The local authority did have some control, particularly with regard to street, housing and sanitary bye-laws, but not much else. The hand of government did not lie too heavily on Victorian enterprise.

Eleven

VICTORIAN LOCAL GOVERNMENT DEVELOPMENTS

When Owen Robinson and his wife celebrated their Golden Wedding in 1905, they were interviewed by the *Kettering Leader*. In the course of a fascinating account of his life, he told the appalling story of how he had the misfortune to lose eight of his children through 'sewer gas' – 'two while we lived in the "Puzzle" and three at the bottom of Queen Street, the cellar being flooded with black sediment. Then I bought the place in Dalkeith Place now known as the Dairy. When we got to that we began to notice smells again, and found three deep cesspools in the yard filled with nightsoil. We lost three children there, and sent the remainder to Scotland while the place was scavenged and made perfect. The four out of the twelve came back all right, increased in health, and I am thankful to say we have lost none since.' Robinson was not a poor man, but that did not prevent the insanitary state of Kettering from killing two-thirds of his children. Improving sanitation was to be the main (though not the only) task of local government in this period.

From the point of view of modernising its local government, Kettering was an awkward size for a town and, until late in the 19th century, Parliament gave little thought to reforming the institutions of such places. Being too small to come under the Municipal Corporations Act of 1835 (and when it grew populous enough to do so, rejecting the idea), Kettering did not gain municipal status until the eve of the Second World War. In the second half of the 19th century, the evolution of its ancient local institutions passed through several phases, each of which was complicated and, Kettering being Kettering, highly contentious.

The Parish Vestry and the Boards

The first was the period from mid-century until 1872, during which the town was governed by a combination of its manorial court and parish vestry, added to which were elected boards brought into being by piecemeal legislation. These were the Poor Law Board, the Burial Board and the Highway Board. Formed in 1859, after the cessation of burials in urban churchyards for public health reasons, the Burial Board raised a loan for the purchase of land for Kettering's new cemetery, which came into use in

50 *Kettering cemetery was started in 1862 after legislation ending burials in town-centre graveyards.*

1862 (and was enlarged in 1870 and 1897). A Highway Board was established in 1863, when the county magistrates adopted the new Highway Act and divided the county into ten districts, of which the Kettering district was one. Additionally, certain services, which were later to come under the aegis of local government, were provided by private utility companies. These were the Gas Company, set up in 1843, the Town Hall and Corn Exchange Company, which had come into existence in 1853, and the Water Company, incorporated in 1872. These were financed locally; the names on their boards of directors were those of leading business and professional men of Kettering. As monopolies providing essential services, they generally made good profits for their shareholders.

Although increasingly archaic, the court leet and court baron of the lords of the manor still had power in certain important respects. The first was in copyhold matters. Despite the conversion of development land into freehold, whenever properties in the old town changed hands they had to establish title by being entered on the manorial roll with appropriate fines paid to the lords. Thus, at the court meeting in October 1865, 21 such properties were processed. Also appointed were manorial officers such as butter-tasters, ale-tasters, chimney-inspectors and meat and fish-searchers, whose appointments were largely a charade, though one enjoyed by the attenders at the court (held in the *Royal Hotel*) because they were always entertained afterwards at the expense of Mr Watson and the Duke of Buccleuch. Another area where manorial rights mattered was Kettering's markets. When a town meeting was held in 1870 to consider moving the cattle market to a new site, Mr Gill, who had been Mr Watson's market tenant for 38 years, was most offended because he had not been consulted. In fact, the market rights were not purchased by the town until after he retired a few years later.

In these mid-Victorian years the parish vestry continued to be the town's main organ of local government – spending the rates, electing church-wardens, overseeing the parish charities, paying for lighting and watching – and had an increasing number of new tasks as the Boards and public utility companies came into existence. As more and more responsibilities were laid on the authorities and the cost to local taxpayers grew, the smaller ratepayers became more active than ever in the vestry. Parish administration became the scene of a running battle between Improvers and Economisers. Scarcely a year passed without some outcry about the sanitary state of the town. For almost a year in 1853-3 smallpox was said to be 'endemic' – foul drains and cesspits were blamed. In October 1853, fear of cholera led to a parish committee being set up to conduct a house-to-house visitation to order the removal of nuisances. Such exercises were, at best, short-term expedients, but that was as far as the majority of ratepayers were prepared to go.

In 1854 the Improver party made an attempt to bring Kettering under the 1848 Public Health Act, the first important piece of public health legislation. In response to their petition, the General Board of Health in London sent an inspector to carry out an inquiry into the sanitary state of the town. William Ranger produced his report the following year. He was in no doubt that Kettering would benefit by coming under the Act and that a local Board of Health was the way forward. He also stated that he was aware that there was no chance of its being agreed to. Local government then being truly local, and the Act being permissive, ratepayers were free to refuse to adopt legislation setting up institutions they were not prepared to pay for.

In 1858, a second opportunity was afforded the Improvers to secure a Local Board, with the passing of a new Local Government Act. Its aim was to allow small towns to secure a local government Act without having to face the cost of a private Act of Parliament. A simple majority of ratepayers, either in public meeting or by a poll of the parish, would be sufficient to adopt the Act. It bestowed all the powers of the Public Health Act of 1848, the Watching and Lighting, the Burial and the Highway Acts on a responsible committee, annually elected. It gave access to government funds through loans repayable over 30 years. Once more, in 1860, the Improvers were defeated in their efforts to persuade their fellow ratepayers to have a Local Board. The Reformers were no more successful in 1868-9, when they lost a parish poll overwhelmingly. So cock-a-hoop were the Economiser party that they presented a silver vase to their leader, George Eldred, a wine and spirit merchant, celebrating their victory as a parochial Waterloo which would settle the question for at least a generation.

They could not have been more wrong. Three years later, Kettering elected its first Local Government Board. The threat (once more) of cholera, the Cattle Plague and the extension of the franchise to many working men in towns, caused Parliament to end the era of piecemeal and permissive legislation on the sanitary question, and to start to pass and enforce compulsory legislation. A Sanitary Act was passed in 1867, followed by a new and mandatory Public Health Act, and a Local Government Board was created. Locally, as Kettering began to grow rapidly, crises developed over water supply and sewage disposal. As early as 1842, Robert Smith had addressed a printed circular to the inhabitants on the water shortage. Every dry summer the issue came up, only to be forgotten when winter rains filled up the wells. In 1858 the worst drought for 32 years occurred, and in 1864 people were at their wits' end to obtain water. There were worries over the danger of fires and businesses sent water carts out into the country to collect water from streams. The year 1868 saw the biggest fire in living memory, when about two acres of buildings behind the *Old White Horse* in High Street, the site of Job's Yard, was destroyed, though no lives were lost. It was the long hot summer of 1870 which finally provoked some local action. At a public meeting, a joint stock Water Company was proposed. Capital was raised by the issue of 2,000 five-pound shares and, within a short time, a deep well and pumping station at Weekley was brought into use, supplying sufficient water for an estimated 19,000 population. However, it was not to be all that long before Kettering found it necessary to make additional efforts to increase the water supply.

The problem of sewage disposal was not solved so readily. It was the greatest local government problem of the age, so it is not surprising that it gave Kettering trouble. Eventually, out of its difficulties over this matter, and at the fourth time of asking, the town came round to adopting a Local Government Board. Various sewage disposal schemes, all opposed by the Economisers, were proposed. After two years' floundering around, it became clear that any plan would need to have the approval of the new Local Government in London, and that Kettering's existing local institutions lacked the legal powers to carry out an adequate scheme. For these reasons, the Improvers called a meeting of owners and ratepayers to consider adopting the 1858 Local Government Act. This was assented to almost unanimously. Considering the result of the poll of the parish three years before, this was a remarkable turn-round. Maybe it had something to do with the recent visitation of the smallpox, when, out of about 200 cases, 19 had died. Their old opponents, alarmed that a Board would be an end to the parish system in which the small ratepayers had power, and would lead to local government falling into the hands of the well-to-do (which it would), petitioned against a Board. In the summer of 1872, a government inspector visited Kettering and considered their case that the parish Sewage Utilization Committtee was competent to manage sanitary matters. He found it wanting, and they withdrew their petition.

The Kettering Local Government Board, 1872 to 1895

The date for the election of a nine-man Local Government Board was fixed for August 1872. To be eligible for election a nominee must possess real or personal estate, or both, to the value of £500, and be rated to the relief of the poor upon an annual value of at least £15. To be an elector, you had one vote if you owned or occupied property to the value of not less than £50 per annum, and further votes for every £50 over £50. At the inquiry, Mr Lamb pointed out that recent legislation extending the franchise had increased the number of voters in Kettering from 545 to 1,515. No wonder the parish Economisers saw it as the end of their period of influence. The nine who were elected to the first Local Government Board were (in descending order of votes cast for them) James J. Roughton, surgeon, William Toller, gentleman, John Wallis, manufacturer, Henry K. Farey, manufacturer, Charles Bayes, farmer, John T. Stockburn, manufacturer, Frank Roughton, gentleman, Frederick Wallis, manufacturer and Henry Church, draper, the majority of whom were Liberals. For the first time the town's economic élite took over direction of its local government. Kettering was entering a new era.

In 1860 it was remarked that Kettering 'still remains in the same state of dirt and discomfort as it was before sanitary science was known, or railways were even thought of'. By 1870 things had somewhat improved. The old

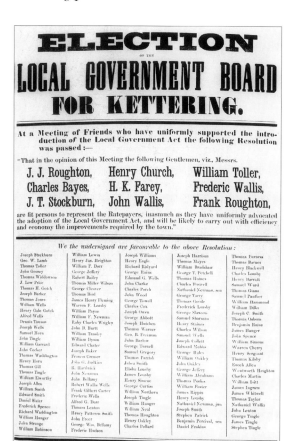

51 *Handbill relating to the first election for a Local Government Board in 1872.*

burial grounds had been closed and a new cemetery was in use, whose lay-out and tidiness was the epitome of Victorian sanitary science. A new Corn Exchange had been erected and became the main venue for meetings of all kinds. The streets, notoriously muddy in winter and dusty in summer, had been improved by the Highway Board. Some of the facilities and the architecture of the town improved with the building of the new police station and the new Grammar School in the '50s, the Grammar School's new properties in High Street, and the opening of the Temperance Hall and a new Wesleyan Chapel in the '60s. Kettering got its first newspaper in the form of the *Kettering Free Press*, though it failed to flourish, moving to Leicester where it became the *Midland Free Press*. However, it continued to report Kettering news informatively. And in 1870 a new telegraph office opened in the town. By then, the factories and streets of new Kettering were beginning to sprout from the old centre. The Local Board would find there was much to keep it busy.

The small ratepayers were suspicious of the Board's powers, and worried that, by being too active, it would present them with heavy bills. However, between 1872 and 1889 the town's rateable value more than doubled, though that did not prevent alarm at the cost of each urban improvement, which seldom came cheap. There were also accusations that Kettering had fallen into the hands of a 'junta'. The Board therefore moved with prudence in its early years. However, with a minimalist approach, problems on which urgent action should be taken at some future point could accumulate. The Board appointed a clerk, Mr Lamb, a medical officer, Dr Dryland, whose task it was to monitor the health of the town and, for the first time, gather 'vital statistics', a treasurer, a surveyor, who was to be responsible for roads, including the former turnpike roads, now unturnpiked, paving and sewering, lighting and fire engines and building regulations, and an inspector of nuisances for sanitary matters.

52   *High Street about 1914, showing the effects of street widening and new commercial building.*

The Board had come into existence to do something about sewage. Within a short time plans for new drains on the east and west sides of the town, and a system of filtration at the outfall into the streams had been drawn up. By 1879 three-and-three-quarter miles of new sewers had been laid and filtration tanks built. It was none too soon. Before the Board came into existence, the Milligan Estate, north of the town (the Buccleuch Street/Upper and Lower Duke Street area), had been started. Unpaved and undrained streets had been laid out and houses built without any means of drainage. In bad weather the streets became impassable and well-water became polluted with sewage from numerous cesspools. The new main sewer provided an outlet for the streets to be properly drained, and the board caused the streets to be paved and drained. It also did the same for the first streets already built on the east side of Rockingham Road. From now on, the Board had to approve plans for all buildings in the town. It came into existence in the nick of time. In its first six years it approved 647 houses, 17 villas, nine factories, three schools, and 95 other buildings.In 1877, the Board began the collection of ashes and refuse in tubs (dustbins). As yet, however, there was no collection of night soil, or emptying of cesspools.

The Board also busied itself in the improvement of the town centre. At various times, Lower Street, Market Street and Gold Street near Toller Chapel were widened. The latter street was further improved with the erection of the Post Office, the Victoria Hall and new shops. In fact, the town centre began to take on the appearance it was to retain until after the Second

53   *The former* Cross Keys Temperance Tavern *and* Temperance Hotel, *now* O'Malley's Irish Bar. *No one can say pub designers do not lack a sense of humour.*

World War. Old relics of Stuart Kettering such as the *Dukes Arms* in Market Street were demolished and rebuilt in the contemporary style. The same year (1877) the Northamptonshire Banking Company's new premises at the High Street end of the market place began the trend for rebuilding banks and other commercial premises. The thirsty of the town who disliked public houses were provided with an alternative in 1880 with the opening of the Cross Keys Coffee Tavern, in Silver Street, under the aegis of the Temperance Society. These years saw the upgrading of the markets. After Mr Gill's death, the Local Board took them over, purchasing the tolls from Mr Watson in 1878, and, as the location of the cattle market in the market place became increasingly inconvenient, it was moved to a new purpose-built site east of the manor house in 1880, where it was to remain for a century. In the last year of the Board's existence (1895) plans were being made to purchase the manor house site from the Duke of Buccleuch, the stipulation being that it should only be used for local government build-ings. In 1894, the Board laid out a new park on Rockingham Road.

In 1885 the *Kettering Observer* made the complacent remark that the Local Board had 'vastly improved the sanitary state of the town without being objectionally crotchetty in its administration'. Not being 'objectionally crotchetty' presumably explains why it was not until 1891 that the reign of the local jerry-builders was brought to an end by the introduction of stricter bye-laws relating to street lay-out and housing. These appeared when the limited nature of the town's sanitary improvements began to be revealed. An outbreak of typhoid in a middle-class part of the town, Broadway, led to a newspaper headline 'IS KETTERING BUILT ON A CESSPOOL?' It became apparent that sanitary inspection had been perfunctory to the point of negligence. Nearly all of the town's drains were inadequate, and the more they were repaired, the more inadequate their original construction appeared. Worse was to come with the revelation that Kettering's sewage had become a major pollutant of the River Ise. In response, the Board tried one of the many patent methods of the time of treating sewage before it went into the river, but this proved ineffective. By 1894, the Board was under severe pressure from the River Nene Commisssioners, the County Council and the Kettering Rural Sanitary Authority to clean its sewage. The County Council gave the Board two months' notice that it would take legal proceedings against it if the matter were not dealt with. The Board was duly taken to court, and an adjournment was made giving the Board 12 months to effect improvements to satisfy the requirements of the River Pollution Acts.

Similar problems arising from the same basic cause – a failure to anticipate the scale of Kettering's growth in the previous two decades – occurred with water and gas supplies. In 1887 there was a serious water shortage; supply needed to be increased as a matter of urgency. The Waterworks Company tackled this through the construction of a new reservoir at Cransley, completed in 1891. Faced with the option of leaving future supplies in the hands of the Company or buying the Company out, the Local Board opted for the latter. A Kettering Waterworks Act was obtained in 1889, the purchase of the plant being one of the first acts of the Local Board's successor body. In the case of gas, friction arose between the town and the Gas Company over its plans in 1891. In order to meet the town's wishes and expand output, the Kettering Gas Act was secured. The old Company was abolished and a new one replaced it, which was to supply Kettering with gas until nationalisation after the Second World War.

These years saw important extensions in health provision. The first was the opening of a new workhouse infirmary in 1884, and two years later a hospital for infectious diseases on a site off Rockingham road was opened, on land given by the Duke of Buccleuch. In 1891 an influenza epidemic led Dr Dryland to propose the formation of a voluntary District Nursing Association. Soon the town was served by three district nurses whose work was especially valuable to the mothers of Kettering. The nurses co-operated well with the town doctors and, within months, a town meeting was called to consider the founding of a cottage hospital, an idea which had come to nothing when first raised in 1887. This time, health was much on people's minds. The idea of a hospital for the town tapped into the charitable instincts of all parts of the community and was taken up with enthusiasm. Doctors gave their services free, the Duke of Buccleuch gave land for the building, the well-to-do subscribed, and they and their wives sat on committees. Working-class organisations such as the Kettering Industrial Co-operative Society, the Friendly Societies, the trades unions and the working men's

54 *John Turner Stockburn (1825-1922), stay manufacturer, Nonconformist, ardent Liberal and Justice of the Peace. Kettering's foremost public figure of the second half of the 19th century.*

clubs raised money, as did the cycling and other sporting clubs. The hospital replaced the old Charity Dispensary, which had served the town since 1801. Its managers generously made over to the hospital £1,000 they had on deposit. The foundation stone was laid in May 1896 by the Duke and Duchess of Buccleuch. A year later, the 25-bed hospital was opened, a new wing being added in 1901 to hold a further 25 beds, mainly for children.

The Local Board dominated Kettering's local government through the two decades of its greatest growth. For most of this time it was a nine-man body, Liberal in its complexion, dominated by some of the town's leading businessmen, with remarkably little turnover in membership, despite three of the seats being up for election annually. Until its last few years, it had long-serving chairmen (Dr J.J. Roughton, 1872-80, John Wallis, 1880-90, and J.T. Stockburn, 1890-98). Conservatives, small ratepayers and working men were successfully kept at bay (with the exceptions of William Fowler Dorr, shoe factory foreman, and Edmund Ballard, secretary of the Co-operative Society – both prominent Liberals). By and large, the Board did a good job, modernising services, if always belatedly, without alienating the ratepayers too much. By the end of the 1880s, the Board found the structures of local government changing around it. Parliament at last faced up to the reform of rural local government. In 1889, the Northamptonshire County Council came into existence, with powers to compel the Kettering Board to take action in certain sanitary areas, as we have seen. Kettering elected three members to the County Council. In 1889 they were J.T. Stockburn and Charles Pollard (Liberals) and H.F. Henson (Conservative).

In 1892 a situation arose which raised doubts about a Local Board as a form of town government. It was pointed out that, as that the population had reached 20,000, the property qualification for members of the Board was automatically raised from £500 to £1,000, and that this would disqualify Dorr and Ballard, the two working-men, from membership. The opinion of learned counsel was that this was correct. Dorr and Ballard at once withdrew. It was proposed that Kettering should consider incorporation, the supporters of the idea arguing that this would be a step in the direction of greater democracy, and would therefore be in tune with the times. A committee was delegated to look into the matter. It reported that a charter of incorporation would cost the shocking sum of £300, that a Kettering Council would not control the police (which the Board didn't anyway) and that the rates would have to be raised one and a half pence in the pound. At a public meeting anti-incorporators won the vote. But they lost the battle. In 1894 the County Council, after an Inquiry, increased the Board from 12 to 18 members. That same year, under the next instalment of rural reform legislation, the Local Board was replaced by an Urban District Council. A new era of local government in Kettering commenced which was to last until the eve of the Second World War.

Kettering Urban District Council, 1895 to 1914

The wider franchise for a UDC, which for the first time included votes for suitably qualified women, offered a challenge to the Liberal caucus which had dominated the old Board for over twenty years. Conservatives were optimistic about their chances, and the Labour movement made its debut on the local government stage, though as yet there was no Labour *Party*. Co-operators considered putting candidates into the field, but decided against to avoid the accusation of becoming political. The Friendly Societies took the same view. Although Kettering's union leaders had been, and still were, Liberals, the Trades Council decided it was time to demand equality. They offered a scenario of an 18-seat Council from the three parties each with six members. The Liberals refused to have this: they were determined to put up 11 candidates in the three wards. The first election (December 1894) resulted in seven Liberals, seven Conservatives and four Trades Council men being elected. Seven were former Local Board members, and continuity was preserved with the election of J.T.Stockburn as its first chairmen. Down to the Great War, Liberals generally kept ahead of Conservatives (except in 1903 and 1913) and could usually count on the support of Labour. The latter never quite achieved parity, but only lost ground once, in 1903. In these years, the size of the Council was twice increased; in 1898 when it was raised to twenty, the three wards being made into five; and in 1904 when the membership was increased to 25. In 1914 the political balance was 10 Liberals, eight Conservatives, six Labour men and one Independent.

The Urban District Council was more fortunate than its predecessor, in that the growth of Kettering's population slackened markedly after 1890. Nonetheless, it inherited unavoidable commitments on the water and sewage-disposal fronts. The compulsory purchase of the Water Company was concluded in 1898, and further work was to be necessary to provide for the town's water needs. In 1904 the construction of a new water main was started and new reservoirs near Thorpe Malsor were completed in 1910 to supplement Cransley's water. On the sewerage front, the Council inherited the County Council's legal action over river pollution, which was suspended for 18 months to give it time to start work. Despite the horrifying cost to

55   *Kettering Public Library, erected through the generosity of Andrew Carnegie, who attended the opening in 1904.*

the taxpayers, the sewage works was enlarged in 1897-8. Ten years later it was further extended and improved. Other essential modernising work on the sanitary front took place in 1902-3, when, following a Local Govern-ment Board Inquiry, a dust-destructor was brought into use. The following year, the Council secured a Local Improvement Act giving it power to open its own electricity plant.

In 1897 the Council took over the powers and duties of the Burial Board. The following year saw extensive street improvements in the town centre, wooden blocks replacing the paving in High Street. Kettering UDC looked at the possibility of providing houses for the working classes. However, the costs of the schemes made them prohibitive: the time for council housing had not yet come. A major concern in the years after the Boer War was unemployment, and a Labour Exchange was opened in 1910. On the health front, in 1902 a temporary smallpox hospital was provided off Rothwell Road. Under the Kettering Joint Hospital Order of 1895 all the local hospitals came under a Joint Hospital Board, whose eight members were elected by the Urban District and the Rural District Councils.

These years saw important developments in education and 'cultural services'. One of the first things the District Council did was to take steps to bring the Public Libraries Act into force. In 1896 a library and reading room was opened in what had previously been the armoury of the Rifle Volunteers. In 1902, Andrew Carnegie, the American philanthropist, gave Kettering £8,000 towards the erection of a public library (and did the same for Northampton, Rushden and numerous other towns). The present building on the Manor House site was opened by Carnegie himself in 1904. Nine years later, the Sir Alfred East Art Gallery was opened next door, a reflection of the interest in art generated in the town by the careers of two of its native sons, Sir Alfred East and Thomas Cooper Gotch. Both sprang from manufacturing families, but abandoned trade to study art and make their livings as nationally respected painters. East was mainly a landscape artist and Gotch a portraitist in the late Pre-Raphaelite style. Too ill to attend the opening of the gallery named in his honour, East died the same year. In his will he made a handsome bequest to the Gallery of his work and that of other modern artists.

56   *Bust of Sir Alfred East, outside the eponymous Art Gallery which he did much to bring into being. The brother of Charles East, he abandoned the footwear business for art, becoming a well-known landscape artist. His example did much to create an artistic tradition in the town.*

If these amenities are seen as reflecting a growth in civic consciousness, a move for municipal status might have been expected. Kettering was to teeter on that brink for another two and a half decades. In 1901 the matter was indeed considered, but once again the ratepayers declined to go for borough status. Those in favour were defeated by anti-incorporators who argued that the rates had already gone up too much, that trade was then in a bad way, and that the last thing that Kettering needed was unelected borough aldermen. In 1914, the manor house site, so long intended for a future town hall, was in fact occupied by a brand new County Secondary School, housing separate boys' and girls' schools within the same building in Bowling Green Road. By then a new era in schooling had begun, and not just in Kettering.

Twelve

RELIGION AND EDUCATION

The Church: Education and other Issues

The 1851 religious census confirmed the numerical supremacy of nonconformity (with its seven chapels to the Anglicans' one). Faced with the burst of urban expansion of the next half century it was only to be expected that, in such a religiously competitive town, both sides would respond vigorously. In 1903, the results of a census of attendance at all places of worship carried out by the *Kettering Leader* indicates that the Nonconformists and others, with their 17 chapels still in a majority, their 'best attended' services attracting 3,039 people, against the Church, with its six places of worship, attracting 2,436. However, it is clear that the gap had narrowed. As in other places, the Church and its supporters had been energetic in responding to the challenges posed by rapid urban growth.

When the Rev. Henry Lindsay became rector in 1863, he found that his predecessor, T.H. Madge, had recently (in 1860) commenced church extension with the opening of the North End National School and plans for a new church close by soon followed. The foundation stone of St Andrew's was laid in 1868, and it was consecrated two years later. It seemed perfectly situated at the northern edge of the old town. However, the immediate reason for its opening was to provide a 'free and open' alternative to the parish church, where only 165 of the 1,135 seats were unappropriated. Lindsay was a 'free and open church' man, but it was not until the restoration of the late 1880s that he was able to apply that principle to his parish church. The status of St Andrew's was that of a chapel of ease: Lindsay had to find the stipend of the curate out of his own income. Fortunately, with £1,095 a year, this was no problem. Nor was there any difficulty over such matters as paying for the land and buildings for church projects in Kettering. There were well-to-do supporters within the town, whilst outside there were aristocrats and squires only too anxious to promote the Church, its schools and the Conservative party in a town where Dissent, the industrial spirit and Liberalism were offensively vigorous.

Lindsay, rector for almost three decades, is a good example of the busy urban Anglican incumbent of the second half of the 19th century. He opened a Church Room (the future St Luke's) among the terraced houses

57   *St Andrew's church, the first of the new Anglican churches in expanding Kettering. Built on land owned by the rector, it was paid for by well-to-do church people in and around the town. The foundation stone was laid by the patron of the living, G.L. Watson, Esq. in 1868, and it was consecrated in 1870. The architect was G.E. Street.*

and factories in Alexandra Street in 1874, and an iron Mission Church (which eventually became St Mary's) in 1887 in the new district off Stamford Road, encouraged by an anonymous gift of £5,000. One of his most successful innovations was the Church Institute and Reading Room, intended to provide a club for church people. From its opening in 1877 it developed into a flourishing organisation. The rector also served as chairman of the Grammar School governors, the Burial Board, the Savings Bank and the Dispensary. A keen Temperance man, Lindsay was the founder of a branch of the Church of England Temperance Society. In his work he was helped by his wife and four unmarried daughters, and his son followed him in the same vocation.

One of the main sources of friction between Church and Dissent was the elementary school issue, and friction became outright political warfare with the passing of the Elementary School Act in 1870. Believing that it was essential both for itself and the country that the provision of most of the nation's elementary education should be given within a Church framework, as it had been since the early part of the century, there was a strong Anglican reaction to the Education Act. A great effort would be made to fill the gaps in every locality so that Board Schools would not be necessary. A meeting called in Kettering was informed that the various National schools provided 513 places and the Nonconformist British School 250 places. Based on a formula that elementary school places required in towns should equal one seventh of the population, the 'shortfall' for Kettering was 237 places. Some

58 *Tower and gable of Stamford Road Board School. Designed by Gotch & Saunders, the school opened in late 1892. It was described as palatial in appearance: after their long wait, the members of the School Board were in no mood to be utilitarian.*

argued that one-sixth was a better calculation, the shortfall, according to that, coming to about 300 places. Churchmen and their supporters made this their target, and the rector informed the Nonconformists that churchmen would not want to provide all of these if Nonconformists were willing to expand the British School. The Nonconformists declined to do so. They were determined to have a School Board, where the 'non-sectarian' religious teaching would be preferable to the Church continuing as the main local provider. The Church then started to raise the thousand pounds needed. The Nonconformists demanded a poll of the ratepayers for a School Board. A tremendous parish battle, the biggest of the century, then ensued. The result was that, in a very high turnout of ratepayers, the votes of those in favour came to 609 and those against 649.

So, in 1871, Kettering became one of the very few towns to come down against a School Board, denting its image as a progressive sort of place. The victory the Church and the ratepayers won proved pyrrhic. As Kettering entered its period of greatest-ever growth, the Church now found itself having to try to meet a growing demand for extra school places. It made heroic efforts to do so. St Andrew's Street Schools and the Boys' National Schools in the Horsemarket were the result. As on the sanitary front, the legislative changes of 1870-71 marked a turning point nationally as well as locally. Legislation was followed by further legislation. Education became compulsory in 1876: not having a School Board in Kettering, enforcement was placed in the hands of the Guardians of the Poor, and ratepayers had no choice but to foot the bills of the school attendance officer. Once again, in 1877, Liberals and Nonconformists made a second bid for a School Board. Another great parish battle ensued. Once again they lost. By 1890, the five Church schools were providing 1,600 places against the British School's 656. However, by now, the estimated deficiency was 900 places. The Education Department in Whitehall issued a notice

59 *Church restoration: a picture taken in 1889 or 1890 when the bells were taken to the Loughborough bell-foundry and retuned. The gentleman in the bowler between the two bells is Canon Henry Lindsay, who died in 1892, just before the last work had been done.*

demanding the shortfall be met. When it was not, Kettering was ordered to elect a nine-man School Board. The result was five Liberal Nonconformists to four Conservative churchmen, and throughout the years of its existence (1890 to 1903) the balance generally stayed that way. The Kettering Board only ever had one chairman, Davis F. Gotch (son of T.H. Gotch), and one vice-chairman, Robert B. Wallis. After 20 years in the education wilderness, Kettering's Liberal Nonconformists (the 'non-sectarian party') entered the promised land.

The School Board era

And what did they do in the promised land? They built the Stamford Road, Rockingham Road, Hawthorne Road, Park Road and Spencer Street Schools, with accommodation for 4,245 pupils, at a cost of £64,000. Four of the five schools were the work of the architectural firm of Messrs Gotch & Saunders, and they were designed to be unlike the Board schools usually put up in industrial towns. With their tall Italianate campaniles, a statement was being

60   *St Mary's district church, off Stamford Road, started as a tin church in 1887, and became St Mary's when it was rebuilt in 1895.*

made. The British School was eventually placed under the Board's aegis, but the Church schools remained independent, funded voluntarily, with no support from the ratepayers (though they did receive some Government funding). This put a strain on the rector, the school managers and their supporters. By the end of the '90s, for them the question was, how could arrangements be made for their schools to receive aid from the rates and yet remain church schools?

In 1887 the Rev. Henry Lindsay started on a major restoration of the ancient parish church, which commenced with the taking-down and re-building of the top 31 feet of the spire. The bells were also re-hung, a complete re-pewing and the removal of the galleries was completed and the pew-rent system extinguished. The cost was around £9,000, and there were plans for a new organ. To general shock and dismay, when it was nearing completion, Henry Lindsay died. He had been rector for almost three decades, years which presented the Church with great challenges. He had defended its interests well, and, though he kept Dissenters at arm's length in the traditional way, he had never been overtly party-political. He was sincerely mourned by all sections of the community.

Lindsay was the last of the Evangelical rectors. His successor was the Rev. Bernard Wilson, a High Churchman, who, in his five years in Kettering, made a big impact. Even before he arrived, he announced his intention of increasing his curates from two to four. By the time he left there were eight. In 1893 the anonymous donor gave another £2,000 for a permanent church to replace the iron mission off Stamford Road: St Mary's was consecrated two years later. The rector opened a new Mission Hall in Brook Street for the northern district in 1893, which in time (1911) was rebuilt as All Saints' church. From the start, Wilson made himself popular by appearing on the platform with Nonconformist ministers at a Bible Society meeting, referring to them as 'reverend brethren'. He forged good relations with the working classes through such events as Co-operation Sunday in 1894, a service for the various co-operative societies. To attract youths, a Company of the Church Lads Brigade was started. For Wilson, Kettering represented the Church's industrial mission, and he carried it out with what would now be called 'a team ministry'. In 1897 he departed for a bigger urban mission, Oxford House, Bethnal Green. Later in his career he became rector of Portsea, Hampshire.

Wilson was succeeded by the Rev. Patrick Murray Smyth, 'an old college friend', in 1898. Smyth was 'an advanced High Churchman' and, like Wilson, he proved to be an active leader. In his time, a new church, St Phillip's, and a new building for the Church Institute were erected. He was notable for leading the Church and its supporters in the struggle for the maintenance of church schools. In the face of a rapidly growing Board School system in which religious teaching was consciously non-sectarian, the Anglicans, like the Catholics, tried to preserve their own distinctive schools, which they saw as an important way of preserving their own future. Nonconformists argued that religion should be taught at Sunday, rather than at day schools. This became Smyth's main concern, and in his time he modernised the old church schools. When he came there were six, all out of date, with a debt of £600 on one of them. The managers were committed to a new school for St Mary's, so there was much money to be raised. By 1911, when Smyth moved on, Kettering's church schools had been improved out of recognition.

Local Authority Education

In 1902 a Conservative Government rescued the denominational schools with a new Education Act, which replaced the directly-elected School Boards by Local Education Authorities based on the County Councils and County Borough Councils. Kettering came under the new County LEA, but the Act allowed for 'retained powers' over education, and Kettering was given its own Education Committee. Ultimately, this arrangement was to benefit education in the town greatly, but the 1902 Act, giving church schools funding from the rates for the first time, generated great anger amongst Nonconformists because it went against the position they had held for seventy years or so. Some resorted to passive resistance, withholding part of their rates. There was a period of severe difficulty working out the basis of the new relationship of voluntary schools to the new education authority, but in the end it was managed.

One of its benefits, a reason why it was enacted, was that it offered the opportunity to reform secondary education. Not secondary education for all (which had to wait until after the Second World War), but the provision of reformed or new Grammar schools with a few scholarship places for a number of bright children, paid for out of the rates. If ever there was a school which needed reform it was Kettering Free Grammar School. As we have seen, in mid-century it had almost faded away under the benign neglect of the Rev. Richard Morton. In 1854 the old Trust collapsed and a new scheme from the Court of Chancery provided for a new start. Fresh trustees were appointed, a new school was built in Gold Street with money raised by public subscription, and an able master, the Rev. Francis Tearle, appointed. For eight years it seemed the school might develop into something promising. On Tearle's departure to Leicester in 1864 these hopes were dashed. Out of a long list of applicants the trustees unerringly picked the wrong one. The Rev. Thomas Widdowson had the mastership for the next 32 years. Under him the School neither fell back nor moved forward. Widdowson remained until 1894, when he resigned to become vicar of Foxton, near Market Harborough. For the whole of this period the number of boys in the school each year remained at around thirty. Periodically, criticisms were voiced, but the fact was that the governors had little or no power over the master, who was irremovable until such time as he chose to go.

In 1897 suggestions were made to move the school from the cramped site in Gold Street, persuading the District Council to exchange it for one on the Manor House site. To bring in funding from the County Council the proposal was to combine it with a Technical School (as in Northampton and other places). These proposals hung fire. Following the 1902 Education Act, a scheme for a County Secondary School was eventually agreed. The town was to have 'a dual' Grammar School for equal numbers of boys and girls on a portion of the Manor House site, which the County Council purchased from the Urban Council. Kettering Old Grammar School closed on 1 September 1913, and, in accordance with a Board of Education scheme, the new schools opened the same month. The schools for boys and for girls were separate, each with its own head teacher, but were tantalisingly contiguous, one of those comic arrangements that only the pure in heart think up. The Old Grammar School trust was managed by a body of seven governors; the schools by a governing body of nineteen. The properties of the old Foundation produced an income of about £1,000 a year, which was to be used for the upkeep of the properties, the balance being handed over to the County Council towards the support of the school. The new Kettering Council School soon became Kettering Grammar School, a name which brought the benediction of a history going back to the time of Queen Elizabeth, a nice illustration of 'the invention of tradition'. If the school ceased to have a close connection with the Church of England and never

61 *The new Grammar and High Schools of 1913, now the Town Hall.*

again had the benefit of clerical headmasters, the politicians who designed the new educational arrangements were biased in favour of the old classical traditions and relegated commercial and technical education to an inferior position in the curriculum. Nonetheless, for the first time, scholarship boys and girls were offered the chance of secondary (and in a few cases) a higher education, though it was the children of the middle class who were the main beneficiaries of the expansion of secondary education at that time.

By then, the Rev. P.M. Smyth had left. In 1911, by now an honorary canon of Peterborough, he had gone to take up the High Church post of Provost of St Ninian's, Perth. Described as 'extremely urbane', he had been energetic and made an impression in Kettering, leaving with a presentation signed by 1,500 people and a speech of appreciation from Frank Mobbs, JP, a Nonconformist. His successor was another Anglo-Catholic, the Rev. C.B. Lucas, who was to stay a great many years. One of his first tasks was to complete the Church re-organistion of Kettering. This he did in 1916 by formally dividing the ancient parish into four.

Later Victorian Nonconformity

The Nonconformists were slower than churchmen to respond to the challenge of urban growth. Their minds were on other things, one of which was their own history. At Great Meeting, the Rev. Thomas Toller completed his half century in 1871, but postponed retirement for another four years in order to complete a century of Toller ministry. The centenary celebration was a grand occasion, a time for much pride in the progress of Dissent. Thomas Toller had yet more years in him, finally passing away in 1885, at the age of 89. Probably he stayed too long for the good of Congregationalism, but it took 12 years for discontent with the Rev. J.M. Watson to emerge. When it did, it was serious. The revolt was not one of immature malcontents; the four deacons and 200 seat holders, the chapel élite, seceded, accusing Wilson of presiding over the church's decline. They took steps to found a new one, and eventually in 1898 London Road church was opened. Beyond

62 *Gold Street, formerly Toller United Reformed Church, Gold Street. The old Great Meeting was radically altered in 1849 and 1875 and became known as Toller Congregational.*

that, Congregationalism failed to spread into new Kettering.

Even the more evangelical Baptists did not begin to do this until the '90s. The confrontational William Robinson moved to Cambridge in 1852 and was succeeded, on the recommendation of the Rev. Dr Frederick Gotch of Bristol Academy (J.C. Gotch's son), by the Rev. James Mursell. Soon after the young minister arrived, it was decided to rebuild the chapel, enlarging it and giving it the distinctive frontage it bears to this day. From the time it came into use, the rebuilt chapel took the name 'Fuller', and the same 'cult of the personality' was adopted at Great Meeting after the retirement of Toller. The young Mursell was energetic, preaching in the Temperance Hall to those who were not church or chapel goers and founding the Fuller Village Evangelistic Society. Much to the regret of his hearers, after 17 fruitful years, he left for Bradford.

When he preached his two trial sermons, the Rev. John Brown Myers so impressed the people at Fuller that he was invited to become the minister by 101 votes to one. He served nine years, before leaving to become Secretary of the Baptist Missionary Society. In Myers' time, new Sunday school buildings were completed, and, when he left, he was sent on his way with a purse containing 50 guineas. In 1884 a major alteration to the chapel increased the number of seats to 1,000. This was during the incumbency of Myers' successor, the Rev. H.B. Robinson, who came in 1880. Robinson's career (as well as the reputations of two young Kettering women) was ruined in 1886 by misdemeanours of a sexual nature. The chapel, however, was flourishing, with 368 members, 796 Sunday scholars (taught by 95 teachers), two Bible classes numbering 133 members, a Band of Hope with 320, and a Mutual Improvement Society with 50 members. In adjacent villages it had six 'preaching stations' attended by 14 appointed preachers, and a mission in Kettering, looked after by a married couple paid by the church.

Understandably, the chapel took its time over a new minister; 18 months to be precise. Then they alighted on an experienced Scotsman, the Rev. S.G. Woodrow, from Charlotte Street Chapel, Edinburgh, who, however, stayed little more than a year. Maybe Kettering lacked the excitement of

'Auld Reekie', and Woodrow fell out with the deacons. For their part, they did not like the decline in numbers (and finances) under the new minister. They then went for a Welshman, the Rev. Phillips, a graduate of University College, Bangor. Kettering was always a good place for a young man to show what he was made of. Phillips was a great success. In his nine years, there was history to celebrate and an urban mission to undertake. The history was the centenary in 1892 of the Baptist Missionary Society's foundation, followed, four years later, by the bi-centenary of the chapel's foundation, both major events. These years also saw the undertaking of the Baptist 'Forward Movement' – establishing a presence in the newer parts of the growing town. In 1890, a mission began in Nelson Street with 51 people 'dismissed' from Fuller. Money

63   *London Road Congregational Church.*

was raised and four years later it became independent, with its own minister. In 1893, a North End mission started in Sackville Street, and the same year the Oakley Street mission room opened. Meanwhile, back at Fuller, between 1891 and 1896, membership doubled. When their minister departed for Norwich in 1899, he did so with the esteem of his people and a Fuller purse containing 50 guineas. In the years leading up to the Great War, the Baptist cause continued to flourish. In the time of the Rev. Henry Davies (1900-11) the biggest alterations to the interior of the main chapel since 1861 were made, with a new organ and choir gallery, and a new Carey Memorial Church was built in 1911 in Nelson Street.

There was always a Calvinistic Baptist presence in the town. Jenkinson's chapel in Ebenezer Place did not long survive its founder's departure to Oakham in 1849. By 1858 it had become a shoe factory. The 1851 religious census records another Calvinist place of worship in Workhouse Yard, though there is no record of it thereafter. In 1868 a new Calvinistic chapel, Jehovah Shalom, was opened in Wadcroft, at the sole expense of Mr William Payne, miller, of Great Oakley. Rebuilt in 1893, it survived for much of the 20th century.

Wesleyan numbers grew steadily in the second half of the 19th century, though the fact that Congregationalists and Baptists outnumbered Methodists persisted as a local feature. A major step was the opening of Silver Street chapel in 1866, which was given a new Sunday school in School Lane through

64 *Fuller Baptist Chapel and minister's house in 1861, after a rebuilding: the woodcut is from the* Illustrated London News, *5 October 1861.*

the generosity of John Tordoff, nine years later. Alert to the northward expansion of the town, the Wesleyans opened a new Sunday school and minister's house on the Rockingham Road in 1879. The project was completed with the opening of a new chapel on the site 13 years later. They also ran a mission in the Victoria Hall in the years after it opened in 1888. Primitive Methodism had a more precarious position. In 1873 they were using the Temperance Hall for meetings, and eventually a little chapel was opened in Grange Road. In 1901, with the appointment of a minister for the first time, numbers grew and the Corn Exchange had to be used for meetings. The following year an iron chapel was opened in Bath Road. This was soon replaced by a brick-built place of worship, to which a Sunday school was added in 1906. In the religious census of 1903 their numbers were small, 24 being their best attended service that day. Nonetheless, by 1916 they had paid off their mortgage.

By the time of this 1903 census, the Salvation Army, the Plymouth Brethren and Seventh Day Adventists had all established footholds in the town, though with only small numbers of adherents (as had that most unevangelistic of creeds, the Friends, with a mere 24). The various missions in Kettering drew greater numbers. Victoria Hall's best attended service attracted 539, London Road (a mission room opened at his own expense by the Baptist, Charles Pollard) had 95, whilst Walker's Lane Mission drew fifteen. The Catholics, whose 'Second Spring' in Kettering was begun, after three and and a half centuries' absence, with a mission by Passionist priests in 1882, drew 60 to Mass in 1903. The gift of land in 1893 made by the Dowager Duchess of Buccleuch, a Catholic convert, was the site for a school-chapel, beside which the later church of St Edward was built.

Though it had its local peculiarities, by the early 20th century Kettering had not lost any of its reputation for being a religious sort of place, displaying the diverse pattern of worship characteristic of the small to medium-sized industrial town. The pattern was still conventionally Christian. Although Unitarian speakers had visited the town, and Kettering's Radicals had supported Charles Bradlaugh in his battles to take his seat in Parliament in the 1880s, neither Unitarianism nor Secularism claimed enough adherents to establish themselves. Nor had Spiritualism yet gained a foothold.

Thirteen

PARTY POLITICS AND THE
RISE OF LABOUR

Conservatism and the Triumph of Liberalism

Between 1835 and 1880 no Liberal ever won a parliamentary election in North Northamptonshire. Having to endure long periods when their best political efforts came to nothing was very trying for Kettering's Liberals and Radicals. However, they did not give up. They were sustained by the belief that national economic and social trends meant that further Reform could not be delayed indefinitely. In this they were correct, but they had to wait four frustrating decades.

On occasions in these years, hopes were raised by Reform Bills introduced in Parliament. In 1859 a town meeting was called over Lord Derby's Bill, which had Joseph Stockburn (J.T. Stockburn's father) in the chair, the main speakers being the Rev. James Mursell and the Rev. Thomas Toller. In the years after the Crimean War, when Lord Palmerston was Prime Minister, prospects for Reform were remote. But Palmerston died in 1865, and it was not long before conditions for Reform revived. That year, Nonconformists were fired-up by the Governor Eyre controversy, which arose out of Eyre's brutal suppression of a rising in Jamaica, an island never far from the thoughts of Kettering's Dissenters. Against a background of general support for the governor, they roundly condemned 'the flagrant and foul acts done in that colony'. Thereafter, events nationally, leading to the creation of a Liberal Party around Gladstone, were mirrored in Kettering, where an alliance between leading Dissenters, Liberal manufacturers and tradesmen, and Radical working men began to form, the latter taking the lead. In October 1866 at a public meeting it was resolved to found a branch of the National Reform League, the first entry of the Kettering working-class into organised politics since the end of Chartism. In the event, it was Disraeli, not Gladstone, who passed the 1867 Reform Act, which extended the franchise to a proportion of the working men in towns for both parliamentary and local elections. But, in the election of 1868, it was a Liberal government which came to power and proceeded to enact the programme of Reform which Dissenters had desired for so long. Church rate soon became a thing of the past.

Whilst these developments pleased Kettering's Liberals, they did little to make the parliamentary seat more winnable. Despite their best efforts to

TOWN'S MEETING

TO CONSIDER THE

New Reform Bill.

WE, the undersigned, Inhabitants of Kettering, do hereby request our Fellow-Townsmen to attend a Town's Meeting, to be held in the CORN EXCHANGE, on *Monday*, the 24*th inst.*, at 8 o'clock in the evening, for the purpose of expressing an opinion on

THE REPRESENTATION OF THE PEOPLE BILL,

commonly called *The New Reform Bill.*

JOHN T. STOCKBURN	THOS. HENRY GOTCH
HENRY GALE GOTCH	J. ALFRED GOTCH
JOHN WALLIS	THOMAS BIRD
WILLIAM TOLLER	ARTHUR LENTON
CHAS. BAYES	GEORGE FOSTER
WILLIAM F. DORR	JOHN PARKINSON
HENRY K. FAREY	CHARLES WICKSTEED
A. JOHN MARGETTS	THOMAS JONES
JOHN GOOSEY	CHARLES POLLARD
THOMAS WALLIS	JOSEPH WELLS
WILLIAM MEADOWS, SEN.	JOHN NEWMAN
JOHN BRYAN	JAMES SPENCE
FREDERIC WALLIS	MATTHEW PAYNE
J. M. WATSON	W. F. LOASBY
H. BERESFORD ROBINSON	J. H. WILMOT
FREDK. SMITH	E. G. WILLS
HENRY COX	RD. PRIDMORE
JNO. T. ILIFFE	J. N. COOPER
EDWARD SMITH	H. T. FAVELL
JOSEPH HUTCHEN	HENRY STANDLEY
THOMAS SALMON	THOMAS LOAKE
EDMUND BALLARD	EDWARD P. TOLLER
WM. GARRARD	WILLIAM SIMONS
R. E. BURGES, M.D.	DAVIS F. GOTCH
JOHN ROBINSON	G. I. WILSON
W. DOUBLEDAY	THOMAS WADDINGTON
W. J. LEWIS	FRDK. SIMCOE

March, 1884.

65   *On the verge of Jordan (for Liberals): a Reform poster of 1884. It carries a check list of Kettering's leading Liberals.*

improve their organisation, it proved no easier than before to prevent Conservative victories in North Northamptonshire. The scattered Liberals of Kettering, Wellingborough, Oundle and those villages not dominated by landowners were outnumbered and outgunned. Until his early death in 1877, the leading Conservative was George Ward Hunt, Squire of Wadenhoe, whose partnership, first with Lord Burghley and then Mr Stopford Sackville, beat the Liberals out of sight.

For the decade after the 1867 Reform Act they did not even think it worthwhile putting forward candidates at elections. When Ward Hunt died, Captain Wyatt Edgell contested the bye-election for the Liberals against a youthful Lord Burghley, who freely admitted that he knew nothing of politics, a confession which did him no harm whatsoever. He was returned with a majority of 900 votes. The gallant captain probably found it scant consolation that two streets in new Kettering were named after him.

Yet, within a short time, Liberalism rose from the ashes. Despite their disappointment in the 1877 bye-election, it proved a turning point. In the election of 1880, a Liberal government returned to power, once more under Gladstone's premiership. Even more remarkably, for the first time for 45 years a Liberal was elected in North Northamptonshire. This was the result of improved Liberal organisation (a new Association having been formed in 1876), and the prestige of their candidate. Perhaps only a Spencer, with all the political clout that his family carried in Northamptonshire, could have won. C.R. ('Bobby') Spencer, Earl Spencer's brother, managed it, though only by 25 votes. Lord Burghley came second; Stopford Sackville lost his seat. If it was a Spencer triumph, it was also a long awaited deliverance for J.T. Stockburn and his friends. In the next instalment of Reform five years later, Kettering was removed from North Northamptonshire, and became, together with Wellingborough, Rushden, Raunds and the other footwear villages close by, part of the new single-member constituency of East Northamptonshire.

Down to the Great War, no constituency was more solid for Liberalism. At the first election (in 1885) under the new arrangements, Bobby Spencer decided to stand for Mid-Northamptonshire, where the family estates were situated. A good candidate for East had to be sought, and was found in the person of Francis Allston Channing. Born in Boston, USA, the son of an an American mother and an English Unitarian minister who duly returned to England, he was educated in Liverpool and at Oxford and became a barrister.When Channing came to Kettering and Wellingborough it was love at first sight; the Liberal activists immediately took to him, and he to them. Channing was to hold the seat in seven elections. Whatever disasters happened to the Liberal party nationally, Channing's seat was never in danger. When he retired, the government rewarded his 25 years in Parliament with a baronetcy. Sir Francis was succeeded by an able Radical with Labour inclinations, Leo Chiozza Money, who was to hold the

66 *Francis Alston Channing, Liberal M.P. for East Northamptonshire from 1885 to 1910.*

seat until 1917. Not only were the Liberals triumphant in parliamentary elections, they ruled the roost in local government. From 1880 to the Great War was the Golden Age of Kettering Liberalism.

Conservatism 1880 to 1914

The political events of 1877 to 1885 turned the world upside down for local Conservatives. The years of effortless supremacy were over. In East Northamptonshire, it was now their turn to be outnumbered and outgunned. They looked to adapt their organisation to the changed conditions. A new Kettering and District Conservative Association was organised. Ten years later a Conservative Club was opened in Montagu Street (followed a month later by the opening of a Liberal Club in Dalkeith Place). The site of the Conservative Club was donated by the Duke of Buccleuch, president of the Conservative Association, who kindly undertook to guarantee the finances of the Club to get it off the ground. In the event that was not needed; the Club paid its way successfully.

67   *The Liberal Club, Silver Street, opened in 1889, by Gotch & Saunders. It has long ceased to be a Liberal Club, was the Trustee Savings Bank and is currently a public house.*

Another Conservative organisation of some importance was the local 'Habitation' of the Primrose League, formed to perpetuate the memory of Lord Beaconsfield (whose favourite flower was the primrose). Designed to widen participation in Conservative activities, most notably by giving women a role, each Habitation had a (male) Ruling Councillor and a female Dame President and a quasi-Arthurian hierarchy. In 1902 Kettering Habitation consisted of 11 'Knights', 20 'Dames', and 508 'associates'. The League gave Conservative women for the first time a chance to work for the party. They proved very useful, especially in rural constituencies, especially at election times. Primroseism proved more successful than the Liberal Women's Association, which saw Liberal women as little more than tea-makers and audience fodder.

As politics became more participatory, and as Kettering became larger, the parties became keen to launch their own newspapers. Although 19th-century newspapers were businesses, virtually all were launched to advocate a political position. As we have seen, the first local paper, the pro-business, pro-Liberal *Kettering Free Press* had commenced in 1855, but had been forced to migrate to Leicester. Kettering news was, however, well covered in the Northampton, Stamford and Leicester press. The first of the new papers was the *Kettering Observer*, set up in 1882. Soon it was faced with a competitor, the *Kettering Leader*, which had begun life in Wellingborough as the *Kettering News*. In 1888 the proprietors brought the *News* to Kettering, where they set up premises in the centre of the town, and changed the name to the *Kettering Leader*. For a while the *Observer* was able to compete, but in 1890 its plant and copyright were bought by the *Leader* and the two were amalgamated as the *Kettering Leader and Observer*. Both were pro-Liberal, pro-Temperance and Anti-vaccinationist. Determined to have their own weekly, the printer Walter Goss, on behalf of the Conservatives, invited J.W. Steff to start the *Kettering Guardian*. Steff was a young man with experience on Lancashire Conservative newspapers, and rapidly became a leading light in Kettering Conservatism, serving as the Conservative Club's first secretary. His death at the age of 34, shortly after the *Guardian* started in 1890, was a great shock in local political circles. The same year the *Leader*'s first editor, P.D. McGowan, a Scots Liberal, who came to Northamptonshire as a teacher, had a breakdown and had to quit after only two years with the paper. Starting newspapers is always stressful.

What must have been hard for local Conservatives to take was that, nationally, the party was in power for almost two decades after Gladstone in 1886 split the Liberals over Irish Home Rule. With the exception of a brief Liberal Government in 1892-4 (when Gladstone tried, unsuccessfully, to pass a second Home Rule Bill), the Liberals did not return to power until 1906. At the election of 1895, all the county seats fell to the Conservatives, except East Northamptonshire; Channing was not for turning. Alone among the county's Primrose Habitations, Kettering's celebrations were muted.

The Anti-vaccinationists

No consideration of the politics of Victorian Kettering would be complete without some account of the prolonged campaign waged against the compulsory vaccination of children against smallpox. From 1838 onwards successive governments legislated on the matter. In general, down to 1853, vaccination was optional; from 1854 to 1871 it was made obligatory, *but not enforced*; then, as a result of the serious smallpox epidemic of 1871-2, further Acts were passed to ensure that compulsory vaccination *was* enforced.

There had always been resistance on the part of some parents to having their children subjected to vaccination. Defiance of the law led first to fines and then distress warrants for those who refused to pay them, and, ultimately, for persistent refusers, prison. The first parent in Northamptonshire to go prison for refusing to pay his fine was Thomas Coleman, a Kettering shoe-maker. Many towns were centres of anti-compulsory vaccination, but the most active were those where religious Dissent and the sort of Liberalism it produced was strong. Leicester was the principal centre outside London, but it was found in Northampton, and, vehemently, in Kettering.

68   *An Anti-vaccination handbill, 1887.*

Opposition to compulsory vaccination arose for several reasons. One was a parental revulsion over infecting healthy children with the 'poison' of a vaccine, and there was circumstantial evidence of children contracting blood-poisoning after vaccination. Another was doubt whether Science's claim that vaccination was eradicating smallpox was factually correct. There were also other arguments suggesting that the virulence of smallpox had declined in the 19th century, and it was believed that improvements in general public health provision rather than vaccination had played the major part in this. Another issue was political; a libertarian hostility to 'the Jennerian Juggernaut' of state compulsion was an issue for many Liberals. This resulted in the demand that exemption should be granted to parents who refused to have their children vaccinated on grounds of conscientious objection. 'Liberty of conscience in the face of unjust laws' was why the issue had such an appeal to many Nonconformists.

As the authorities sought to apply the law more effectively in the 1870s and 1880s, opposition grew. The more people were fined and imprisoned, the more vehement the anti-vaccinationists became. In places where resistance was strong, the numbers of children being vaccinated dropped alarmingly. The Kettering Board of Guardians sought to enforce the law, and this led to attempts to elect an anti-vaccinationist majority to the Board, whose intention was to suspend compulsory vaccination by refusing to appoint vaccination officers. Serious conflicts in meetings of the Board arose, with Conservative rural guardians, some of whom were also magistrates, trying to defeat these attempts to obstruct the law. In 1889 the government set up a Royal Commisssion. Anti-vaccinators then argued that until the Commission reported, compulsion should be suspended. The report of the Royal Commission was published in 1896. In outline, what it proposed was keeping compulsory vaccination but allowing exemption to those parents who had objections on grounds of conscience, and the law was changed. Although the anti-vaccinationists had won, there were numerous troubles in applying this and anti-vaccinationism continued to be contentious until the Great War.

In the early years the leading resisters were Owen Robinson, Charles Wicksteed, Charles Pollard and the Rev. H.B. Robinson, who joined forces with shopkeepers such as Benjamin Percival, and working men such as Coleman. Indeed, most resisters were working men and their wives. Some were fined repeatedly; public appeals from their friends and admirers raised funds to help them pay. A Kettering Anti-vaccination League was founded in 1884 and soon most of the town's leading Liberals, including their Member of Parliament, lined up behind the banner of Anti-vaccination.

The Rise of Labour

In 1895, as a token of the esteem in which he was held in Labour circles, Leonard Bradley was presented with a handsome illuminated address. As well as carrying the names of those who had contributed towards it, it listed those of Labour men who had recently been elected to such public bodies as the School Board, the Board of Guardians and the Urban District Council. If the rise of Labour can be summed-up in a single document, this must surely be it. President of the Kettering and Rothwell Branch of the footwear union and president of the District Trades Council, Bradley was honoured because he, more than any other individual, had acted as catalyst to the emergence of a local Labour movement. As already noted, when he came to Kettering in the early 1880s, wage levels were lagging behind those in other footwear centres, the chief reason being the lack of organisation amongst the workers. This began to be rectified by the formation of No.1 branch of the footwear union in 1885, which recruited riveters and finishers: membership was soon extended to Rothwell men. In 1890, No. 2 branch was started for clickers and rough stuff men and Kettering activists took a lead in spreading unionism to Higham Ferrers, Rushden and Irthling-borough, to Wellingborough and to Earls Barton. The formation of No.1 branch was soon followed by the creation of a Trades Council on which sat the representatives of other unions in the town – bricklayers, carpenters, tailors and typographical workers. In the highly fragmented labour scene, trades councils brought local unions together to discuss matters of mutual interest, though at this stage in their history they studiously avoided party politics. But they did promote the idea of a 'united Labour interest'. Each year the Trades Council organised a demonstration in Feast Week, which always began with a great procession through the streets, in which trades unionists were joined by other working-class organisations, providing a highly visual reminder of the growing presence of organised labour.

In terms of numbers, a more powerful labour association than trades unionism, and one which had emerged earlier, was the Kettering Co-operative Industrial Society, which started in 1866. There had been earlier

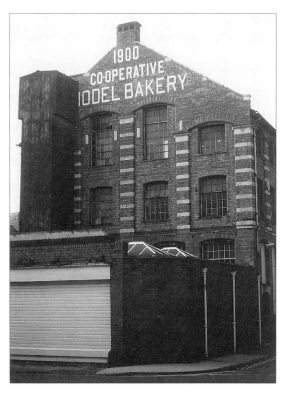

69   *The Model Bakery, erected by Kettering Industrial Co-operative Society in 1900.*

co-operative ventures in the town, none of which had lasted very long. The first was in the 1820s, suggested by John Jenkinson and friends, but the poverty-stricken conditions of the times were not propitious. Co-operation took off generally in 1858-9 and there was soon a Kettering Working Men's Self-supporting Society, but it did not long survive a court case brought in 1861 against its treasurer and acting agent, to recover a sum of money placed in his hands. Three years later, John Plummer concluded that 'in Kettering, co-operation has proved a miserable failure'. He wrote it off too soon. Another attempt was made in 1866, and, despite much hostility towards the co-operative idea (the committee being sneered at as 'shoe-making grocers'), this time the venture survived: the Kettering Industrial Co-operative Society came into existence. From modest beginnings, it grew into one of Kettering's major institutions.

Launched with a membership of about seventy, its first store was the front room of a house in High Street, later occupied by Winterhalder, the jeweller. Two years later, 'No. 1 store' was opened on Bakehouse Hill. The Society was lucky in the men who made up its first committee, men who were prepared to give years of service to the ideals of co-operation as an alternative to the prevailing economic system. Prominent among these men were Edmund Ballard, who served on the committee for 23 years, and George Eyet Smith, secretary for 25 years (to be succeeded by William Ballard, Edmund's son). After an anxious start, the K.I.C.S. took off in the boom years of the 1870s. By 1881 it had about a thousand members and four stores. In the next decade, membership doubled, and by 1892 the number of stores stood at seven. A Penny Bank had started in 1873 and by 1895 had over 4,000 depositors. At first, the Society concentrated on groceries, but eventually moved into breadmaking, butchery and the coal business. In 1893 a new drapery store was opened in Newland Street, and six years later a 48-acre building estate on the north side of the town was purchased and laid out with 445 two-house plots. Co-operators did not live by bread alone. An educational department was started to teach people the workings and potentialities of co-operation. Over the years, most of the labour leaders of the time came to Kettering to address its meetings, and the department also ran ambulance classes, a choir and a string band, and held summer meetings in the villages around. K.I.C.S.'s first village store was at Corby, opened in 1898. One important educational development was the formation of a Co-operative Women's Guild. With votes for women an emerging political prospect, the Women's Co-operative Guild was of importance in widening working-class women's horizons. In 1916 the K.I.C.S. celebrated its jubilee. By then it had 9,000 members, share capital of £200,000 and in the past year its sales had amounted to £230,000.

Besides the distributive K.I.C.S., by then a number of *productive* co-operative societies had come into existence. The first was the Kettering Co-operative Boot & Shoe Manufacturing Society Ltd., which began in 1888, a direct result of the bitter

70   *The new premises of the K.I.C.S. in Newland Street in 1895.*

labour dispute of the previous year. It was launched with share-capital subscribed by 140 workers and its manager and secretary was Frank Ballard, another of Edmund Ballard's sons. Two years later it moved to new premises in Havelock Street. As the factory system took over and as industrial disputes became more prevalent, the idea of productive co-operation became more attractive to the more committed trades unionists. However, it was harder to make this type of co-operation work than the retail version. In the economic conditions of the 1880s and 1890s, many newly founded co-operatives proved short-lived. Not so in Kettering. By 1909 the Boot & Shoe Society was selling its footwear to 250 retail co-operative societies up and down the country, but was a typical Kettering business, employing a workforce (in 1926) of 250.

The Kettering Clothing Manufacturing Co-operative Society Ltd. was destined to become an altogether bigger enterprise. Starting in 1893, it began with capital of £500 and a dozen workers. Two years later, it was doing well enough to open a factory on the corner of Dryden Street and Field Street, destined to be extended several times in the future. In 1911 a second factory opened on the other side of Field Street, and by then the society had another factory at Barton Seagrave. By the 1920s the Clothing

71 *The opening of the Kettering Co-operative Clothing Company's new factory on the corner of Dryden Street and Upper Field Street in 1895.*

Co-operative Society, 'Kaycee', had become Kettering's biggest employer. The same year as Kaycee began, 'the Union', another Boot and Shoe Co-operative Society, was started by the National Union of Boot and Shoe Operatives, in reaction to the great 'Boot War' of that year, in a small factory in Tanner's Lane. The vision was work without bosses, productive co-operative businesses selling their goods to distributive co-ops, creating an alternative economic system. Although only a smallish concern, 'the Union' survived a good number of years, though it was to have a hard time after the Great War. In 1895 the Co-operative Building Society was launched, a response to labour troubles in the building trade. Employing about 30 men, its first jobs were on the Co-operative Clothing factory, alterations to the Drapery stores and a band room for the Rifle Band Club. Yet another clothing co-operative, the Corset Society, was established in 1898. It too survived: by 1926 it had 189 employees. So extensive and inter-meshing were the activities of co-operation in Kettering that it was becoming noted in the world of Labour. One respected writer in 1898 described the town as 'the worthy Mecca of Co-operation'.

Trades unionism and the burgeoning influence of co-operation by no means encompasses all the organisations of the working class in Kettering in the later 19th and early 20th centuries. There were, for instance, the network of Friendly Societies and working men's clubs, and the activities they promoted, but these will be looked at in the next chapter. What has to be considered is the entry of Labour into the political life of the time. We have already seen how, in local government matters, the election for seats on the first Urban District Council in 1894 damaged the relationship between the Trades Council and the Kettering Liberal party. At each annual Council election therafter the two groups put up their own candidate. For the first time, in 1902, a labour councillor was elected chairman of the UDC. Down to the Great War the Liberals always had a majority, usually being able to count on the Labour councillors as fellow 'progressives' on most issues. This was Liberalism's golden age, but it was made possible by the existing electoral system. When the franchise was democratised after the Great War, Liberalism would be swept aside by the Labour Party in Kettering, as in other places.

In the period under consideration, however, there was a Labour movement before there was a Labour Party, and trades unionists such as Bradley and his comrades were Liberals, or 'Lib-Labs' as they were subsequently named. The sharp quarrel with the Liberal caucus over the first UDC election (which led to Bradley resigning from the Liberal party) was the beginning of a rift, and there were other sources of tension. The great footwear dispute of 1895 and the imposition of the factory system caused bitterness between unionists and their Liberal employers. Another was the attempt of Socialists to wean Kettering workers away from Liberal belief that capitalism could be reformed: it was something they never quite managed.

72 *The first Labour men to hold public office in 1895. They were elected to the Urban District Council, the School Board and the Board of Guardians. Leonard Bradley is seated in the middle.*

The 'Socialist Revival' began in the mid-1880s with the formation of the Social Democratic Federation and the Fabian Society. The Social Democrats took their socialism from Karl Marx and the American Henry George. Speakers from their branch in Northampton first came and addressed an open-air meeting on the Market Hill in 1888. Their revolutionary rhetoric and contempt for such respected labour institutions as trades unions, savings banks and other thrift bodies made them few converts. Attempts to establish a SDF branch in Kettering failed. Nonetheless, with the visits of such people as Tom Mann and Keir Hardie, as well as for local reasons, the 'socializing of politics' began to take place. In 1895, shortly after the first UDC election, a Kettering branch of the Independent Labour party, a socialist body, but one markedly less sectarian than the SDF, was established. Bringing notable speakers to Kettering over the next few years, it did recruit members, spread Socialist ideas, and became a permanent presence in the local Labour scene.

Nationally, Socialism and Liberalism took a battering in the jingoistic mood of the Boer War era (1899 to 1901) but recovered in the serious depression which followed. At a demonstration against unemployment jointly organised by the Kettering Trades Council and the ILP in 1905, reviewing the Unemployed Workmen's Bill before Parliament, Keir Hardie said that the agitation for the measure 'had brought out the people of England in a way that they had not been brought out for at least half a century'. From that time on, demonstrations organised by the Trades Council and the ILP branch became annual events. At the general election of 1906 the Liberals gained one of their greatest victories, and the return of so many Lib-Lab representatives led to the formation of a Parliamentary Labour Party. A proposal in the Trades Council that a branch of the new Labour party should be established in Kettering was deferred, but a Kettering Socialist Club and Institute was founded.

Most of Kettering's Labour leaders remained Lib-Labs, who thought the way forward lay in increasing their influence within the Liberal party, which itself recognised the need to address the concerns of Labour though such issues as unemployment relief, old age pensions, trades unions legislation, and health and unemployment insurance in their great legislative programme of the next few years. A second factor was that whenever the Trades Council considered putting up a candidate at an election it lacked the funds necessary to do so, though putting up candidates with the backing of the footwear union was much talked about. A third was that, although attempts to forge a united Labour interest were slowly having some effect, key organisations were against becoming too involved in party politics. The Friendly Societies, and to a large extent the working men's clubs, had a policy of banning political discussion in case it destroyed the spirit of unity and conviviality. The most important obstacle was the long-standing refusal of the Co-operative movement, the one organisation which had the funds to fight elections, to become directly involved in politics. Nonetheless, Kettering's Co-operative societies increasingly saw themselves as a united body, and were prepared to organise meetings with the Trades Council. It took the Great War to bring the Co-operative movement into party politics.

These weaknesses showed clearly in December 1909, with a general election due the following month. When the Trades Council discussed putting up a Labour candidate, there was a split over whether it should be the Socialist, Ben Tillett, or the Lib-Lab, Whitehead, who was supported by Bradley and his allies. Tillett was chosen, but withdrew because of the continuing opposition of Bradley and the Trades Council. In the January 1910, Channing was returned to Westminster for the seventh successive time. However, having served for 25 years, he gave notice that this would be his last election. Embroiled in their epic struggle with the House of

Lords, the Liberal Government called a second election in December that year. Released from their loyalty to Channing, Bradley and others gave their support to the candidature of T.F.Richards from Leicester, General President of NUBSO. Kettering's first Labour candidate did reasonably well. Richards polled 1,431 votes, most of which he gained at the expence of the winning Liberal, Leo Chiozza Money (born in Genoa). Chiozza Money's majority was well down on Channing's in January. At a Trades Council meeting in January 1911 to thank Richards for his efforts, there was post-election bickering. Nonetheless, the lesson of the election was that in constituencies such as East Northants the Liberal party was threatened by Labour's entry into national and local politics. No one foresaw how much and how soon.

Fourteen

INDUSTRIAL CULTURE:
ASSOCIATION, LEISURE AND SPORT

Temperance

If the characteristic Kettering Liberal could be said to be a Nonconformist chapel-goer, a businessman and an anti-vaccinator, it is a racing certainty that he would also have been a Temperance supporter. 'The principal manufacturers, tradesmen, Sunday School teachers, local preachers, and the active workers in every good movement, were abstainers', declared Charles Pollard at a tea party in 1874 given to celebrate Thomas Bird's 'Twenty-first teetotal birthday'. Pollard was Kettering's leading Temperance man. By the time of Bird's 'coming of age', the Temperance movement had been active in Kettering for over three decades, having been launched in 1837. In the depressed conditions of the Early Victorian years the propagation of its message had been difficult. But, from about the time of the opening of the Temperance Hall in 1864, it began to prosper.

Convinced that drink was the source of all evil, and that abstinence from it was the only sure and certain way an individual (and society) could be reformed, Temperance people saw their movement in quasi-religious terms. In practical terms, the objective of Temperance was the reconstruction of the working classes. Not of course all of them, but the minority who could be brought to a sense of their own sinfulness. A Band of Hope was formed in 1853 for young people. As befitted a revivalist movement, Temperance put over its message to the sound of music. The first of Kettering's bands was the Temperance Saxhorn. In the early days, Temperance meetings with their music and colourful confessions of reformed drunkards added considerably to the entertainment of the time. Ensembles such as the Hallelujah Band (which visited in 1866) always found a warm welcome.

In August 1872 it was claimed that Kettering, with its membership of a

73 *Plaque to Charles Pollard on London Road Mission Hall.*

167

thousand or so, contained more total abstainers than in any other place in Northamptonshire. In 1837 a 'Tent' of the Independent Order of Rechabites, the Temperance Friendly Society, was opened. It failed in the 1860s, but was successfully refounded in the 1870s. Rather like Co-operative zealots, Temperance people sought to create parallel institutions with those in the regular world. As an alternative to the public house, the *Cross Keys Temperance Tavern* in Silver Street was opened in 1880. Kettering, like other towns, also had its *Temperance Hotel*. In 1882, 'Gospel Temperance', in the form of the Blue Ribbon Army, whose followers proclaimed their allegiance by wearing the ribbon, arrived.

Until 1889, Temperance people were generally Methodist or Nonconformist, but in that year a branch of the Church of England Temperance Society was established. With virtually all religious leaders on side, 'Temperance Sunday' was widely observed in Kettering's places of worship in 1892. By then, a considerable Temperance network had developed. In addition to the Kettering Temperance Society there was the Fuller Temperance Society, the Church of England Temperance Society, the British Women's Temperance League, the General Band of Hope, the Toller Band of Hope, the Wesleyan Methodist Band of Hope, the Young Abstainers Union, the Independent Order of Rechabites and the Salvation Army, all fighting the good fight against alcohol.

Despite all this earnest activity, the successes of Temperance should not be exaggerated. If it managed to limit the number of places serving drink in 'new Kettering', it could do little about the old town centre. In 1884 there were 19 public houses, eight beer houses, nine others with 'out-doors' licences, and 17 of the 69 grocers and other shopkeepers were beer retailers as well. The Temperance movement looked to Parliament to legislate against the easy availability of drink. Gladstone had limited the hours of opening somewhat in 1872, but when, in 1893, it looked as though the Liberal government were contemplating a Local Veto Bill, under which local authorities could shut public houses if two-thirds of the ratepayers voted in favour, the drink trade organised. A Kettering and District Licensed Victuallers, Indoor Beer-house Keepers and Off-licence Protection Asociation was formed. The Local Veto did not materialise: Parliament always recognised that the drink trade was a legitimate business and that if laws were passed closing businesses down there would have to be an enormous amount of compensation paid. Above all, politicians knew that there was a public demand for alcoholic refreshment.

In a letter to the *Northampton Herald* in 1863, the local working-class writer, John Plummer, pointed out that 'the public house forms the alpha and the omega of a working man's pleasure'. Most men went to the pub not to get drunk 'but for the pleasure of joining in social converse and sharing the pleasure "of a bright fire, a joke, song, or story"'. Noting that the Temperance movement had little appeal, his solution was Working Men's Clubs, which, he thought, would offer all the attractions of pubs '*minus the drink*'.

Working Men's Clubs

This was the view of others keen to promote clubs for working men. In October the following year, a meeting was held at the Temperance Hall to air the idea of a club for Kettering. It was attended by clergy and other interested parties. A committee was set up to further the scheme. Plummer advocated the idea in the press, and described visits to clubs in Lancashire and Yorkshire. However, the committee failed to get a club off the ground. Despite the prospect of reading, smoking, bagatelle and refreshment rooms, Kettering's working men were just not interested. The reason was simple – refreshments were to be non-alcoholic.

The next development was the attempted formation of a Working Men's Club and Institute under Church and Conservative auspices. With the support of the Duke of Buccleuch, and of other local landowners, the idea of a club was carried one step further. One was promoted and met in 'the new room adjoining the Royal hotel', which the Duke owned. At its first annual meeting the committee, however, were none too pleased with the members' indifference to the lecture programme offered, and deplored their fondness for smoking (despite the fact that this was allowed under the rules). After that, nothing more is heard of the venture, though something very like it reappeared in 1877, in the form of the Kettering Church Institute and Club, which, as already noted, did develop into a successful institution.

It was to be another decade before the first recognisably modern Working Men's Club was opened in Wellington Street, the foundation stone being laid in 1887 by F.A. Channing, MP, supported by the Hon. and Rev. C.J. Vernon, Captain Tibbits of Barton Seagrave, J.T. Stockburn and Dr J.J. Roughton. The reason for all this cross-party goodwill was clear. Times had changed: significant numbers of working men now had the vote. There was no prohibition of beer in Wellington Street. By the time of the formal opening a year later, it already had 500 members. Having bestowed its blessing, upper- and middle-class influence disappeared: the club was run for working men by working men. Very soon it had become 'the popular resort of the Kettering workers of all opinions'. Within the club, all the features that make late 19th-century (male) working-class life so appealing developed: conviviality, the love of horticulture and sport, mutual support. From the start it had a 'harmonic room'. Music and other entertainments were provided by the members themselves, local bands and other musicians. In 1898, a purpose-built concert room was added, with a skittle-alley underneath. Despite official denials that the bar was not a prominent feature, two-thirds, and sometimes more, of total annual receipts were for refreshments and tobacco: these provided the funds which enabled the club to flourish. Its seventh annual report (in 1895) outlined the activities which went on – a cricket club with two teams, a cycling club with 90 members, and a football club founded 'in connection with the cycling club'. There was an ambulance class, a mutual aid club, annual bird and flower shows, and a whist class. The club had a library and reading room (though

there is no mention of lectures). Donations were made to the Town and the
Rifle Bands, to the club's own relief fund and to the Kettering Centre
ambulance. Two years earlier, the club gave £26 5s. to the Kettering and
District Hospital, and took out shares in the Kettering Productive Co-
operative Boot Society and Rothwell Working Men's Club, and made a loan
of £50 to the Club & Institute Union. Aiding causes of concern to the
working classes became a regular feature.

With the growth of the town, other clubs soon followed. In 1894 the
North Park Working Men's Club was started in a corner of the Park gardens.
The United Trades club followed four years later, in premises in Mill Road
and Thorngate Street. The next year, 1899, in the great burst of patriotism
created by the Boer War, the Kettering Rifle Club was formed 'for the
encouragement of rifle shooting'. Money for a firing range was soon raised,
and one was made in Geddington, the club itself being in Havelock Street.
The late Victorian club scene was completed with the founding of the Town
Band Club in Rockingham Road.

Kettering's Friendly Societies

Some, possibly many, of the members of working men's clubs were in Friendly
Societies. The coming together of artisans and tradesmen to form clubs to
provide benefits in time of sickness and funeral expenses after death, had
a long history. In Kettering, the earliest known are three which date from
the 1790s: a Tradesmen's Benefit Society, a Junior Tradesmen's Society and
a third known simply as the Friendly Society. All were based in public houses,
as were most of the subsequent Benefit Societies. The practice was to hold
their annual meetings and club feasts on Easter Monday and these were
often reported in the newspapers. In 1850 the *Northampton Herald* noted
that there were 13 Kettering societies, comprising upwards of 500 members,
of which the Provident Friendly Society (started 1836) was the most
flourishing. The failure of the Gotch Bank was a severe blow; six of the
clubs lost the funds they had deposited. The biggest loser was the Caledonian
Lodge of the Manchester Unity of Oddfellows, with £395 in the bank at the
time.

Friendly Societies emerged in various ways. If some were tradesmen's
clubs, others were founded by the patrons of individual public houses (such
as the Old Angel Club, established in 1815, still going strong 50 years later).
Places of religious worship had their own Benefit Societies; additional to
the Baptist Meeting and Great Meeting clubs, the parish church ran the
Union Friendly Society. Others were part of the world of the 'national
affiliated orders'. Perhaps the earliest was the 'Caledonian' Lodge of the
Manchester Oddfellows. When 'Court Mystery' of the Ancient Order of
Foresters opened in 1842, it was launched with a splendid procession, with
Foresters from Oundle, Rothwell and other places taking part, carrying
banners and decked out in their regalia. Friendly Society processions became
a colourful part of town life.

In the course of the 19th century, other national affiliated orders opened branches in Kettering. 'Shakespeare' Lodge of the Nottingham Order of Oddfellows in 1844; the Ancient Order of Shepherds (connected with the Foresters) in 1864; and the next decade 'Blue Violet' Lodge of the Free Gardeners. As already noted, the Independent Order of Rechabites, a Temperance Friendly Society, had an early presence but faded away, to be restarted in 1871. Another Temperance Order was the Good Templars, which had two lodges in 1873. This started in America, as did the Buffaloes, under whose rules 'Lodge Lyric' opened in 1889. The following decade saw the 'Campbell Praed Encampment' of the Knights of the Golden Horn established in the town.

These various forms of benefit society had different levels of contribution, rule books, initiation ceremonies and lodge customs. A man would choose whichever he fancied or could afford, often choosing a club his workmates recommended. The aim of all was essentially the same; the avoidance of the workhouse in sickness or old age and of a pauper's funeral. The means were thrift, the pooling of resources, and the sharing of risks. Generally, the bigger your contributions the better your benefits. Some covered the illness or death of dependents: you chose your Society with these in mind. With regard to ceremonies and customs, they were often based on masonic models. By the later part of the century, despite the masculine thinking which lay behind their ethos, Female Friendly Societies had come into existence for working women (of which there were plenty in Kettering) and widows.

At the local level, the rich network of the clubs played a part in the public life of the town. By the last decade of the century, Whit weekend had replaced Easter for the annual meetings and celebrations. In 1893 there was a church parade which saw a thousand or so members process through the streets to Fuller, where they were treated to an appropriate sermon from the Rev. Phillips. Soon, the Amalgamated Friendly Societies Fête and Gala was established. Sport, music, dancing and other entertainments combined to provide conviviality and raise money for good causes.

If the Friendly Societies were the 'freemasonry of the working-classes', conventional freemasonry existed in the form of the Kettering Lodge of Free and Accepted Masons (No. 455, 'Perseverance'). From at least 1871 its major meetings, particularly those at which a new Worshipful Master was elected, were reported in the newspapers. From the lists of names provided it is clear that the brethren were drawn largely from the Conservative side of Kettering's professional and business élite. Almost all were churchmen, though a few were Wesleyans. Few, if any, names of leading Nonconformists appear. Before the opening of the new Masonic and Drill Hall in York Road in 1895 the Lodge's larger meetings were held in the Conservative Club.

The Rifle Volunteers

Rifle Volunteering was a patriotic development starting in 1859, when there was a war-scare caused by the Emperor Napoleon III's invasion of Italy.

74   *Warren East, boot merchant, Rifle Volunteer, bandsman and keen local photographer at Geddington Cross.*

Faced by a widespread desire to do something towards national defence, the idea of forming local companies of volunteer riflemen to act as a 'citizen reserve force' was suggested. It was taken up enthusiastically, with the leading landowners such as Lord Spencer, Earl Pomfret and the Duke of Grafton taking a lead in Northamptonshire. Because Volunteers had to buy their own uniforms (which cost three guineas), though the government supplied their weapons, they were drawn from the ranks of the better-off. Those who joined were mainly Conservatives, though there was a sprinkling of officers from Liberal families, such as Henry Gotch and E.P. Toller. The Kettering Company's first Captain was Captain Eden, agent to the Duke of Buccleuch, but the rural influence soon waned. From quite early, its officers and NCOs were professional men and the sons of manufacturers in Kettering, though for twenty years a leading light was Warren East, shoe repairer and bandsman, who rose from Private to Captain, finally retiring in 1890. Because (so it was said) of the strength of Nonconformity and Liberal opinion (which was generally against a warlike foreign policy), the town was slow to come forward, the 9th (Kettering) Company of the Northamptonshire Volunteers not being formed until 1861. There was perhaps another reason why Volunteers were drawn from the ranks of the better-off. Working men had for a very long time enlisted in the county Militia, the older reserve force whose history went back to the previous century.

Once the war scare of 1859 passed, despite much rhetoric about being 'the third line of defence', 'the most unique military force in the world' and the absurd claim that 'without the volunteer movement there would probably have to be conscription as on the continent', for forty years there was little chance of the Volunteers seeing action. Volunteer Companies were local clubs for men who liked to shoot and enjoyed dressing up in the grey uniform, with its black frogging and American-style forage cap. Other benefits were practising at the rifle range at Broughton, regular shooting contests with other Rifle Companies, an annual seven-day summer camp in the grounds of a country house, often Althorp (the 5th Earl Spencer being an ardent Rifle Volunteer), enjoyable annual dinners, and, for marksmen, visits to the National Rifle Association's annual Wimbledon meeting, which moved to Bisley in 1890. For Kettering, the best thing about the Volunteers was their Band, responsible for establishing the town's reputation in the brass-band world.

Festivals and Holidays

As Kettering became an industrial town, the holidays characteristic of an old market town did not disappear, but were changed and modified. By mid-century the old winter Assemblies were replaced by 'County', 'Yeomanry' and 'Yeomanry and County' Balls in January and February. The opening of the Corn Exchange provided a popular new venue for these and other meetings. For the general populace, the fun-fairs associated with the cycle of agricultural, cattle, and statute fairs and Mops persisted, though it went into decline in the last quarter of the century. Kettering's traditionally boisterous celebration of the Fifth of November declined about the same time. In 1855 an estimated three thousand people witnessed a re-enactment of the recently-fought Battle of Inkerman, after which a seven-foot effigy of the Tsar was burned in place of Guy Fawkes, adding patriotism to protestantism. The following year, long before dawn on the Fifth, the inhabitants were wakened by the incessant noise of guns, pistols and other firearms being discharged. All day the noise was deafening, supplemented by 'merry peals' on the church bells. In 1870, when the banning of the firing of guns and pistols came into force, the *Mercury* remarked that 'it has evidently found compensation in the greater spirit of the other demonstrations', by which was meant a huge bonfire on Market Hill which burned all day, and, as night fell, hooligans of all ages rolled burning tar-barrels and let off squibs and rockets. Thereafter, in keeping with the times, the event became more decorous.

One custom seems to have started (or been re-invented) in mid-century – the Christmas Waits. These at first were carols sung by the church choir

75   *Sanger's Circus comes to town, c.1900. Notice the lion and the lamb together on top.*

at midnight, but in 1861 Kettering 'No. 1 Band' began playing at 10 p.m., and the Temperance Band took over at midnight. On that occasion, out of respect for the recent death of Prince Albert, only solemn music was played. Christmas morning was greeted by the pealing of the church bells. In 1888, it was reported that the Waits were performed with more than the usual zest, the number of choirs and bands traversing the streets between 9.00p.m. and 6a.m. being greater than ever before. The Town Band, the Rifle Volunteer Band, the Salvation Army Band and that of the National School, plus several companies of vocalists, saluted the happy morn.

Apart from Christmas, the fairs and Guy Fawkes Night, the weekends and Mondays of Easter, Whitsuntide and Kettering Feast were the principal holidays. For reasons of religious solemnity (and the weather), there was more of a holiday atmosphere on the Mondays of the latter two, than at Easter. Sundays were given over to attendance at church or chapel, though concerts of religious music became increasingly popular with the expansion of music-making. Whit Monday and Feast Monday and Tuesday saw more secular pleasures. The coming of the railway had a transforming effect, particularly on the Feast. Hitherto, the tradition was that Kettering exiles and country cousins came to visit, and pleasures were taken within the town or on outings to Barton Seagrave Hall, Boughton Park or Rockingham Castle. Travelling showmen brought their attractions, and innkeepers laid on food, drink, music and dancing, the two bowling greens being customary venues for these entertainments.

The railway made visits easier and added the exciting possibility of excursions. Thus, on Whit Monday 1858, people had the choice of Pell's Celebrated Opera Troupe performing 'the songs of the slaves and free blacks of America', Ginett's American Equestrians (who processed the town before performing in a field off Northampton Road) or a railway excursion to Matlock. By 1890, excursions were available to London, Cromer, Hunstanton, Yarmouth and Blackpool. By then, both Whitsuntide and Feast Week had been extended into Tuesday, Wednesday and even Thursday, and the factories had taken to closing for the week. Over the years, the list of attractions greatly expanded; in addition to excursions, there were now band contests, flower shows, cricket matches, other sporting events, open-air Temperance and other meetings, and the annual demonstration of the Trades Council.

From 1871 Bank Holidays were introduced, the August bank holiday being popular from the start. Somewhat puritanically, in 1888 the Trades Council tried to persuade the town that the August bank holiday and the Feast were too close together and interfered with 'the convenience of the trade'. Their recommendation was that the Feast should be held over until August bank holiday. Whilst the closure of the factories for a whole week meant that working men lost pay, the idea proved a non-starter. The truth was, the manufacturers were not interested in working in Feast week because it fell conveniently 'between seasons'. The Trades Council tacitly accepted their defeat by undertaking to sponsor what soon became Feast Monday's chief event, their sports meeting for Athletics and Pony races. Unusually amongst English towns, down to the Great War, Kettering's Feast never lost its attraction. Not even the celebrations of the Queen's Jubilees in 1887 and 1897, coming just before the Feast, lessened the jollifications.

The holding of horticultural shows in market towns was traditional, going back well into the 18th century, but it was not until the 1880s that the organising of flower, vegetable, animal and bird shows on an annual basis became firmly established. These shows, spread throughout the year, added another element to the calendar of events open to the Kettering public. Interest amongst the fanciers was raised in 1868 both when the Kettering and District Horticultural Society held an Horticultural and Poultry Show, and also by the stimulus of the Northamptonshire Agricultural Society's annual show coming to Kettering in 1873. The Show left a surplus in the hands of the local committee and a portion of its members determined to revive the Kettering Poultry Show. By the middle of the next decade a plethora of societies and clubs had established their own annual events –

the Kettering & District Horticultural Society, which held its flower show in Feast Week and its chrysanthemum, fruit and vegetable show in November, the Dog Fanciers and the Ornithological Society, who eventually combined as the Kettering Ornithological and Canine Society (whose show was on Boxing Day), the Conservative Club with its flower show, the Working Men's Club Ornithological Club, the Rifle Band Club Ornithological Club, the United Trades Club & Labour Institute, with its annual exhibition of poultry, pigeons, rabbits and cage-birds. In 1895 the first show of the newly constituted Kettering & District Fanciers' Association in Victoria Hall was pronounced 'an unparalleled success'. When the County Show returned to Kettering in June 1899, it provided agriculturalists, horticulturalists and the fanciers with a much appreciated bonus to their year.

Music, entertainment and the arts

If later Victorian Kettering became well-known for its footwear manufacturing and Co-operative Societies, it also became notable for its brass bands. As already recorded, the first of these was the Temperance Saxhorn Band in the 1850s. The other early band was 'Mr Mobbs' Brass Band', which eventually became Kettering Rifle Band. If Temperance and the military connection were important influences on the emergence of banding, so was the greater availability of sheet music and musical instruments. The Town Band was formed in 1871 and soon became the Rifles' rival. If these were the top two, there were soon to be others: the Kettering Albert Band was formed in the workroom of Mr Foster, Albert Street, in 1873, and by the end of the century the Victoria Mission, the Salvation Army, the United (1895) and sundry church and chapel ensembles had appeared.

The Victorian public loved brass-band music. No event was complete without a band. Working men being what they are, it was not long before competition came on the scene. The first Kettering brass band contest, sponsored by the Rifle Band, was held in Feast Week, 1883, attracting six bands from outside Northamptonshire. First prize was take by Irwell Bank from Lancashire, the second by Burslem, Staffs, and the third by Colne, Lancs. They enjoyed their visit so much that they came back the following year, only to be bested by Black Dyke Mills. The band contest became one of the major attractions of the Feast, competing bands processing the town before the competition, attracting thousands to hear the music. After the competition pieces there was a concert, and the evening was rounded off with dancing. Soon, there were competitions for more local bands. One of the first (in 1888), organised by the Town Band, attracted entries from Earls Barton, Little Bowden, Rothwell, Walgrave and Desborough, all of which had benefited from the tuition of Randolph Ryan, bandmaster of the Town Band. In 1898, the first contest in connection with the recently formed Northamptonshire Brass Band League (First Division), resulted in the Rifle Band winning and (to general disbelief) the Town Band coming last, behind Earls Barton Old and Finedon Old.

Kettering bands were soon doing well in contests outside the town. In late 1891, the Town Band won 14 'firsts' and three 'seconds', and was invited to play on a bigger stage. In 1894 it took fourth prize at the annual contest at Belle Vue, Manchester. By now, the rivalry between the two main bands had become keen. Under the leadership of Thomas Seddon, the Rifle Band came to the fore. Appointed bandmaster in 1886, at the age of 24, he made it one of the best bands in the Midlands. Perhaps its greatest moment came when it was selected by the Town Council of Dieppe to represent England at an international band contest there on 3 July 1898, alongside bands from France, Belgium, Germany and Austria. The Rifles won three prizes. The judge, incidentally, was a M. Saint-Saens, 'the celebrated organist and conductor'. Later that year, the Rifle Band came fifth out of 20 at Belle Vue. At what was virtually the national championship at the Crystal Palace in 1901, the Rifles came fourth and the Town Band fifth.

Brass bands contributed much to life in Victorian towns. By providing readily available music they added to the *joie de vivre*. As well as keeping up the older tradition of religious music, they introduced people to the classical repertoire. They provided opportunities for boys with talent to make a name for themselves. They offered opportunities to travel – to local village fêtes or taking part in competitions further afield. Their clubs became part of the local club scene, and they were part of a national banding network, finding a welcome wherever they went. Moreover, they could always raise money for good causes. When severe weather led to unemployment and privation for the 'out-door workmen' in February 1895, bandmasters Seddon and Ryan suggested a street collection to supplement the efforts of the Kettering Relief Committees. The idea caught on, the two bands being joined by those of the United and of Fuller church. Playing in the streets, accompanied by four conveyances, money and provisions in kind were collected and distributed to over a hundred of the unemployed and their families.

There was plenty of other music-making besides that of brass bands. Kettering had a long tradition of performing sacred music. A notable concert was given in the Corn Exchange in 1868 by the church choir, assisted by instrumentalists, the principal feature of which was Mozart's 'Twelfth Mass'. This was the inspiration of the choirmaster, C.H. Ogle, departing for Brighton, who conducted an orchestra of 46 performers, led by J.F. Mobbs. A choral society started in 1880, arising out of a choral class run by the parish organist, Brook Sampson. For the first nine years of its existence its conductor was Henry Gale Gotch. In his time the society gave 23 concerts. In 1893 the Kettering Orchestral Society, formed with the object of 'further developing instrumental music in the town' gave its inaugural concert in Victoria Hall. The following year saw the promotion of a Grand Evening Concert 'given by Mr Percy Notcutt's talented company of vocal and instrumentalists'. It was said to have been the finest concert ever staged in

Kettering, and attracted a crowded audience in Victorian Hall 'from all parts of the town'. The hall was crowded two years later for a Complimentary Concert to Mr Charles Lawrence, 'a popular tenor vocalist during the past twenty-five years', where the star of the evening was Mr Harry Bailey, 'the popular baritone from the Albert Hall Concerts', a native of Kettering.

The entertainment in the working men's clubs provided 'turns' similar to those in music halls, if in an amateur way, though these were not open to the public at large. Eventually, in 1903, a Music Hall, The Coliseum, was opened in Russell Street. In this period there seems a lack of professional dramatic productions, though there were occasional visits to test the market. One such was the visit of the London Comedy Company in 1871, who performed for two nights at the Corn Exchange, with the popular comedy 'Still Waters Run Deep' on the Monday, and 'Don Caesar de Bazan' on the Tuesday, each performance concluding with 'the musical and humourous burlesque "Cinderella"'. Presumably those who craved more of these delights had to seek them out in Northampton or Leicester.

On the fine art front, Kettering followed with great interest the artistic careers of Thomas Cooper Gotch and Alfred East and local painters, notably W.T. Wright and J.T. Nettleship, whose new works were reported in the local press. Within the town, a development which took root was exhibitions of the work of amateur painters started by Harry Stannard RBA, a teacher of painting, who organised the first Kettering exhibition at the Corn Exchange in 1896. It contained over 200 pictures by local people and some woodcarving, art needlework and other craft exhibits. At the second exhibition the following year there were pictures by Gotch, Nettleship, Harris Brown the Northampton portraitist, making a name for himself at the time, and Hugh Watts. In 1898 the judging was done by East and Gotch, happy to be of help in their native town, Gotch exhibiting one of his best known pictures, 'Death of the Bride'. First prize was won by Harry Dorr, a rising young Kettering artist, and George Harrison also was a prizewinner. A tradition was created which lasts to the present. East was particularly keen to do what he could to stimulate interest in art. As we have seen, the result of all this was the founding of the Kettering Art Gallery and the generous bequest of pictures by East, by then Sir Alfred.

Sport in Victorian Kettering
The oldest continuous sport was, perhaps, bowling and there are newspaper references as early as 1797 to meetings on the Bowling Green, which was located on what later became the new cattle market, and left its name on Bowling Green Road. There was a second green belonging to Mr Harradine and, for much of the century, these were the only venues in Kettering for open-air events, such as those connected with Feast Week. Later, the Lodge Bowling Club was formed and met for twenty years or so on a ground at the rear of Lonsdale House, moving in 1901 to a new green and clubhouse on Northampton Road.

If bowling was the oldest, cricket was the second oldest sporting pastime. In 1855 there is a report of Kettering beating Higham Ferrers, and the following year two teams are mentioned, one 'Club' and the other 'Town', playing against Broughton and Wellingborough, both on a Monday. A decade later, two teams are mentioned – Kettering United and Kettering Albion. By 1877 the Albion had become Kettering Town Cricket Club, and by then trade-based matches were being arranged as the game spread. It was in the 1880s that the game became less occasional. In 1881 the Town played nine games, opponents including Oundle School, Wellingborough, Old Leysians, Mr Broadbent's XI and Mr Rokeby's XI. Its president was Dr J.J. Roughton, and a bat was presented to the Rev. G. Thurston for his feat in scoring a century. In 1888 Kettering Town went to Northampton to play a Northamptonshire Club and Ground XI. At this stage, the players were mainly the sons of professional men and manufacturers and such names as Dryland, Gotch, Stockburn, Toller, Bird and Hutchen appear, the Newman family being severally represented. That season the team played 24, won eight, lost nine, drew six and tied one. The following year the Club moved to a new ground and pavilion near Headlands Road. In 1896 the town club was the moving force behind the formation of the Kettering and District Cricket League, which had 20 teams, organised in three divisions.

By 1870, athletics had arrived on the scene and from the start reflected differing class perspectives towards sport. Working men had no rooted objection to competing for cash prizes and saw races as something to bet on. The middle classes had objections to both: their ideal was amateurism untainted by cash incentives, as reflected in the rules of the Amateur Athletic Association, although valuable prizes such as silver cups were offered to the winners of their competitions. Under these rules an athletics meeting was established in Feast Week in 1871, and soon became a major event in the Kettering year, especially when pony racing was added to it. Parallel with amateur athletics was 'pedestrianism', in which working men ran foot races for prize money. In May 1873, 62 competitors were 'on the card' for the heats for Mr Frederick Turner's 100-yards handicap, for prizes ranging from £2 10s. (about double the average weekly wage) for the winner, to five shillings for the fourth. In 1878, it was complained that 'professionals' were entering the Feast Week sports under fictitious names, and that money was being won because, even if they were later disqualified, betting was 'first past the post'.

In the decades before the Great War a widening range of annual athletic events was promoted by various Kettering clubs. The Football Club put on their first meeting in 1878, the Rifle Club in 1886, and the Amateur Cyclists Club started a cycling and athletics meeting three years later. One of the most popular was the annual sports meeting to raise funds for the new General Hospital. At its third meeting in 1898, 4,000 people paid for admission. By then, Kettering Town Football Club had its own athletics and cycling event, and cross-country running was organised by the Harriers' Club, which had been founded in 1896.

76   *Kettering Amateur Cycling Club in 1890, the year it was founded. Standing on the right is Harry Palmer, who became a champion wheeler and was a noted ice skater as well.*

In 1878, a Mr Farrar of Gas Street caused a sensation by riding round the Market Place on a tall-ordinary. In doing so, he introduced Kettering to the pleasures of cycling. Although machines were not cheap, through the blessings of hire-purchase ownership soon spread. Kettering Amateur Cycling Club was founded in 1890 and soon had 150 members. On August Bank Holiday Monday that year it held its first open athletic and cycling sports meeting on the Town Cricket Ground, Headlands Road. The following month, the Club's own athletics and cycling sports drew 2,000 spectators; in all there were four race meetings in the year, including a 40-mile handicap (Stamford and back). Soon, Kettering produced a champion, in the person of Harry Palmer whose career started when he was fifteen. He was the son of William Palmer, of Messrs Reesby & Palmer, the High Street Restaurant, himself a leading figure in the formation of the Club. By 1895, the 19-year-old had won 80 prizes at events all over the Northamptonshire, Huntingdonshire, Bedfordshire and Rutland district, the area affiliated to the National Cycling Union's Northampton Centre. Harry Palmer was also an excellent skater when the fens were frozen and 'no mean exponent of the game of billiards'. Sadly, he was to die young.

In that decade, two other clubs came into existence; the Kettering Thursday Cycling Club (presumably shop workers with a Thursday half-day) and the Wellington Street Working Men's Cycling Club. It was not long before the latter were holding their own athletics and cycling sports. Cycling was always as much about pleasure as competition. In June 1894, the Working Men's Club joined up up with the Northampton and the Rothwell Working Men's Clubs for an outing round the villages, ending with a convivial evening at a hostelry. Cycling was the most important extender of mobility since the coming of the railway; it took only a few minutes to be out of Kettering into unsullied countryside.

Alongside new sporting activities, old ones carried on, despite the best efforts of the law (and evangelical opinion) to stop them. 'Hush Hopper' of Kettering lasted 18 rounds in a prize fight in the open air against Bridgeford of Higham Ferrers in 1887. The following year, the police got wind of a 'supposed prize fight' between Cecil Hopkins, shoe hand, and Edward Powers, gas man. They were bound over by the magistrate and caused to enter into recognizances of £10 each to keep the peace and be of good behaviour for six months. In 1894, at a quiet spot near Kettering, there were reports of a prize fight between 'Kilrain' of Kettering and 'Whiskers' of Uppingham, which went 28 rounds in 40 minutes before the Kettering man's seconds threw in the towel. At the other end of the social spectrum, those who took their pleasure from horses could enjoy the Kettering races, 'a pleasant little meeting' for Hunters, Galloways and Ponies every Feast Week Monday from 1880, and from 1891 there was another pony racing, trotting, jumping and athletic Festival in North Park. With the widening of membership of the Pytchley hunt in the later part of the century, a few in Kettering availed themselves of the pleasures of horse and hound. The most surprising, perhaps, was J.T. Stockburn, who, having handed his business over to his sons in 1887, bought a farm. A great lover of the open air, he began to hunt with the Pytchley, a somewhat unusual pastime for an ardent Nonconformist and Liberal. It must have done him good; he lived to be ninety-seven.

For the middle classes, new sports came along in the '90s. Golf started in 1894, the local pioneer being Dr Allison. To publicise the game a 'championship match' was arranged between a Scots professional at Oxford University golf club and the pro at the Winchester club. The first Ladies golf championship was at Kettering in 1896, for the Goodyear Challenge Bowl, 'played under handicap by lady members of golf clubs in the county of Northampton over 36 holes'. The winner was Mrs C.W. Phipps of Northampton. Another sport destined to be largely the preserve of the middle classes, which also gave women the opportunity to participate, was tennis. In 1889 a team of Kettering ladies and their partners played Oundle at mixed doubles.

The game which had the most democratic appeal was, of course, football. It was said to have started in the district about 1869 when the Hon. and Rev. Henry Marsham came to Barton Seagrave and started a club there. A match was played against a Kettering scratch team under Eton Rules (on which soccer was to be based), which became an annual fixture. In 1871, G.W.

†KETTERING v. RUSHDEN.
C. DIXON'S BENEFIT.
A PRESENTATION.

For 14 years C. Dixon has been an active member of the Kettering Club, and during that time he has never absented himself from an engagement except through illness or other unavoidable causes. He played as centre with considerable distinction throughout the season in which the Kettering Association Eleven secured the Wellingborough and District Cup—seven or eight years ago—and did some useful work for the Rugby fifteen two years earlier, when they passed through the whole season without a reverse. In earlier times he was seen principally at the Rugby game, but of late he has gone in more for the dribbling code. He had been captain of both Kettering teams, and has represented the county at either. He is now about to retire from the football field, and very properly a benefit match was arranged as a parting tribute to his worth. It was played, in beautiful weather, on the Town Ground on Saturday afternoon, between

KETTERING AND RUSHDEN WANDERERS,

and was very fairly patronised. After an excellent contest the visitors proved victors by three goals to two. Prior to play the Kettering team were photographed, and at the close of the game an adjournment was made to the old Coffee Tavern, where about twenty members of the club and friends of Dixon, including Messrs. W. Freeman and W. Burgess, of the Rushden team sat down to tea. Afterwards, Mr. N. Newman, who presided, referred to the pleasure it gave them to gather together and do honour to Dixon, whom he had known during the whole of his football career; no member being more respected by colleagues and opponents alike. (Applause.) Dixon was only a small man (laughter), but he had grown with the game in the district (laughter and applause), and he had always played it thoroughly and fairly. (Cheers.)—Mr. H. T. Favell, as one of the committee, then handed Dixon a handsome silver English stopwatch, a gold albert and star, and also a purse containing six sovereigns — the result of the "gate" — amid cheering. Mr. Favell bore testimony to Dixon's unassuming and gentlemanly bearing, and said no player was held in greater esteem, especially by the local clubs, to whom he had given material help and advice. (Cheers.) By his good play and excellent behaviour Dixon had gained the post of captain of both of the teams, having been

CAPTAIN OF THE RUGBY TEAM

for the past four years, Mr. Favell, in concluding, thanked the Rushden men for their hearty co-operation; they responded to the invite of the Kettering committee to play the match with the greatest good will and warmth of feeling. (Applause.) They had generously given their services without fee or charge for expenses. (Cheers.)—Dixon was loudly cheered on rising to reply, which he did most briefly; and later on thanks were passed to the teams for playing, and to the committee for the benefit.—The proceedings were enlivened by a number of songs, and at the end of the entertainment Mr. Newman was thanked for presiding.

77   *Account of a presentation to an early Kettering footballer. Dixon was adept at both soccer and rugby.* Northampton Mercury, *13 April 1889.*

Roughton came to live in Kettering and under his captaincy a club was founded, its first match being against Uppingham School. The first away game was against Leicester 'where Rugby rules were played for the first time'. Until 1889, Kettering Football Club played under Rugby, Uppingham and Association rules, as the opposition wished. The unofficial club motto seemed to be 'You name it, we'll play it'. As in many industrial towns, in the '80s rugby was overtaken in popularity by soccer. In the end, the problems of trying to field teams who could play either form led to a decision in 1889 to make the club an Association one. By then there were several other football teams in Kettering – the Alberts, the Almas, the New Town Wanderers, the Hawks and the Revellers. Kettering became a soccer town at the time when soccer nationally was beginning to take on its modern shape. Kettering rugby faded away until 1902, when a new club was founded.

In 1884, Kettering Town won the Northamptonshire Senior Cup in the competition's first season, but, from 1889, the club widened its ambitions. Two years later it went professional, paying the players ten shillings a week, and joined the Midland League in 1893-4. In the next few years the club progressed steadily. The 1895-6 season was its most successful so far, coming first in the Midland League, winning the Kettering Charity Cup (which it had started in 1888-9 to attract a bigger 'gate' and raise funds for good causes. Clubs within fifty miles of Kettering were eligible to enter). Kettering Town also won the Luton Charity Cup, were runners-up in the Northants Senior Cup and had a run in the FA Cup ended by Newton Heath, the team which eventually transformed itself into Manchester United.

Down to the Great War, Kettering Town did all the things small-town clubs did to rise in the professional game. In 1897-8 it moved from North

78   *The Yeomanry assembling on the market place in 1913.*

Park to its present ground on Rockingham Road, won the Midland League again the next season and decided to widen its horizons. From 1900-01 it had three seasons in the Southern League. In the end, after coming bottom in 1903 and being £600 in deficit, it withdrew. The Club then played three seasons back in the Northamptonshire League, winning the championship in 1904-5, and acquired the nickname 'the Poppies'. Kettering then played in Division II of the Southern League (1908-9 to 1912), and then joined the Central Alliance, where it played until the coming of the Great War.

Intimations of War: Rifle Volunteers and the Army
In 1872 the Liberal government began a series of reforms of the organisation of the British Army, the essence of which was the linkage of old regiments with counties. It was announced that two line regiments, the 48th and the 58th, were to be linked to Northamptonshire and Rutland and to have a joint depot in Northampton, and the Northamptonshire & Rutland Militia was to be augmented to make two Battalions. At first, there was no place for the Volunteers in the new arrangements. In 1881 it was announced that, in

future, the 48th and the 58th Regiments were to be known as the Northamptonshire & Rutland Regiment and that recruiting for the line Battalions under ordinary circumstances was to be confined to those two counties. Thus was 'a territorial connection' established. Further reforms began to give the Militia and Rifle Volunteers a more modern role as 'territorial reserve forces'. By 1888 Kettering Company had become 'M' Company of the Northamptonshire Volunteer Battalion, and soon there was an 'N' Company as well. As a body they expressed themselves ready to undertake active duty, and from this time on training was much more concentrated and serious. By now their numbers had risen, and they got a new drill hall in 1895. In the Boer War, 160 officers and men of the 1st Volunteer Battalion served for a year in South Africa, 16 of whom were from 'M' and 'N' Companies. One, Private Cooper, lost his life there. If the role of the Volunteers in the Boer War was not a major one, it did establish their credentials as serious soldiers rather than a mere Home Guard.

The Boer War revealed the limitations of the British Army, which was stretched to beat what, after all, were irregular units of farmers. It was not as if the German or the French Army had been the enemy. It fell to the Liberal politician, Haldane, to modernise the forces from 1907. For the first time a County Territorial force was established which incorporated the old Militia, the Volunteers and the Yeomanry. The first two became the 4th Battalion, The Northamptonshire Regiment (Infantry), the Kettering Volunteers becoming 'F' Company. The Kettering Yeomanry, which had survived the general disbandment of 1828, and later in the century became the Kettering Troop of the Royal Bucks Hussars, became 'C' Squadron of an expanded Northamptonshire Yeomanry. The County Territorial Force, organised by a County Association, was equipped with its own Royal Field Artillery and Army Service Corps and the Officers' Training Corps at schools such as Oundle and Wellingborough Grammar was also part of it. By the time of the Great War the country had a proper Reserve force. It was to be tested to destruction.

Fifteen

THE GREAT WAR AND AFTER

Kettering at War

Kettering soldiers, in common with those of the other six nations and empires involved, went to war with smiles on their faces. 'F' Company of the 4th Battalion of the County regiment (the former Volunteers) went off to Northampton to train and the 120 officers and men of 'C' squadron of the Yeomanry departed for Bedford.They were soon to learn that war was no smiling matter. Into Kettering came the Scottish Horse for a six-month stay, and, by early October, Belgian refugees arrived, fleeing the invasion of their country by the German army.

In late 1914 the Yeomanry were sent to the Western front. Their first taste of battle came the following March, at Neuve Chapelle. The regulars of the 1st and 2nd Battalions, as part of the British Expeditionary Force, had gone to France at the outbreak, and were involved in the Retreat from Mons and the Battle of the Aisne. In November the 1st Battalion were invoved in the 17-day battle of Ypres: of the 700 men a mere 82 survived.The role of the 3rd Battalion (the former Militia) was to act as reserves. By October 1915 they had been providing drafts, on occasions at the rate of a hundred men a week, for 14 months. By that time, the Northamptonshire Regiment had grown to 10 Battalions. As well as those who were serving in France, where Sgt William Boulter of the 6th Battalion won the Victoria Cross at the Battle of the Somme in 1916, the 1st/4th Battalion were in the Dardanelles.

Almost immediately the war started it became apparent that it was going to be on a scale never seen before. Another army – Kitchener's Second Army – would have to be raised. Conscription then being unthinkable, local advisory committees were set up to encourage recruiting. In an amazing burst of patriotism, young men did not need much encouraging. By the end of September 1914, 20 per cent of the boot operatives of Kettering and district had enlisted. This was the era of 'Pals Companies'; famously, Edgar Mobbs of Wellingborough, Northamptonshire's former international rugby footballer, recruited some 250 of his friends. Mobbs was killed in 1917, and by then many of his pals were dead too.

By March 1915, a Kettering & District Volunteer Training Corps had been formed, and those who volunteered were in uniform by July. In

185

79   *The Reservists march off to join the British Expeditionary Force in August 1914.*

June 1916, the War Office gave sanction to the formation of the Northamptonshire Volunteer Regiment, the first Battalion consisting of men in the
Northampton, Kettering, Wellingborough and Towcester Companies, the
2nd from Higham Ferrers, Rushden and the other districts up to and
including Peterborough. The demand for yet more men was, however,
inexorable. By mid-1915 the idea of conscription first began to be aired. In
Kettering it was strongly opposed by 'progressive opinion', particularly the
Trades Council and the Liberal *Kettering Leader.* The way for conscription
was prepared by 'Lord Derby's Scheme'. A National Register of every person,
male and female, between the ages of 15 and 65, not serving in the forces,
was drawn up. When the register was complete, all single men of military
age were to be made the object of 'special visits' from recruiting officers to
persuade them to join up. The object of this 'canvass' was to induce men to
enlist – a plain 'yes' or 'no' would not be sufficient. The first men enlisted
under Lord Derby's scheme left Kettering in the second week in January
1916. A Local Appeals Tribunal was formed to adjudicate in cases of men
'starred' as being necessary for certain essential industries, and therefore
exempt from the scheme – for the time being.

With the government and a jingoistic popular press working in tandem, public opinion was steadily moved towards accepting conscription. In January 1916, Parliament gave a first reading to the (Compulsory) Military Service Bill. Leo Chiozza Money, Kettering's Member of Parliament, now pronounced himself in favour, and the *Kettering Leader* also came out in support. In July, it was estimated that in pre-war days 3,600 males of all ages were employed in Kettering's factories. Up to the present, 1,134 had enlisted and 2,823 were currently employed. An agreement had been reached that boot makers were needed more in the factories than at the Front. But, in October, the news was received that ten per cent of the 'eligible' workers were to be 'released for the army'. In January 1917 it was announced that *all* men in the boot trade under the age of 31 were to be called up.

There were those who opposed conscription on the grounds of conscientious objection. Early in 1916, the Kettering Urban Appeals Tribunal was set up to listen to appeals against military service on those grounds. Some were upheld, but hostility and ostracism was usually the fate of 'conchies', popularly seen as cowards or 'Pro-Germans'.

On the economic front, the War did wonders for Kettering's industries – footwear, clothing, engineering and iron-making. The footwear manufacturers were quick to send a delegation to Paris in August 1914 to secure their share of contracts placed for the French army and came back with orders for a quarter of a million pairs of army boots. They received double that from the War Office in London. In October, Kettering was turning out 90,000 pairs of boots a week and there was never a time in the Great War when demand lessened. The biggest order ever placed in Kettering came in April 1916, when the Russian government requested three million infantry boots and three million Cossack boots for the cavalry. In December 1918, it was estimated that, in the previous four and a half years, ten million pairs of boots had been made in the town's 34 factories. Clothing businesses such as Wallis & Linnell and the Co-operative Clothing Company received huge orders for khaki uniforms and other items of clothing and equipment. To cater for the insatiable demand for munitions placed on Kettering engineering firms, a separate Kettering Munitions Company was launched by Charles Wicksteed, E.F. Wallis and A. Wallis in July 1915.

The demand for expanded boot production brought orders in what had hitherto been slack times in the working year, such as the autumn and early winter, and in 1916 firms even stayed open in Feast Week. Record output brought record profits. But there were problems as well as profits. Manufacturers were not very enthusiastic when the government demanded they cut-back on production for the domestic market, but were forced to agree. Faced with a shrinking male labour force, overtime became routine, the working day running from 6.00 a.m. to 7.30 p.m. From the middle of 1915, the idea of allowing women to work the 'automatic machines' in the factories was voiced. It soon became reality. Most onerous of all for employers was 'War Socialism'. Key industries such as the Railways and the Coal Mines

80 *Land Army volunteer, Miss T. Wells, working at Aldwincle in 1917.*

were nationalised. In late 1914, the government took authority to exercise control of all branches of the leather and boot trades. The following year the government took over the direction of skilled labour, and trades union rules were relaxed. A Joint Board of Control and Arbitration, chaired by A.K. Bryan of Kettering, was imposed for the county (exclusive of Northampton), in place of the former local Arbitration Boards. Businessmen did not like War Socialism but accepted it as a patriotic duty – for the duration.

By mid-1915 the call was for the 'three Ms' – men, munitions and money. The latter was in the form of 'silver bullets', war loans. From the start, Kettering proved extremely patriotic. War Savings Associations sprang up in almost every factory and were eventually merged into one Central Association. By February 1917, the town had taken out more than £1 million of war loans, and, by the end of the War, an additional £½ million. For its efforts in raising war loans in 1920 the town was thanked by being given a 28-ton tank, which stayed on display for some years. In addition, Kettering proved notably charitable in raising money for the Prince of Wales' Fund, the Red Cross, the YMCA and the Blinded Soldiers Fund. Another outlet for helping the War effort was through the Voluntary War Workers Association, which aimed to produce socks, gloves, pyjamas and dozens of other articles for the comfort of soldiers at the Front. During its existence the Association turned out an estimated 50,000 items of this description.

Women played a crucial part on the home front. Despite trades union misgivings, the large-scale use of women in industry came in following the establishment of a Women's War Employment Committee in July 1916. Recruitment began in November when it was announced that there were vacancies for hundreds of females in boot production. From that year women were also employed in considerable numbers in the munitions industry and on the land. About a hundred worked at Wicksteed's; it was estimated that, by November 1918, between them they had produced about 85,000 shells. From September 1914 to April 1919 the Voluntary Auxiliary Division, under

Commandant Mrs Farmer, cared for wounded and sick soldiers at Kettering V.A.D. Hospital. This was supported by a ladies' Equipment Committee and by the Kettering Association for the Administration of War Work, which helped by contributing articles of clothing. Individual women from Kettering also served as V.A.D. nurses, one of the first being Miss Brindley, a teacher at the High School for Girls, who went off to a Serbian Field Hospital soon after war started.

The brunt of the hardships of life on the home front was largely borne by working-class women. Feeding families became difficult when food prices started to rise in the autumn of 1915, and price controls were brought in, beginning with sugar. Their difficulties were added to by the blizzard of March 1916, the worst since 1876, which came at a time when there was a coal crisis. Largely because of the vulnerability of food supplies (most of which were imported) to the German U-boat campaign, food shortages intensified in 1917. Increasing the acreage of land under cultivation and the King's proclamation on food economy of May that year would not have prevented the country being starved into submission had not the navy begun to defeat the submarine campaign. By Christmas 1917 the food shortage became acute. Public anger at profiteering and the Black Market was growing. Somewhat late in the day, in January 1918, rationing was introduced. Another major domestic issue was housing. Protests against rent increases began in 1915. By early 1916, a Kettering Tenants League had 1,000 members and they were strongly supported by the Trades Council. The declining quality of the housing stock and the failure to build new homes to keep pace with the rising population over the past decade or so was another factor. That August, the District Council announced plans to purchase land on Stamford Road for a 'Garden City' of Council houses.

The War brought important developments in Maternity and Child Welfare. As in all wars, children – the nation's future – came to be seen as precious. The idea for a Maternity and Child Welfare Centre for Kettering originated with a 'School for Mothers', started in May 1914 by the Citizens' League, who established the Kettering Health Society Welcome Club. Fortnightly lectures were given to young mothers, the project being funded by voluntary contributions. Eventually, the Sanitary Committee of the District Council agreed to take over the work. One result was that Kettering's first Health Visitor, Mrs Rawson, was appointed. At the beginning of 1916 the Local Government Board made the notification of measles and German measles to the local Medical Officer of Health compulsory. In 1917, the 'Save the Babies' movement was advanced by 'National Baby Week'.

The Great War reached its climax in the winter of 1917-18. The terrible battles on the Western Front in 1917 had failed to achieve the 'breakthrough' the generals on both sides had hoped for. At home, the prospect of being starved into submission was only narrowly averted. King George called for a 'Day of Intercession'; on 6 January 1918 the churches and chapels of Kettering, as in other places, were filled. In their Spring Offensive of 1918,

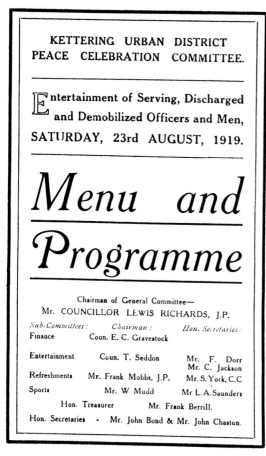

KETTERING URBAN DISTRICT
PEACE CELEBRATION COMMITTEE.

Entertainment of Serving, Discharged
and Demobilized Officers and Men,
SATURDAY, 23rd AUGUST, 1919.

Menu and

Programme

Chairman of General Committee—
Mr. COUNCILLOR LEWIS RICHARDS, J.P.

Sub-Committees :	Chairman :	Hon. Secretaries :
Finance	Coun. E. C. Gravestock	
Entertainment	Coun. T. Seddon	Mr. F. Dorr
		Mr. C. Jackson
Refreshments	Mr. Frank Mobbs, J.P.	Mr. S. York, C.C
Sports	Mr. W Mudd	Mr. L. A. Saunders
Hon. Treasurer	Mr. Frank Berrill.	
Hon. Secretaries ·	Mr. John Bond & Mr. John Chaston.	

81 *Kettering's official entertainment for servicemen in 1919.*

the Germans seized the initiative and broke the stalemate on the Western Front. For the first time since 1914, the War became one of movement. However, the German Spring Offensive was held, and, as rapidly as it had advanced, the German army was forced back towards the Rhine.

On Armistice Day, 11 November 1918, Kettering celebrated the end of the War with joy tempered with relief and near-exhaustion. Flags and bunting appeared everywhere. People thronged the streets, wearing red, white and blue favours. The bells of the parish church rang out. Factories closed. Wounded soldiers 'were the recipients of special recognition'. At the Board of Guardians, all present ('save one') stood and sang 'God Save the King'. The 4th Battalion (the old Volunteers) had always been in the front line, Gallipoli, Hill 60, Egypt and the battle of Gaza and so on. When the 2nd Northamptons, 'the Steelbacks', were given a big welcome in Northampton it did not escape notice that all there was left of the famous Battalion was a cadre of seven officers and 75 other ranks. Kettering's Roll of Honour revealed that 4,568 men and women served, of whom 833 were killed. Grandiose plans were made for a War Memorial in the form of a domed hall to seat 4-500, together with a large Cross in a garden at the corner of Sheep Street and Bowling Green Road. For the time being, however, a temporary wooden Cenotaph designed by J.A. Gotch, who lost his only son in the War, erected outside the Library, had to do. In the end, the planned Memorial Hall was never built, though the garden was laid out. A stone Cenotaph of modest proportions was erected in 1921, and the names of the dead were recorded on stone plaques on the walls of the Art Gallery. Eight decades later, the sheer number of names recorded there still has the power to shock.

The end of the War did not end human suffering or discord. By the time of the Armistice the great influenza epidemic was in full swing. In all, it was to kill more people than the Great War. In industry there was discontent over rising prices and arguments about the government's idea for Whitley Councils. In the autumn of 1918, serious discontent broke out in the form

82 *Kettering's Memorial to the Great War. The Cenotaph was erected in 1921, replacing a temporary wooden one. On the walls of the Art Gallery are the long lists of the names of those who lost their lives.*

of 'strike fever'. In Kettering, a demand for a 50 per cent pay-rise to offset the rise in the cost of living led to the first 'unofficial' strike in the footwear trade, with about 4,500 out in Kettering and another 1,500 or so in Burton Latimer and Rushden. The workers did not get all they demanded but were awarded a substantial rise of over 20 per cent by the Arbitration Board. At the same time, 50,000 ironfounders struck nationally, and there was a rail strike which went on for two weeks. There was also discontent amongst employers, who wanted an end to state direction. Most active locally was Charles Wicksteed, who gave lectures attacking bureaucracy and nationalisation, particularly of the coal industry.

Wartime Politics and the 1918 Election
Asquith's Liberal government, in power when the War started, was replaced in 1915 by a Coalition under Lloyd George – 'the man who won the War'. Party politics were suspended for the duration. Nonetheless, it was recognised by the more acute that, after the War, politics would never be the same again. Democracy – the extension of the vote to all adult males, and possibly to all or some women as well – would be irresistible if the country survived undefeated. The prospect of democracy posed a threat to the two political parties. The Member for Kettering was very well aware of the danger. Leo

83 *Leo (later Sir Leo) Chiozza Money, Liberal M.P. for East Northants from 1910 to 1918.*

Chiozza Money had a good War, being knighted in 1915 and becoming a member of the government, as Shipping Controller, in 1916. But his coming out for conscription in 1916 brought opposition from the left. That year, he declared that he would not stand in the next election because of the risks of a triangular contest. In fact, he was moving left, with other Liberals. In 1918 he resigned from the government and formally applied for membership of the Labour Party.

In 1914, the Kettering Labour scene was as highly fragmented as ever. By then it consisted of the Trades Council, the Independent Labour Party, the British Socialist Party (the Social Democrats under a new name), the Women's Labour League, a Labour, Church and various Co-operative bodies. The I.L.P. and the British Socialists were soon in opposition to the War. By 1915 they were the main supporters of the idea of a Peace, which brought down the wrath of the patriotic majority, convinced that the War was about Right versus Might, upon their heads. Labour supporters were deeply affronted when Councillor Haynes, the vice-chairman of the Urban District Council in 1915-16, failed to be elected to the chair in 1916, apparently because it felt Labour was 'unreliable'. Councillor Gravestock, a Liberal, carried on as chairman, a position he filled for the whole of the Great War.

It was in 1917 that events led to the formation of a Labour party. In April a meeting of East Northamptonshire labour organisations reviewed the prospects for the next election, which would come at the end of the War, and decided to support a Labour candidate. Things were clearly moving Labour's way. July 1917 saw the reorganisation of parliamentary constituencies, with Kettering moved to mid-Northamptonshire. The following month the Kettering & Wellingborough District Co-operative Association decided on direct representation for the movement in Parliament and resolved to put up a Co-operative candidate.

Separate from that development was the formation of a Mid-Northamptonshire Labour Party in November. Councillor J. Haynes was elected chairman and J.E. Chapman secretary *pro tem*. In January 1918 a Mid-Northampton-shire Co-operative Council was formed and names were forwarded to the Co-operative Union for placing on the roll of prospective Parliamentary candidates. The following month, the Mid-Northants Labour Organisation set up a selection committee, but agreed to 'exchange opinions' with the Co-operative Council. In July, the Labour Party agreed to joint action with the Co-operative Council. By the late summer, the choice for a candidate had narrowed to Howard Marlow, a Desborough man working in Oldham, and A.E. Waterson, president of Derby Labour party. A Derby Councillor, a keen Co-operator who believed in a 'Co-operative Commonwealth' he was also a Friendly Society man. A Primitive Methodist, Waterson was a life-long abstainer and a supporter of equal rights for women. He received the strong endorsement of the Women's Labour League and the Women's Co-operative Guild, and won the nomination.

By now, the Liberal Party was becoming seriously worried. At the end of May 1918 there was a meeting to wind up their association with East North-amptonshire and start a new one with the Mid-constituency. Harry Manfield, the sitting Member for Mid-Northamptonshire declined on health grounds to stand in the next election and Captain Leland Buxton was invited to become the candidate. Buxton pronounced himself in favour of the League of Nations, women's rights, co-operation and the Labour Party. However, he argued that there was still a political truce and that this was not the time to play party politics. In November, as supporters of the Coalition Govern-ment, Mid-Northamptonshire Conservatives threw their lot in with Buxton. However, shortly before the election, the National Party decided to contest the constituency, their candidate being General A.F.H. Ferguson, J.P., of Polebrook Hall, Oundle, twice wounded in the War. The policy of the National Party was 'nation before party'. It supported Lloyd George and hoped to see him at the head of a government composed of the 'best men of the nation'. What the candidature of Ferguson achieved was to confuse the Conservatives, some of whom were bewildered by their Party supporting a Liberal Coalition candidate.

The electorate for the new Mid-Northants constituency was 20,877 men and 13,747 women, women of the age of 30 and over having the franchise for the first time in parliamentary elections. In Kettering itself there were about 16,000 male and 3,500 female electors. In the first election for eight years, Waterson won, with 10,299 votes (45.7 per cent), Buxton came second, with 7,7761 votes (34.4 per cent) and General Ferguson was third, with 4,486 (19.9 per cent). Nationally, Lloyd George's Coalition got its vote of approval. Sir Leo Chiozza Money, standing as a Labour candidate, lost to a Coalition Unionist in South Tottenham: he must have wished he was still in Kettering. That year, Sir Francis Channing published his *Memories of Midland Politics*. He must have been glad he wasn't in Kettering. After 1918 the place was no longer Liberal-friendly. Down to the end of the Second World War the Liberals contested only two of the seven elections and came last each time.

In 1918-19, Labour people were cock-a-hoop, believing there was a real prospect of the command economy of the War Years being carried forward into 'reconstruction'. There was a certain amount of welfarism, notably on the 'Homes fit for Heroes' front, but Liberals and Conservatives were united in their opposition to 'government interference', nationalisation and, because of the rash of strikes of the time, against strong trades unionism. Labour was to find that under Lloyd George and his government the ideological clock was indeed going to be turned back to 1914.

The government did not find it easy to go back to the sort of capitalist system that existed before the War. Leaving aside the serious international problems which faced it, the British economy was in trouble. After a very short-lived post-war boom, the great staples of the Victorian economy – textiles, coal, iron and steel and ship-building – all went into decline, mainly because of the destruction of the network of international trade which had had Britain at its centre. Footwear and clothing, producing basic require-ments of the domestic market, were not as badly hit as the above-mentioned sectors, but their export markets were. Kettering and other footwear towns did not suffer the same as the North of England, South Wales and Scotland, but they did not escape the serious unemployment which came to charac-terise the inter-war years.

Politics and Elections 1918 to 1940

If the balance of the political parties in Kettering had tipped in Labour's favour, the vicissitudes of national politics affected the Party's fortunes in inter-war elections. Following the Unionist revolt against Lloyd George's Coalition, Waterson was defeated at the election in November 1922 by Owen Parker, a Unionist, though it was a very narrow defeat (129 votes out of a total of over 28,537). The following year, when Baldwin called for a general election over the Protectionism versus Free Trade issue, largely for tactical reasons, S.F. Perry, a trades unionist from Stockport, was returned for Labour, defeating Parker and a Liberal. For the first time, a Labour government found itself in power, though it relied on Liberal support in the House of Commons. The government did not last long. In the election of 1924, which saw the return of Baldwin to No. 10 Downing Street, Perry lost to Sir Mervyn Manningham-Buller, Bart., but narrowly – by 1,241 votes out of a poll of 30,000.

Perry, the father of Fred Perry, the noted tennis player, remained Labour candidate for Kettering and was rewarded in 1929 with a victory over a Conservative, Col. John Brown, well known as an officer in the Northamp-tonshire Regiment, and a Liberal, in an election which saw the return of a second Labour Ministry to power, again led by Ramsay MacDonald. The new government was unlucky; almost immediately it ran into the effects of the world-wide depression triggered by the Wall Street Crash. By 1931, a Labour government was forced, following Treasury advice, to make cuts in public expenditure, including unemployment benefit. This split the cabinet.

Out of the crisis, a National government was formed under MacDonald's premiership. MacDonald, like Lloyd George after the election of 1918, found himself the head of a National Government consisting mainly of Conservatives. Labour was thrown into confusion. At the 1931 election, Perry lost easily to a Conservative, J.F. Eastwood. Kettering was not to have another Labour Member of Parliament until 1945. A Co-operative and Labour man lost the election of 1935, and in a bye-election in March 1940 another Conservative, John Profumo, defeated an Independent. Thus, for over 14 years, Kettering was represented in Parliament by a Conservative.

Local Government between the Wars

The election for seats on the Urban District Council in April 1919 revealed how the balance had shifted in Labour's favour. Seven Conservatives, eight Liberals, six Labour and three Co-operative councillors were returned, together with one Independent, in the person of Mrs Frank Wilson, the first woman to be elected. By 1926, the number of Labour and Co-operative councillors had risen to 14 out of the 25 seats. Also that year, three of the five county councillors for Kettering were Labour men, and six out of the 15 guardians of the poor. However, Co-operative and Labour lost their majority on the UDC after the General Strike that year and did not regain it until after the Second World War.

In the 1920s the Council busied itself with housing, an urgent political as well as social issue, as R.T. Smith, the Council Engineer and Surveyor, frankly admitted in his *Municipal Work in Kettering* (1925). 'During the last four years the Kettering Council have undertaken a number of works, some of which would not have been dealt with so soon, but were specially put in hand with a view to the relief of unemployment ... new roads, highway improvements and recreation and athletic grounds ... and a little over twelve months ago the Council started a building department for the erection of houses on their housing estates.' The decision to purchase land on Stamford Road had been carried out in 1919 and the development of the first council estate was planned on the model of the Cadbury estate at Birmingham, complete with Central Avenue, circular outer road and connecting roads. Kettering workers were offered suburbia, and this type of low-density new housing (12.4 to the acre in this case) became the national post-war norm. By 1923, 281 houses, mostly 'parlour-type houses with three bedrooms', had been completed. Accompanying this were three new roads 'completed as works for relief of unemployment, the Ministry of Transport contributing half the cost' – Windmill Avenue (the Stamford Road end of which was the western boundary of the new Council estate), Gipsy Lane and Southfield Avenue which, as Smith observed, 'forms a bye-pass route connecting three main roads'. In addition, the Council had also improved the water supply. It needed to provide a higher pressure in the mains and greater storage facilities. At Clover Hill it installed larger pumps and enlarged the reservoir. In this burst of activity, a new Fire Station was also built.

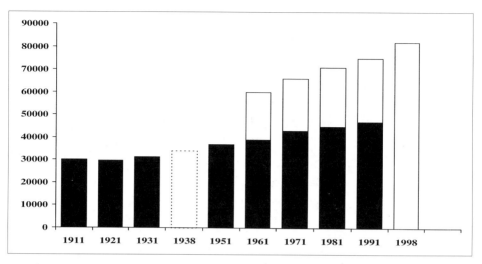

84 *The population of Kettering, 1911 to 1998. There was no census in 1941, but there is a 1938 estimate. From 1961 the higher figure is for what became the new Borough of Kettering.*

In all, between the wars, 1,572 new houses were constructed on the edges of the town along such roads as Gipsy Lane, Windmill Avenue and St Mary's Road, the majority by builders other than the Council. The Co-operative Society was quick off the mark in 1919 with the construction of 32 semi-detached houses on its Neale Avenue estate. Most were built in the '30s when deflation and low interest rates led to a building boom, an important factor in the economic recovery of the time.

Economic Developments between the Wars

Kettering's 'great leap forward' had come to a halt just before the Great War. As the population statistics indicate (growth in the 40 years from 1911 being a mere 7,000), in the first half of the 20th century, Kettering's economy was in a 'steady state' situation. No other significant industrial developments came along to keep Kettering's economy dynamic. Down to the 1960s, the staple trades of the later 19th century continued to serve Kettering well and to employ much of the labour force, both male and female. In 1935 the number of boot and shoe manufacturers had fallen from the 1916 figure of 34 to 26. Kelly's 1940 *Directory* lists 26 firms, 17 of which were still in being in 1951. In addition are listed four last manufacturers, boot heel makers and shoe-filler manufacturers, and 24 firms in the leather business. Of the 15 engineering firms, five made boot and shoe machinery, and a fifth produced boot and shoe-repairing machinery. The others had a range of specialities, from tool making, agricultural implements, ball bearings and flexible shafting, to printers' machinery, the business of Timsons Ltd, of Perfecta Works, Bath Road, successors to Owen Robinson's old firm.

Clothing, chiefly the firms of Wallis & Linnell and the Kettering Clothing Manufacturing Co-operative Company, remained major employers until after

85 *Factory life: the 'Gentlemen's Fashions' machine room at Kettering Co-operative Clothing Company factory in the 1920s.*

the Second World War. By 1919, the Co-operative Company had a thousand workers in its Field Street and Cobden Street factories and had become the town's major employer.

The coming of such transformers of 20th-century life as the cinema, radio and the internal combustion engine did much to change social life in Kettering, as elsewhere, but did little to alter the basic pattern of Kettering's economy. The provision of buses made it easier to move around locally, especially for country people, and the motor car did the same for the middle classes, to whom motor car ownership was largely confined in the inter-war years. The sale and maintenace of vehicles led to the establishment of firms in the motor car business, the 1940 *Directory* listing some 25, the great majority being agents or engineers (or both) though there were four car-hire firms and one (motor vehicle) body builder.

Stability and Change − Social Life in Inter-War Kettering
This period in Kettering's history has its own local chronicler in the late Tony Ireson. Born in Kettering in 1911 and educated at the Grammar

School, except for his war service years Tony spent his life in the town, much of it working as a journalist on the *Evening Telegraph*. In the 1960s he became involved in resisting the Council's plans for demolition and rebuilding the town centre and in 1984 published an account of this in *Old Kettering and its Defenders*. Four years later he published *Old Kettering – A View from The 1930s. Book 1*, which arose out of the previous book and the experiences which led him to write it. Thereafter, at intervals of two years or so, another five *Old Ketterings* appeared. At the time of his death in 2002, a seventh was almost ready for the printer. These books took a picaresque approach to Kettering as he knew it in the 1930s and to what happened since. Essentially, they are hymns to localism. His point is that, 50 years ago, local life was more truly local than it is now, and was the better for it. Kettering's businesses were locally owned and operated, its Council provided most essential services, local endeavour had built and maintained the local hospital and much besides. These services, he says, absorbed the talents and the abilities of townspeople in every walk of life. 'They were needed, they were working with and serving their fellows, their jobs gave satisfaction and most never thought of migrating. Kettering prided itself on its remoteness from London and its resistance to outside influences.'

Ireson's *Old Kettering* volumes touched strong feelings of local patriotism. In each subsequent volume he printed information and photographs sent in by readers which added to the story. No outside historian could possibly recapture Kettering in the '30s (and earlier) with quite the same degree of intimacy. Nonetheless, they viewed the past through rose-tinted spectacles and their approach, darting from one story to another, gives a cumulative rather than an analytical account of the town. Moreover, they see Kettering as an island entire unto itself. Few are the references to what was happening in the world beyond. The problem is that Kettering has always been affected by outside influences – the coming of the railway or the introduction of the workhouse system, to name but two.

One of the reasons why Kettering fascinated Tony Ireson was that the town was physically and institutionally still Victorian-Edwardian, give or take such additions as motor garages, cinemas, the opening of shops such as Montague Burton the tailor, Marks & Spencer and so on. And it remained essentially Victorian-Edwardian until the urban renewal of the 1960s, when the rapidity of economic and social change, so characteristic of the modern era, began to sweep away Kettering's old economic, social and institutional bases.

In 1940, the Victorian pattern of the Friendly Societies was still there, despite the fact that old-age pensions and national insurance had to some extent replaced or undermined them. The five old brass bands were still there, but had been joined by a newcomer, Munn & Felton Works Band which, within a year or two of its inauguration, had the temerity to come first at the Crystal Palace. The pattern of the places of religious worship remained as in 1914, with the addition of such latter-day denominations as

86   *The expansion of K.I.C.S. The opening of the Brigstock stores, 1920s.*

the Seventh Day Adventists, the National Spiritualist Church and the Company of Jehovah's Witnesses. Kettering was no longer 'the Holy Land' of a century before, but religion was still strong and religious rivalry was still there. But the connection between religion and politics was not so important. Politics in the 20th century revolved around class, not religion.

Kettering remained 'the very mecca of Co-operation'. On the eve of the Second World War the K.I.C.S. had 24 branches; no part of the town lacked a store. It had an optical department for spectacles, and its own house-decorating business. The four manufacturing Co-operatives were still producing boots and shoes, clothing and corsets. The teeth of co-operators were looked after by the Co-operative Dental Association Ltd., and they could buy their houses through loans on mortgage from the Co-operative Permanent Building Society. The Co-operative Insurance Society Ltd. insured them against sickness and provided funeral benefit, and the Co-operative

87   *Wicksteed Park: the paddle boat lake and miniature railway. By 1921 Wicksteed had spent £50,000 on his park.*

Funeral Service was available to bury them. On the political front, the Co-operative Party retained the upper hand in its partnership with Labour. On the Working Men's Club scene, the pre-war network was augmented by several new ones – the Miniature Rifle, the United Services, the Windmill Working Men's Club in Stamford Road and the Argyll in Argyll Street.

On the educational front, by 1940 the Boys' Grammar School had grown, 70 places having been added to the original 211 and the Girls' High School had expanded by 56. The latter also had a Junior School in Headlands, opened in 1918. Kettering now had a County Boot & Shoe School in Thorngate Street. Proud of the record of its School Board in the later 19th century, Kettering felt a similar pride in the record of its Education Committee in the first half of the 20th, regarding itself as the most progressive authority in Northamptonshire. Taking advantage of the Fisher Education Act of 1918, it had opened a Central School two years later, the only one in the county. At a time when secondary schooling for all was a distant pipe-dream, this was a post-elementary school for 12- to 16-year-olds. What the Kettering authority would also have liked was a Technical College, but that did not come into being until after the Second World War.

In some respects, Kettering's traditional sporting and recreational patterns resumed in the inter-war years, but there were new developments. If the popularity of radio, from its beginnings in 1925, created a new form of entertainment inside the home, and the B.B.C.'s policy of making the nation feel that it was one big family was influential, the arrival of the moving pictures provided potent and reasonably priced entertainment outside the home. By 1940 there were six well-established cinemas in Kettering – the Empire in Eskdaill Street, the Electric Pavilion in High Street, the Odeon in Gold Street, the Savoy in Russell Street and the Regal in High Street. The Victoria Hall was the first to show silent films, and talkies when they came along in 1927. 'The Vic' was eventually purchased by the Odeon chain and rebuilt as a luxury cinema in 1936. In the inter-war years the weekly visit to the cinema transported people out of their mundane everyday world. It was one of the things which made the Depression years bearable.

For Kettering people, and those within reach of Kettering, they were also made bearable by Wicksteed Park. Although not a local man in origin, Charles Wicksteed became one of the most characteristic of Kettering businessmen of the later Victorian era. After having to struggle to make his business successful, eventually he made a good deal of

88 *Charles Wicksteed (1848-1931). The son of a Unitarian minister, from an early age he showed mechanical talents. He built up a successful engineering firm in Kettering, and played a full part in local politics, being an ardent disciple of Gladstone. Passionate, irascible and individualistic, having failed to persuade the Local Board to open a public park, in the end he made one of his own.*

money. In 1911 Wicksteed purchased 400 acres of the Barton Hall estate and in 1916 formed the Wicksteed Village Trust, which was endowed with shares in his firm. It was somehow characteristic of him to risk his business for a project he believed in. His original plan was to develop a model village of low-cost pre-fabricated houses, but with the arrival of council houses after 1918, this idea was abandoned. Some land was sold for private housing. With the remaining 140 acres Wicksteed embarked on plans for what was to evolve into the first children's recreational park in the country. He started with a boating lake in 1919 and a huge programme of tree-felling. Two years later, the park was officially opened. By then, he had already spent £50,000. At regular intervals, new features were added. The park became popular with children and adults alike, one of its great virtues being that there was plenty of space to absorb the largest crowds. Wicksteed, always accompanied by his dog, was a familiar figure there. In 1928 he spent another £6,000 on the purchase of Barton Hall, which eventually became a hotel and later an old people's home. Most popular at the weekend and at holiday times, the park is open every day for people to walk in. Nowadays, entry is free but there are charges for motor cars. Wicksteed placed its

89   *Fourth generation: the four sons of T.H. Gotch. Standing, right, John Alfred Gotch, architect and writer on the history of architecture, Kettering's charter mayor. Next to him is Thomas Cooper Gotch, artist, in Kettering for an exhibition of his works (shown on the walls behind). Seated, left, Davis Frederick Gotch and, right, Henry Gale Gotch.*

future in the hands of a charitable trust and each year donations are made to charities out of the profits. Charles Wicksteed died, sadly by his own hand, in 1931. His body lay in state in the pavilion in his park, the continuing existence of which keeps his memory alive.

The '30s were coming to a close when, in 1938, Kettering acquired a borough charter, a corporation and a mayor. The first to don the chief magistrate's chain and robes of office was John Alfred Gotch, the architect who left his mark on Kettering through the buildings his firm designed. And who better, as a representative of the fourth generation of arguably Kettering's foremost modern family, to inaugurate a new era in Kettering's local government? The event coincided with Neville Chamberlain concluding the Munich Pact with Hitler. The country soon found itself having to fight the Great War all over again.

Sixteen

THE SECOND WORLD WAR AND AFTER

Kettering in Hitler's War

If Britain came closer to defeat and invasion in 1940 than at any time in the Great War, the cost in casualties was far less terrible, though it was bad enough. The town's War Memorial carries the names of 297 servicemen who lost their lives, just over a third of the number in 1914-19. Kettering men serving in the Northamptonshire Regiment and the Yeomanry saw action in most theatres of the war. At the outset, the 1st Battalion was in India, where it stayed until 1943, when it was sent to Burma to fight the Japanese for the rest of the War. The 2nd and 5th Battalions were with the B.E.F. and took part in the retreat from Dunkirk. Subsequently they served in North Africa, the invasion of Sicily, in Italy and then took part in the Normandy Invasions and the subsequent campaign in Europe. The 2nd Battalion suffered so many losses in Normandy that it was disbanded and the men allocated to other units. The Yeomanry, which had gone over to tanks and armoured vehicles in the 1920s, was also involved in Normandy, the battle for Antwerp and 'the Battle of the Bulge' in the Ardennes. In their amphibious troop-carriers they ferried infantry over the Rhine for five days in the invasion of Germany. Kettering men also served in other regiments in the army, and in other services. Marine William H. Mills took part in the 'Cockleshell Heroes' attack on German shipping in Bordeaux, being in one of only two canoes to reach their target. After blowing up enemy shipping, he was, like nearly all the rest of his comrades, captured by the enemy and executed. News of this did not come out until November 1945. When he died he was only 20, the age at which so many others lost their lives in the War.

From 1942, Britain became the base from which the United States' Air Force, alongside the Royal Air Force, launched massive and continuous air-raids on Germany and German-occupied countries. The Americans had the use of airfields all over Eastern England. Close to Kettering were Grafton Underwood, Harrington, Deenethorpe and Benefield. Between August 1942 and the end of the War, the Americans flew more than 9,000 sorties from Grafton Underwood alone, dropping over 23,000 tons of bombs on enemy targets. On these missions, 1,500 young Americans lost their lives. From

90 *The North African campaign: men of the 5th Battalion, Northamptonshire Regiment march into Tunis, May 1943.*

Harrington more than 2,500 sorties were flown, many of them to supply the French Resistance, which often involved making dangerous landings in France. The War was an unforgettable experience both for local people and those young Americans, some of whom took brides from the Kettering district back to the United States. In 1980 it was American ex-Servicemen who paid for the restoration of the bells of Kettering parish church, 28 of the veterans coming over for the ceremony.

The experience of the Great War meant that this country was better organised on the home front in Hitler's War. Conscription and rationing came in from the start. Farming, as in the Great War, was directed by the government and people were urged to 'Dig For Victory'. By the end of the War, 2,306 Kettering 'allotmenteers' occupied more than 232 acres in and around the town. Women played an even bigger role than in 1914-18 – in the services, in factories, driving vehicles and on the land. A major role was played by the Women's Voluntary Service for Civil Defence (WVS), founded in 1938. Their work was invaluable in the reception of refugees and in the

91   *The young and the brave: U.S. airmen at Deenethorpe.*

38 branches of Civil Defence. In Kettering, the WVS ran a canteen for
servicemen in the Cornmarket Hall for five and a half years from June
1940, staffed by 300 local women, some of whom did the work in addition
to working full-time. In the last two years of the War, the County WVS ran
a highly organised 'rural pie' scheme, delivering over nine million meat
pies and sausage rolls and two million jam tarts from three factories which
produced the food in WVS vans to their representatives in the villages, who
sold them to residents. On the Civil Defence front, there were 300 (male)
Air Raid Wardens in Kettering.

   As in the Great War, Kettering's footwear industry played an important
part in the war effort, producing around 75 million pairs of boots for the
armed forces, including three million pairs for the Russians. The whole
footwear industry was directed by a Government Footwear Controller, Major
F.J. Stratton, from his office in The Headlands, service contracts being
allocated on a quarterly basis to a range of manufacturers. Because of the
scarcity of leather, one achievement was the salvage (a great Second World
War word) of old boots. Special machines took worn-out footwear apart and
what leather could be re-used went towards boot 're-building'. All this was
accomplished with a greatly diminished labour force and without those
footwear factories taken over for other purposes. As in 1914-18, Kettering's
other industries played their part in the War effort, ranging from the

92   *The Duchess of Gloucester visits Wicksteed's, December 1953. The firm was mainly producing industrial sawing machines, which were widely used in the war effort.*

manufacture of 100,000 'silk yellows' by the Corset Society factory, to be worn on the back of their uniforms by allied troops 'for identification purposes' had the country been invaded in 1940, to tens of thousands of more conventional military uniforms, to the miles of steel tubing for 'Pluto', the fuel pipeline across the Channel used in the invasion of Normandy in 1944, made at Corby works under conditions of the utmost secrecy.

Northamptonshire soldiers took part in the Normandy landings and pushed on with the 21st Army through France, Belgium and Holland. In February 1945, the editor of the *Kettering Leader* visited and reported his meetings with local men serving in Belgium. The Germans fought a fierce retreat, but R.P. Winfrey was there for the *Leader* when the Rhine was crossed early in April. For the Germans, the war was almost over. Hitler committed suicide on 1 May and a few days later his armies unconditionally surrendered. VE (Victory in Europe) Day brought a great burst of relief and joy. 'For two days [8 and 9 May]', reported the *Leader*, 'thousands of revellers gave the town an atmosphere of a swift-moving and colourful Mardi Gras.' People danced in the streets throughout the night to music from radios and radiograms and almost every street had its bonfire and open-air tea party for the children. There followed a United Service of Thanksgiving on the Wednesday attended by thousands, some wearing black armbands in mourning. A sour note was sounded by the rector of Kettering declining, on behalf of the four Anglican churches, to take part. 'If they did so it would convey a false impresssion of a unity which did not exist', he said. The rector of Barton Seagrave, however, took part in the United Service, remarking, 'I cannot understand the attitude of my brethren'.

It took another three months and the dropping of atomic bombs on Hiroshima and Nagasaki to force the Japanese surrender on 14 August. Seven thousand people attended the open-air Service of Thanksgiving in the market place to mark VJ (Victory in Japan) Day. In attendance was the Mayoress, Mrs Hilda Tew, whose husband had been killed in Italy in May 1944.

On the War Savings front, Kettering proved itself as patriotic in the Second World War as it had been in the First. In September 1945 Kettering easily exceeded its target of £250,000 in aid of 'Thanksgiving Week', just as it exceeded its targets for 'War Weapons Week' in 1941, 'Warships Week' in 1942, 'Wings For Victory Week' in 1943 and 'Salute the Soldier Week' in 1944, each time by over £100,000. Even before the end of hostilities, the first determined efforts to return to normality began. In January 1945, the Council affirmed pre-war plans for a Civic Centre on the Cattle Market; in April, for the first time since 1940, the Kettering and District Eisteddfod was held; in May the Kettering Arts Association held its annual exhibition; and in November, the Woodland Pytchley restarted foxhunting with a meet at Rockingham Castle.

Brave New World

When the Rev. T.P. Adler, vicar of Rothwell, returned home from four and a half years as an army chaplain in Egypt, he observed that 'the people at home look very thin, hard-worked and underfed'. How right he was. Life had been hard and 'Austerity' was to remain official policy for some years. But immediately after the War ended, attention turned to politics: there was a general election to be fought.

John Profumo, Kettering's Member of Parliament, had a good War. In fact, in 1945, he seemed to have everything: a Lieut.-Colonel on Field-Marshal Alexander's Staff, at 25 years of age he had youth, wealth, good looks and intelligence. In the event, none of this proved enough to win again in Kettering. All over the country, Labour candidates were returned in a remarkable victory. Profumo was beaten by G.R. Mitchison, who won with a majority of 6,444 votes. Profumo indicated that he would remain Conservative candidate, but in 1950 found the safest of safe Tory seats in Stratford on Avon. He became a cabinet minister in Macmillan's government, but his career was ruined by his involvement in the Christine Keeler/Stephen Ward scandal. Mitchison remained Kettering's MP until 1964 when he was succeeded by Sir Geoffrey de Freitas, another Labour politician of impeccable bourgeois credentials. Kettering remained 'a safe Labour seat' until 1983 (de Freitas being succeeded by Bill Homeward, a steel union man, in 1979).

Once the peace celebrations and the general election were over, there was little euphoria. People were short of almost everything – food, coal, even water. There was a housing crisis, the state of the nation's health caused concern and on the industrial front there was an acute shortage of labour and raw materials. The wartime system of the rationing of coal, food and clothing continued. Plans were hastily made to improve Kettering's water supply and housing. Builders rushed to erect 600 houses, including some pre-fabricated dwellings, on a new Council estate on Stamford Road. On the health front, the immediate concern was the incidence of tuberculosis, especially among footwear factory workers. A mass-radiography programme was started; by 1951 the extent of the disease had, according to the authorities, 'drastically declined'. By then, the National Health Service, the cornerstone of the 'Welfare State', had come into being. In 1945, 'Kaycee' reported that it had 'lost' 800 women and girls since 1939. New female workers were attracted from Scunthorpe and South Wales. In the ironstone mines and ironworks, foreign workers were recruited, and many of the war refugees – Poles, Czechs, Ukrainians – never returned home. In footwear, there were grumbles that the army was slow to release workers. More disturbingly, there were fears that the trade was no longer attractive to school-leavers, though, in November 1945, there were substantial wage rises. Manufacturers felt that the hand of government control lay too heavy on them and they were beset by other problems, not least leather shortages. But there was optimism. It was assumed that Kettering's future would be like its past, only better.

And for nearly twenty years it was. There was good demand from export markets for footwear, the government was encouraging about the prospects of the industry and hopes for a Footwear Research Centre were fulfilled with the establishment of the Shoe and Allied Trades Research Association (SATRA) in the town. The post-war era was better than the '20s and '30s because of full employment and the introduction of the Welfare State. Full employment was achieved partly by government policy, partly because of the labour shortages, partly by the unions being much stronger than in the past, and, significantly, by the effects of the Cold War, the Korean War and the Malayan Emergency. British industry benefited from all these, though, in the longer run, this featherbedding of government contracts took industry's collective eye off the importance of exports.

In its determination to avoid a repetition of the disappointments after the Great War, the Labour government was committed to massive social welfare and industrial projects. On the social welfare front, compulsory national insurance, unemployment and other benefits, old-age pensions for all (of a certain age) and a National Health Service free at the point of access, were brought in. On the industrial front, the railways, the coal mines and the steel industry were nationalised. Most contentious was steel nationalisation. In 1951, 12 local companies became part of British Steel, including the Kettering Iron & Coal Company, Cransley Furnaces and Stewarts

& Lloyd at Corby. Ten thousand workers were affected. The government were much impressed by schemes of rationalisation and economies of scale in the public utilities; Kettering Gas Company became part of a large regional Board, as did Kettering Council's electricity and water.

Immediately after the War a major isssue in Kettering was the implementation of R.A. Butler's 1944 Education Act. There was much sorrow about the ending of Kettering's Education Committee and pride in its record, and there was ill-feeling over the constitution of the new divisional executive to replace it. In the end the new executive consisted of Kettering, Burton Latimer, Rothwell and Desborough. The aim of the new Act was to create secondary education for all, the school-leaving age was raised, and, joining the Grammar School, the Girls' High School and the old Central School, Rockingham Road and Stamford Road Schools were designated secondary schools. Few at the time foresaw the contentiousness of the 'Eleven plus' and the failure of 'parity of esteem' of Grammar and Secondary Modern schools to be accepted by parents. What was appreciated was free secondary education, the increase in the number of places to be competed for in the Grammar Schools, and the access these schools offered to higher education and upward social mobility.

Housing was the other crucial issue facing the Council in the immediate post-war years. When plans were announced for a crash programme of 600 new houses the housing department received 2,000 applications. As we have seen, the first tranche of new houses was completed in a year on the new estate on Stamford Road. By the time of the Festival of Britain celebrations in 1951, 450 houses on the Grange Housing estate on the opposite side of that road were ready for occupation. By 1956, 1,500 new homes had been added to Kettering's housing stock.

In these years Kettering found itself with a cuckoo in its nest. Even before the end of the war Corby was making bold plans for the future. Interestingly, at first, it looked to new light industries; 'Will Corby be a Young Sheffield?' was one *Kettering Leader* headline in April 1945. It seemed not. A few weeks after, it was announced that Corby works was planning another tube mill and more furnaces. And a few weeks later the Corby Joint Planning Committee announced a ten-year plan to increase its population to 30,000. In 1946 Corby was given New Town Status, and British Steel was soon making plans for a big extension of Corby Works. By 1950 Corby Development Corporation began the work of building the New Town.

Kettering and the Festival of Britain
'The Age of Austerity' can be said to have been brought to an end, symbolically at least, by the holding of a Festival to celebrate the achievements of post-war Britain. If the idea was derivative of the Great Exhibition of 1851, and was carped at, it proved a great success. It cheered the nation up and lightened a little the gloom and the grimness of life since the War. The main events, as in 1851, took place in London. But pretty well every place

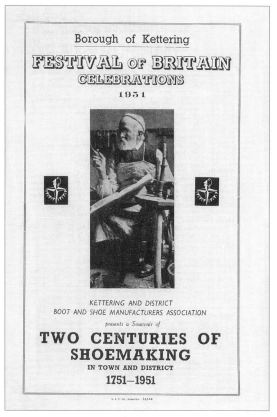

93 *Kettering celebrates the Festival of Britain, 1951.
A pamphlet given over entirely to footwear, perhaps
because Kettering was still given over to footwear.*

in the country marked the event. Kettering's celebrations, arranged in co-operation with the Arts Council of Great Britain, consisted of a Celebratory Concert, a visit by the Three Arts Ballet, and a Pageant of Kettering (in ten scenes), all at the Savoy Theatre; three Variety Concerts and a Festival Dance at the Central Hall; and a Folk Dance Festival at Wicksteed Park. In what was a great year for exhibitions, there was also a Festival Exhibition of Products of Local Industries. A few weeks earlier a Science in Local Industries Exhibition, organised by the Kettering and Corby Scientific Societies, which aimed to show what was manufactured or produced within a ten-mile radius of the town and the part science played in this, was held.

Inevitably, footwear was much to the fore. In 1951, Kettering's 23 factories, together with four in Burton Latimer, employed six thousand workers, who turned out six million pairs of shoes per annum. There was optimism about the industry's future. When Munn & Felton brought all their work under one roof in their new 'Emmaneff' factory in Wood Street that year, so many people turned out to witness the formalities that the scenes were, in the words of the *Leader*, 'reminiscent of VE and VJ Days'. The year 1951 also saw the introduction of the two weeks' holiday with pay, a development which became so much part of the pattern of life that people have forgotten when it first came in. It was not long before Harold Macmillan was to coin the phrase 'You've never had it so good', and it was, for the majority of people, true – for the first time in history.

By that year, the social and sporting networks were well on the way to being reconstructed after the long hiatus of the War. After having its notoriously sloping pitch levelled Kettering Town Football Club resumed fixtures in 1946. A new Limited Company was formed in 1950 and for 26 years the 'Poppies' played in the Southern League, enjoying most success under Tommy Lawton, player-manager from 1955-7. Kettering Town fans had the unexpected pleasure of seeing one of the soccer legends of the 1930s scoring for their team. Under him they won the Southern League

94   *High Street, about 1963.*

title twice. Lawton soon moved on to manage Notts County, but later said leaving Kettering was the worst move he ever made. The Town Cricket club resumed activities, but it was not until 1951 that a Northamptonshire League got going, and the County Club only managed to raise the funds to start first-class cricket that summer. The old established Amateur Cycling club was soon joined by a new one, Kettering Friendly, in 1946, a club which proved very popular amongst the fraternity of wheelers. On the musical front, the Kettering and District Theatrical Group was formed in 1956. The Regent Players, an Operetta Group, fond of performing the works of Gilbert and Sullivan, started two years later, and the Kettering Symphony Orchestra was formed in 1963. All of these were to have an existence of twenty to thirty years. Working Men's Clubs and the Bands resumed. When Munn & Felton were taken over by Great Universal Stores in 1960, the band's name was changed to GUS, the firm supporting its activities for 26 years, until financial stringency forced its withdrawal. GUS, as was its pre-War habit, won national titles in 1964, 1966 and 1981.The band then found sponsorship from the Desborough-based Rigid Containers Ltd.

During the War, part of the Pavilion in Wicksteed Park was requisitioned by the military, but the park remained open for use by the public. It was the venue for 'Holidays at Home' weeks and dances were held 'when accommodation permitted'. After the War, improvements were made – the canteen kitchens were rebuilt and fitted with modern equipment, children's paddling and bathing pools were constructed. Following concern about accommodation for visitors in showery weather, a large hall was planned and eventually opened in 1954 as the Coronation Hall. It was fitted up as a cinema, with seating for 750. By the 1950s the park was drawing in visitors from as far afield as Aylesbury, Doncaster, Derby, St Albans and Yarmouth. The biggest-ever attendance at Wicksteed was on 8 August 1965, when an estimated 60,000 children and their parents turned up for the Tingha and Tusker (TV Puppets) annual meeting.

The cinema in Wicksteed's Coronation Hall opened just as commercial cinema began to feel the cold draught of television, which almost killed it. The showing of the Coronation of Queen Elizabeth II in 1953 led to a huge increase in the sales of television sets. Television provided a hypnotic new form of home-based entertainment, and no people on earth fell more in love with it than the British. Cinema declined almost overnight. The Empire in Eskdaill Street closed in 1954, the Gaumont in 1959. Kettering's last picture house (Studio 1 and 2), formerly the Savoy Theatre, hung on until 1985. It has revived recently, but, compared with the pleasures of going to a picture-palace, a Multiplex lacks ambience; it is like watching a big television in a small barn. Television was merely one of a range of new developments which were to transform economic and social life in the '50s and '60s. At the time people did not fully appreciate how much, but Industrial Kettering and its institutions were to be blown away by the Gale of the Western World.

PART THREE
Post-Industrial Kettering

Seventeen

KETTERING SINCE 1974

The Collapse of Kettering's Staple Industries

Despite optimistic feelings at the time of the Festival of Britain that Kettering's future would be something like its past, this was not how things turned out. The next twenty years saw the decline of its industrial base and a policy of urban renewal which did much to sweep away old Kettering. The failure to diversify its old economic base was not peculiar to Kettering. From the early 1960s the County Council and the Government began to formulate strategies to bring growth to Northamptonshire. This was the golden age of post-war planning. New Town strategies were set in motion for Northampton, Wellingborough, Daventry and Peterborough. Conspicuously absent were plans for Kettering's future. The reason almost certainly was that nearby Corby was selected for New Town status.

In these twenty years, Kettering's footwear trade had, for a variety of reasons, steadily declined. Fewer businessmen saw much prospect of making profits under modern conditions, fewer young people were attracted to work in boot and shoe factories, there was greater competition both in foreign and the home markets, and becoming part of larger conglomerates did not in the end save Kettering's firms: Sir Charles Clore worked no miracles. Ironically, it was Free Trade (the ark of the old Liberal and modern Tory covenant) which did for footwear what it had done for silk a century earlier. When Timpson's factory in Bath Road was abruptly closed in August 1972, with a loss of 580 jobs (and another 70 in Yorkshire) the writing was on the wall. It mattered little that the workforce at Timpson's had recently been cut and yet had improved output by 30 per cent. The reason was the flood of cheap (and comfortable) foreign shoes allowed into Britain by a government unwilling to apply import quotas. From then on, Kettering's staple industry withered. In 1975 the Trades Exhibition, held annually for the past 20 years, was cancelled, an admission that the basic trades were in decline. By 2002 the 200 million pairs of shoes made in this country in the 1960s were down to 34 million. Now only one per cent of shoes sold in Britain is made here. The Kettering footwear industry is reduced to one firm, Loake Bros., plus a small outfit that makes specialist shoes for people with disabilities. Loake Bros, like other manufacturers including Start-rite,

95   *The Old Grammar School building and the Odeon Cinema, Gold Street, before 1964. From* Lost and Hidden Kettering.

Clarks and Doctor Marten, have their uppers made abroad and shipped here for finishing, in Loake's case from Chennai, India.

The decline of the Co-operative businesses accompanied that of footwear. When the K.I.C.S. celebrated its centenary in 1966 its fortunes had never seemed higher. It had a membership of 40,000, its trade stood at over £4 million a year and it had greatly extended its central store on the corner of Montagu and Newland Streets. Yet there was growing concern about falling profit margins and the fact that the fragmented nature of the individual Societies was going to make it increasingly difficult to compete in the changed world of retailing. The solution was for old Societies to amalgamate and move into supermarket mode. This did not go down well in Kettering. But faced with the inevitability of terminal decline, late in 1977 the Kettering Industrial Co-operative Society voted to amalgamate with the Leicestershire Co-operative Society. On 30 January, 30,000 members of the KICS, with 500 employees, 31 food shops, two department stores, two garages, seven pharmacies, dairy and fuel supply departments, the King Street headquarters, the Central Hall, and an annual turnover of £9 million, were transferred to the enlarged Leicestershire Society.

The manufacturing side of Co-operation had also been brought low. The once great Clothing Company, faced with the challenge of Marks & Spencer and the other multiple national clothing enterprises, had ceased trading in 1975 and the two footwear productive enterprises had closed as a result of rapid shrinkage of the boot and shoe industry. The year 1975 saw the end of another major wholesale clothing business, with Wallis & Linnell, Kettering's oldest firm, going into liquidation. Seven years later, their factory in School Lane was demolished: a Health Centre now stands on the site.

Urban renewal

At the same time, the Council began a policy of urban renewal – the demolition of town-centre buildings to provide modern shopping facilities. In the '60s almost every town council in the land was seized by the desire to Americanise, to have shopping malls where Boots, Sainsbury's, Tesco and other muliples could be brought together under one roof. Kettering Borough Council was no exception. To make way for a shopping centre (like Northampton's and Wellingborough's), an extensive site had to be cleared. If that meant demolition on such a scale as to alter the appearance and character of familiar town-centre streets, so be it. This was precisely what some planners and politicians wanted; 'the Shock of the New' – the very definition of modernity. This, however, ran counter to the truism that what gives places such as Kettering their character is the quality of their buildings, often designed by local architects. The shock of the new, the loss of the familiar, can be deeply upsetting to people who have lived their lives in the place. On the other hand, old buildings, old shops, become outdated. Every town gets to be rebuilt, in a piecemeal way, every century or so. Moreover, modern people expect modern shopping.

In 1964 the old Grammar School building on Bakehouse Hill was demolished. A familiar and visually pleasing Victorian building was replaced by a row of nondescript shops. When the next and much larger-scale demolition was signalled, a struggle between Renewers and Preservers commenced. In 1969 a Kettering Civic Society was founded by Arthur Heath, John Steane, Tony Ireson and others, whose view was not that progess should be denied, but that, in the process of renewal, what was distinctive should, if possible, be preserved, and, if not, what was new should be in harmony with its surroundings. To make their point about preserving the character of the town, the Civic Society published two well-illustrated and informative booklets: *A Walk Round Kettering* (1972) and *Lost and Hidden Kettering* (1974). A question which always faces Preservers is, of course, if a building is saved, who pays and how can it earn its keep? The old Grammar School building had ceased to be a school in 1913 and Kettering Education Committee, which used it afterwards, had moved to new accommodation.

The major piece of urban renewal was further up the hill in Gold Street. The extensive frontage of the Post Office Buildings (designed in 1887 by Gotch & Saunders), the Odeon Cinema and the Victoria Hall were all to go. This frontage, together with the buildings on an extensive area behind, including Georgian Beech House, were to be demolished. The whole site was to house a large new shopping centre, Newborough Mall, and was to cost an estimated £1.25 million, which the Council was to fund. The aim was to make Kettering 'the second shopping centre of the county'.

96   *Present shops on the site of the old Grammar School. In the background is the Telecom building, the ugliest thing in Kettering.*

The new shopping centre took over twenty years to complete. It was built in three phases and each brought a new name. Newborough Mall of 1969 became Newborough Centre in 1975, and in 1983 Newborough Centre became Newlands, partly because the complex was extended to a new frontage on Newland Street, and partly because the Council, in the flush of Conservative local government privatisation, sold the Centre to a consortium for £4.7 million in 1987. Newborough smelt of local government; Newlands had the commercial fragrance of history. The Newborough Centre (Phases 1 and 2) was opened for business in late 1977, with Boots, Sainsbury's, Smith's and a range of other shops under one roof. The public liked it and it was profitable. Even an economist from Leicester University in 1984 admitted he had been wrong (in 1972) to doubt its viability.

The Civic Society and other opponents regarded it as an ugly monstrosity. Tony Ireson, who lived in Beech Cottage in Tanner's Lane in the demolition zone, fought the compulsory purchase order on his house, and won, proving that Beech

97   *Tony Ireson in old age, photographed with an old school friend, Stephen House.*

Cottage's demolition was not actually necessary for an access road to the rear of the Newborough Centre. Ireson was a proud upholder of the old Kettering tradition of defying the powers-that-be. But if Beech Cottage was saved, 70 feet of his front garden was sliced off and the new view from his window was of the service area (i.e. the back end) of the shopping centre. Nonetheless he stayed put. Ireson's pen was his sword. He wielded it to some effect in telling the story of the redevelopment of Gold Street and other aspects of Kettering's urban renewal in *Old Kettering and its Defenders* (1985), which he published himself. When Tony Ireson began all this, the Newborough story was not yet com-

98 *'The commercial fragrance of history'. The Newborough Shopping Centre refurbished as Newlands: the Gold Street entrance.*

plete. The new owners commenced with Phase 3, converting Newborough into Newlands. The project was ready by 1989. The interior was refloored with marble tiles and refurbished and, in the course of considerably extending the shopping area, it now had a second frontage in Newland Street (which the Civic Society blasted as 'a garish Las Vegas Casino'). It was a blow when, in a unilateral declaration of independence, Sainsbury's quit the Centre and built a large new supermarket close by, on the corner of Rockingham Road and Northall Street. The Civic Society was just as unimpressed, naming it 'Fortress Sainsburys'. The Society also kept its collective eye on other pieces of renewal. In 1982 it had its differences with the Council over proposed changes to the Victorian façade of the *Royal Hotel* and three years later protested against the rebuilding of Barclays Bank at the bottom of Market Street. The Society wanted the old Westminster Bank frontage retained. In the event, it wasn't.

Local Government since 1974

In the early stages of the building of the new shopping centre, Kettering's local government was re-cast in 1974 by the general reform of local institutions by the Conservative government. The new Borough of Kettering is geographically very different from the old. If the word 'borough' means (as it always had up to then) 'an urban district', then New Kettering is that oxymoron, a *rural* borough. It consists of 58,000 acres of Northamptonshire, Kettering being joined by three neighbouring small towns – Rothwell, Desborough and Burton Latimer – plus 22 villages, with a total population, in 1987, of only 72,000. Corby, which might have been part of this new

Welland ward includes the parishes of Weston by Welland, Ashley, Sutton Bassett, Dingley, Brampton Ash, Stoke Albany, Wilbarston and Bray-brooke.
Buccleuch ward consists of Rushton, Newton, Weekley, Warkton, Grafton Underwood and Cranford.
Queen Eleanor is the Geddington parish and Slade consists of Harrington, Orton, Thorpe Malsor, Loddington, Cransley, Broughton and Pytchley.

WELLAND (1 seat)

DESBOROUGH (4 seats)

ROTHWELL (4 seats)

QUEEN ELEANOR (1 seat)

BUCCLEUCH (1 seat)

KETTERING (28 seats)

SLADE (2 seats)

BURTON LATIMER (4 seats)

99   *Map of the new, post-1974, Borough of Kettering.*

hybrid, was not having any of it. Corby is lord of its own district both for local government and parliamentary elections. New Kettering Borough was divided into 22 wards to elect the 45 members of the new Council, 28 for Kettering, four each for the three small towns, and five for the villages.

Local government changes broke with the past and brought unforeseen problems. Until 1974 Kettering's Library and Art Gallery were the responsibility of the Borough's chief librarian. The new arrangement was that the Library became part of the County service, while the Gallery remained under the Borough. Mr Burden, the librarian, who had successfully broadened the acquisitions policy with modest resources, now lost responsibility for the Art Gallery. The new Borough resurrected Kettering's Museum. Housed in Westfield, an old mansion, it was so old-fashioned, it should have been, in Dylan Thomas's words, '*in* a museum'. Westfield was closed, and a new District museum was opened in the Manor House, together with a tourist information bureau. In the museum was lodged the Robinson motor car, made in Kettering in 1907, purchased by the Car Rescue Committee, who raised the money to buy the vehicle. Amongst other local government improvements were the refurbishing of the market place (though Kettering market is a pale shadow of its former self), the closing in 1992 of the cattle market, which became a town-centre car park with a swimming pool to one side of it, and the useful Cornmarket hall was give a complete overhaul.

As a consequence of both new educational orthodoxies and the effects of social change, the years since 1974 have brought a range of developments in education. In 1976, the Grammar and High Schools became comprehensives. The boys' school had been a successful town Grammar, numbering H.E. Bates, the novelist, and A.H. Halsey, Professor of Sociology at Oxford, among it former pupils. It became nationally well-known when, in 1957, under the guidance of an outstanding physics teacher, Geoffrey Perry, and Derek Slater, a chemistry teacher who was an enthusiastic radio ham, a team of boy space-watchers became the first to inform the world that the Russsians had launched the Sputnik space-probe. Three years later they were the first to record signals from Sputnik 4, the first Russian satellite. Under the headship of John Steane, the school also did valuable archaeological work in the vacations. Steane, however, resigned when it became comprehensive; he and his wife, Nina, a poet and water-colour painter of talent, left for Oxford, where he joined the museum service. They were a loss to Kettering. The school closed in 1993 because of 'falling rolls'. Kettering got a much-desired Technical College in 1978, but around it the old industries which it was opened to serve were collapsing. Like many another College of Further Education, Tresham has had to cast about to find a new role for itself, no easy task in the face of bewildering changes in governmental expectations.

Party Politics Since 1974

The hiving-off of Corby meant that in parliamentary elections Kettering was no longer a 'safe Labour seat'. There were also other reasons. As in other places, Kettering's Labour Party was beset by tensions between left and right. When Sir Geoffrey De Freitas, a Social Democrat in all but name, announced he was quitting to stand for the European Parliament, there was a five-sided battle to be the next Labour candidate in 1978. The nomination went to Bill Homeward, a steel union man, who had narrowly lost to de Freitas in 1964. The issue split the party. In early 1979, on the Borough Council, in addition to the 20 Conservatives, six Independents and five Liberals, there were six Labour and eight 'rebel' Labour councillors. In the parliamentary election of that year Homeward beat Rupert Allason, a Conservative, but Labour's majority toppled from 11,170 to 1,478. Mrs Thatcher began her amazing run of four election victories, and a strife-torn Labour Party became unelectable. Homeward lost his seat in 1983 to Roger Freeman, a merchant banker, who was to be elected twice more in the years of Mrs Thatcher's hegemony. In the 1992 election Freeman had a majority of 12,187. Yet, under John Major, the divided Conservatives contrived to make *themselves* unelectable. New Labour, renouncing socialism and embracing capitalism, stole the political middle ground. Yet Freeman only lost Kettering to Phil Sawford in the election of 1997 after four re-counts. Born and raised in the constituency, Sawford (no Blairite) had served on the Borough Council for twenty years. In 2001, by a narrow majority, he was re-elected. The constituency, however, was now 'a knife-edge marginal'.

Late Twentieth-Century Economic Developments

To add to the anxieties caused by the Newborough Centre and the decline of Kettering's staple industries, in 1979 the Council faced the biggest economic crisis to hit the Midlands in sixty years, a direct result of Thatcherite fiscal policies. By 1982 nearly one in five male workers was unemployed. If the situation in Kettering was bad, that in Corby was disastrous. In the summer of 1979 British Steel announced losses of £327 million. Shotton and Corby works were to close. In the previous forty years Corby had grown from a village to a New Town of 50,000 inhabitants. Even before the announcement of the closure of the Steel Works with the loss of 5,000 jobs, unemployment stood at seven per cent. In July 1982, it was up to 22.3 per cent. By then, a massive effort to help Corby was under way, with funding coming from every conceivable agency in this country and the EEC.

Corby bounced back, placing its future in food production, retailing, small industrial units and service industries. Kettering did much the same. With the retirement of Ken Butler, its first Chief Executive, who had been Borough Treasurer to the old Council, one of the new breed of CEOs, experts at 'managing change', was brought in in 1984. This was Martin England, a Yorkshire man, who commuted during the four years of his time in Kettering. The Government had axed the New Towns Commission, cut back local government spending and was busy smashing the trades unions. The cleansing powers of Capitalism and local self-help were invoked. Kettering (like Corby) was by then already one of Sir Geoffrey Howe's New Enterprise Zones, and an industrial strategy was set out in *Building on Achievement*. A Kettering Business Venture Trust was formed by the Council and the Chamber of Commerce; by 1988 it was claiming that 50 companies had been helped under its small firms scheme. In 1985 the same partners set up the Kettering Enterprise Agency. The Morse Report, commissioned by the Council, argued that Kettering was well-placed to attract firms by virtue of its geographical position and good communications. This was set out in *The Perfect Centre*, a 100-page booklet. By 1989, the severe depression was at last over: unemployment in Kettering was down to three per cent, and a series of initiatives was launched to renew Kettering's economy. As usual, the best-laid plans of politicians, planners and entrepreneurs were thwarted: not all initiatives were pushed through to their expected conclusion because of the failure of the national economy. Another slump came along; by 1993 one in eight shops in the town centre was said to be closed.

The *Perfect Centre* arguments were, however, essentially correct. Kettering is geographically well-located in the national economy. A major improvement to the town's communications was the A1/M1 link (now the A14), the building of which greatly improved communications between the West Midlands and the East Coast. In 1991 five miles of it, the southern by-pass, were completed and a northern by-pass was opened two years later. These years also saw a general improvement in Northamptonshire's wider road network. Eighty miles from London, the virtual incorporation of the Kettering area into the aegis of the prosperous South East and the relative cheapness of its housing meant that people who work in London were attracted to Kettering, with which rail access is good. By 1990 it was estimated that 500 a day were commuting by rail.

New roads by-passing towns yield-up land for industrial and other developments. The 'managers of change' love to give these rural-sounding names – 'business parks', 'leisure villages'. In 1981, four acres in Northfield Avenue became a new site for business. The Co-op closed its central stores and opened a new supermarket there in 1985. An important out of town development was the Telford Way Industrial Estate, on land formerly belonging to British Steel. The largest project was on the Pytchley Lodge

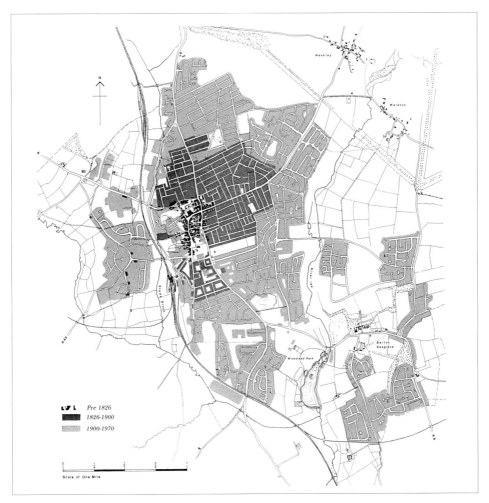

100 *The outward expansion of Kettering by 1970, a map by Peter Taylor.*

estate, now Kettering Venture Park. Located between the south end of old Kettering and between the railway line and the new A14, one of the major developments was the Tesco supermarket, opened in 1989, a veritable cathedral of shopping. There are also motor car agencies, other commercial enterprises, the prize-winning *Kettering Park Hotel*, an Odeon Multiplex cinema and a post-modern 'traditional' pub. Also, between the old town and the new A14, Kettering Leisure Village has grown up.

The outward spread of Kettering was not caused by these developments alone. Virtually all new housing projects – some of them very extensive – have been on the periphery, notably on the Barton Seagrave side of the town. One of the largest is Ise Lodge, which began in 1965 on 82 acres of the Hall Farm estate. In twenty years it had grown into what has been claimed to be 'the second largest private estate in Europe'. After the post-war years, little of the new housing has been Council housing, buried as a concept by the Thatcher government, along with New Towns. Moreover, the year 1989 saw the privatisation of £2.5 million-worth of the Borough of Kettering's Council Services. The spreading out of Kettering had other social causes and social consequences. Everywhere, the middle classes are migrating to or beyond the suburbs. In the era of 'relocation, relocation' the dream is of a nice job in the city and a home in a village. The corollary is always inner-city decay. As the years pass, the terraced streets and old factories of Kettering seem more depressing and the people poorer.

In the last 30 years of the 20th century, in common with a hundred other towns, the old industrial and employment patterns of Kettering have been largely replaced. People now work in commerce, shops, food processing, local government, the health service, banking and insurance rather than in factories. There were always plenty of women employed outside the home, but now there are more. Prosperity is widespread, but much of it depends on the fact that in many households there are two incomes. Moreover, since 1979 the gap between the prosperous and the poor has widened, in Kettering as elsewhere.

Against all this social change, something of traditional Kettering survives. There are still working men's clubs, though some old ones – such as the Rifle Band – have gone. As noted, there is still a brass-band tradition, though works' bands are no more. The business of Munn & Felton was taken over by Grand Universal Stores and the band became the GUS. After some years, GUS ended their sponsorship. This was taken on by Rigid Containers of Desborough and the band's name was changed accordingly. When Rigid Containers became part of a Belgian concern at the start of the new century, sponsorship passed to Travelsphere Holidays of Market Harborough. At the time of writing (2003) the band is still competing. The only other old one to survive is that of the Salvation Army, though there are some associated with evening classes, and it is good to note that the brass-band tradition is kept alive in Northamptonshire schools. Wicksteed Park is still there, though it was losing money in 1979 when Robert Wicksteed, grandson of the founder, became chairman of the Trust. Crowds had fallen to 350,000 a year and the Park's attractions were falling behind those of Alton Towers and Thorpe Park. Over the next twenty years the Trust spent about £2 million modernising the facilities. After the installation of the first of the big rides in 1983, attendances rose again to 750,000 a year. With its ability to absorb large numbers and not feel overcrowded, and its mixture of the traditional and the new, the Park is still a good place for parents and grandparents to bring children. Sport in Kettering flourishes in its various modern forms. There are rugby and cricket clubs, and Kettering Town continues its battle to resolve the financial problems of being a small-town professional soccer club, the clashing egos of owners and managers, and the expectations of the fans. Sad to report, towards the end of this, the 2002-3 season, Kettering Town was at the foot of the Nationwide Conference, and relegated from English League football.

Eighteen

CONCLUSIONS:
KETTERING PAST AND PRESENT

The long span of Kettering's history is perhaps seen most clearly in terms of economics. For six centuries pre-industrial Kettering evolved from an Anglo-Saxon village into a market town, under the aegis of the Benedictine Abbey of Peterborough. Its business was farming and providing its market area with essential goods and services. In the final century and a half of its pre-industrial life the power of the medieval church was brought down by Henry VIII and England was protestantised. The land, the town and the manorial and rectorial assets of Kettering passed into lay hands. In the late 17th century the town's rural and marketing economy was supplemented by the rise of woolcombing and worsted weaving on a substantial scale. The two trades, together with spinning, became the chief occupation of the poor. Kettering became a 'proto-industrial' town and remained so for rather more than a century. The collapse of the woollen textile business in the 1790s left Kettering with a severe pauper problem, and the arrival of silk weaving and the establishment of the pioneering footwear business did not offset the collapse of the town's older staple industry. When Queen Victoria came to the throne Kettering was in a bad way. It was not until the middle decade of the 19th century that modern industrialisation slowly began to take off. When it accelerated, as it did from 1870, it led to the greatest period of expansion the town had known. Kettering became well-known as one of the centres of boot and shoe manufacturing in England, and it had other industries as well. When these staple trades were undermined in their turn in the 1960s and '70s, the town's economy was rebuilt on a post-industrial basis, partly by a re-emphasis on its ancient role as a shopping and service centre, and partly by replacing manufacture with food production, light industry and 'white collar' employment in financial, health, education and local governmental services.

Although in essential outlines Kettering's economic history is like that of some other small industrial towns, its trades had their own peculiar historical patterns. No two industries are the same. The evolution of the manufacture of footwear was not the same as the manufacture of, say, cotton cloth, or iron making, or pottery. In particular, the domestic, or putting-out, form of production lasted far longer in footwear than textiles. However, once machinery was adapted to all the processes in boot-making, working in a footwear factory was not all that different from working in a cotton mill or on a motor car assembly line. Nor, in its social patterns, was Kettering entirely different from other industrial towns.

The history of any place is not just a matter of economics, though how people earned their daily bread is fundamental. Cultural patterns have an economic base, but other roots as well. One which many country towns share is the relationship, at once symbiotic and oppositional, with their rural hinterland. The forebears of most Kettering people originated in the local countryside. Migrating to the town was not always happy; there is a long history of opposition to the feudal and post-feudal powers of big land-owners, well illustrated by the presence of Kettering men among the hedge levellers of 1607. Another basis of opposition was that of those Protestants who, as well as their hatred of Catholics, were never satisfied with the Eliza-bethan definition of the Church of England. For them, Kettering was a safe place to resort to when their dissent made life too uncomfortable in the villages. One result was that Kettering was one of those places where, by the early 19th century, Dissenters outnumbered Churchmen. The consequences of that were influential, especially on the political front.

Kettering was always a place for the Awkward Squad. The radical tradition found political expression in the 19th century through Chart-ism, which arose out of the tribulations of the time. If, before the emer-gence of a Labour Party in the Great War, a political alliance between plebeian and middle-class Radicalism developed in party politics, some Kettering workers decided that the way to a better material life was through Co-operation, supporting an alternative to the individualism of 'free enterprise'. Because of the pecularities of boot-making, trades unionism came late, and there were bitter disputes as the trade transformed itself into a factory industry. But once industrial peace returned and political democracy arrived in the 20th century, Kettering became a safe Co-operative and Labour constituency, though the vicissitudes of the Long March of Labour had their local effects between the Wars, and indeed after. The transformation of Kettering from a safe Labour seat to a 'knife-edge marginal' since 1979 is as much a result of changes in society as constituency boundary changes.

The main social asset of Kettering was its smallness, even when its population multiplied by six in half a century. It remained compact enough for almost everyone (above the level of the poor) to know of one another. Victorian Kettering was a face-to-face sort of place, in which everyone knew what your religion, politics and opinions on a range of issues (except perhaps sex) were, because you expressed them openly. It was like a little city-state: it had its senators, sooth-sayers, poets and orators. But so did most towns. In the 20th century, for all sorts of reasons (including the way houses were built) society became semi-detached, and, for some people, fully-detached.

The rapidity of modern technological and social change has meant that the spreading-out of towns has been accompanied by other horizon-expanders. Ours is a motorised society and we range wide. It is common-place to go on holiday in once impossibly exotic places. International communications have made the world a village. Homogenised American culture – Hollywood films, fast-food outlets, Disneyland and the world according to CNN – all seem to militate against localism. Industry is dead, but shopping is life. Puritanism is vanquished by hedonism; the *Cross Keys Temperance Tavern* is now *O'Malley's Bar*. But is Old Kettering completely gone? 'The past is never dead', said William Faulkner, the American novelist, 'It is not even past.' But in a Kettering where the old offices of the once-mighty Kettering Industrial Co-operative Society are now a Sikh Gudwara, it is hard to agree.

NOTES

Abbreviations

Bull *History*	F.W. Bull, *A Sketch of the History of the Town of Kettering Together with some Account of its Worthies*, London and Kettering, 1891
Bull *Supplement*	F.W. Bull, *Supplement to the History of the Town of Kettering Together with a Further Account of its Worthies*, Kettering, 1908
Bridges	J.Bridges, *The History and Antiquities of Northamptonshire* (ed., P.Whalley), 2 Vols., 1791
Hist Par Ch	*A History of Kettering Parish Church*, Kettering Civic Society, 1977
KCL	Kettering Central Library, Northamptonshire Libraries and Information Service
NCL	Northampton Central Library, Northamptonshire Libraries and Information Service
NM	*Northamptonshire Mercury*
NP&P	*Northamptonshire Past & Present*
NRO	Northamptonshire Record Office
PRO	Public Record Office
VCH	*The Victoria History of the County of Northampton*, Vol.3, 1930, ed., W. Page

2   The Origins of Kettering, pp.5-12

This is based on the following: *The Anglo-Saxon Chronicle*, ed. G.N. Garmonsway, 1967; Glenn Foard, 'The Administrative organisation of Northamptonshire in the Saxon period', in *Anglo-Saxon Studies in Archaeology and History 4*, 1985, pp.185-222; A.E. Brown and Glenn Foard, 'The Saxon Landscape, a regional Perspective', in *The Archaeology of Landscape*, ed., P. Everson and T. Williamson, 1988, pp.67-94; Bull *History*, pp.1-5 (charters); The Royal Commission on Historical Monuments, *An Inventory of the Historical Monuments in the County of Northampton*, II, 1979, pp.xliv and xlvi and pp.101-5; *VCH*, pp.221-4; J. Gover, A. Mawer and F.M. Stenton, *The Place Names of Northamptonshire*, 1933, pp.184-5; Dennis Jackson and Brian Dix, 'Late Iron Age and Roman settlement at Weekley' and Brian Dix, 'The Roman Settlement at Kettering, Northants, Excavations at Kipling Road, 1968 and 1971', *Northamptonshire Archaeology*, 1986-7, pp.44-71 and pp.95-108.

3   Manor, Market and Church, pp.13-24

Manor: Domesday and charter information from *VCH* and Bull *History*, *passim*; for the medieval fields see D.N. Hall, *The Open Fields of Northamptonshire*, 1995, pp.302-3; for the Compotus, C.Wise, *The Compotus of the Manor of Kettering for the 20th year of the Abbot Richard London A.D.1292*, 1899, and an unpublished essay by R.A. Martin in 1970 analysing this; for the 1301 Tax, see PRO E179/155/31; for later farming changes, Edmund King, *Peterborough Abbey 1086-1310*, 1972, p.150 *et seq*.

Market: the most important source on medieval Kettering is Glenn Foard's work in the County Council's 'Kettering Extensive Urban Survey' of 2002, funded by English Heritage. This contains a very full analysis of medieval Kettering, which deserves publication in book form in its own right. For the medieval forest, B.Bellamy, 'The Rockingham Forest Perambulation of 1299', *NP and P*, VI, 1978-83, p.303.

Later Middle Ages: Norman Groome, 'The Black Death in the Hundred of Higham Ferrers', *NP and P*, VI, 1978-83, pp.309-11; the Lay Subsidy of 1524 is at PRO E179/155/123. For the Lane family, see Bull *Supplement*, 46-48.The will of John Lane, 1546, is at PRO Prob II/ 31 and that of Richard Alderman (1542) is at PRO Prob II/29.

The Church: this account is based on Bull *History* and Bull *Supplement, VCH, Hist Par Ch* and N. Pevsner, *The Buildings of England, Northamptonshire*, 1961, pp.262-3. For medieval wills the source is R.M. Serjeantson and the Rev. H.I. Longden, 'The Parish Churches and Religious Houses of Northamptonshire, their Dedications, Altars, Images and Lights', *Archaeological Journal*, 70, 1913, pp.351-3.

4   *The Reformation and Kettering, pp.25-38*

The Stripping of the Altars: the principal sources used are Bull *History*, Bull *Supplement* and *Hist Par Ch*. For post-Reformation rectors, see the Rev. H.I. Longden, *Northamptonshire Clergy, 1500-1900*, 1939-43, *passim*. For Elizabethan Protestantism, W.J. Shiels, *The Puritans in the Diocese of Peterborough 1558–1610*, 1979, *passim*.

The Free Grammar School: Bull *History*, pp.114-20 and *Supplement*, pp.32-9; B.A. York, 'The Origins of Kettering Grammar School', *NP and P*, VI, 1978-83, pp.21-7.

The Stripping of the Assets: Bull *History*, pp.83-98 and pp.172-3 and *Supplement*, pp.15-25; C. Wise, *Rockingham Castle and the Watsons*, 1891; the quotation 'Thus had one incumbent …' is on p.191; Treswell's map of Kettering is at NRO FH 272. For the Sawyer family, see Bull *History*, *passim* and *Supplement*, pp.45-58.

Manorial Courts: Bull *History, passim*, and C. Wise's series of articles 'Glimpses of Kettering in the Sixteenth and Seventeenth Centuries' which first appeared in the *Kettering Guardian* in 1901 and are reprinted in *Northamptonshire Notes and Queries*, New Series, Vol.IV, pp.173, 186, 194-5, 200, 210, 215 and 225, Vol.V, pp.234, 241, 246, 255, 265, 269, 275, 278, 295, 285 and 289, Vol.VI, pp.297, 303, 309, 315 and 322.

5   *Kettering in the Seventeenth Century, pp.39-49*

Economic developments: The quotations from Leland is in Bull, *History*, p.13, and Camden in *Britannia*, 1610 edition, p.510. For the Sessions House, see Bull, *History*, p.16, and Wise, *Northamptonshire Notes and Queries*, New series, IV, p.151. For the hedge levellers the best account is that of E.F. Gay, 'The Midland revolt of 1607', in *Transactions of the Royal Historical Society*, 1904, pp.214-17. The names of those who admitted taking part are listed in NRO Montagu Papers, Letters Volume 13, 1600-1612, no.118. For relief of the poor, Janet Meads' unpublished essay 'Bequests to the poor 1512-1700', based on a study of the many wills of the period, is the source. The will of John Pettiver the rich mercer is in NRO, Second Series Wills, E 261. For Richard Alderman, see Wise, *Northamptonshire Notes and Queries, op. cit.*, pp.201-5.

Puritan Kettering: The list of popish recusants is found in NRO, Fermor Hesketh Baker, 719. For the attempts at enforcing conformity and the combination lecture, *Hist Par Ch.*, p.13. The state of the church in 1631 is at NRO, Diocesan Records, church surveys 1631, fo 3v. For the Laudian survey of 1637, see NRO, X 2159, p.141-3.

The Civil Wars: Francis Sawyer's resistance to Ship Money, *Calendar of State Papers Domestic*, 1638-9, pp.5, 34, 36 and 45. For the Petition of Freeholders, *Cal S P D 1640*, 7. For the Etcetera Oath meeting, *Hist Par Ch.*, 14, and for the Civil Wars generally, Bull, *History*, pp.17-22. For Sir Gilbert Pickering, *Strapetona*, No5, 1978, pp.2-5 and for John Browne and other members of the Committee, *Northants Notes and Queries*, III, pp.63-4. For Boteler, see *Biographical Dictionary of British Radicals in the Seventeenth Century*, ed. R.L. Greaves and R. Zeller, 1981, p.93.

6   *Nonconformity and the Church, pp.50-64*

This chapter relies on Bull, *History* and the *Hist Par Ch*. Biographical information on clergy and schoolmasters in the 17th and 18th centuries is drawn mainly from Henry Isham Longden, *Northamptonshire and Rutland Clergy, op. cit.*, and for 19th-century clergy from contemporary newspapers.

Early Nonconformity and the Church: Archdeacon Palmer's report on conventicles is at NRO Hesketh Baker MSS, 708. For the Declaration of Indulgence see *Calendar of State Papers Domestic 1671-72*, pp.305-6. Robinson's 'bilious pugnaciousness', the Rev. Edward Craig used the phrase in a pamphlet war between the Church and the Baptists over 'infant sprinkling', or baptism.

The Evangelical Revival: for Jenkinson, see this author's 'Baptist as Radical, the Life and Opinions of the Rev. John Jenkinson of Kettering', *N.P. and P.*, VIII, 3, 1991-2, pp.210-26. For the early Wesleyans, 'Kettering Eighty Years Ago',by the Rev. Benjamin Gregory, in a volume of newspaper cuttings for 1889-93 in KCL. Abraham Maddock's diary is in the British Library, Add Ms 40,653, but extracts are available in 'Antiquarian Memoranda 1889-1913', in KCL. The struggle between Lord Sondes and the Rev. B.W. Fletcher can be followed in the *Northampton Mercury* from June 1820 to May 1828, *passim*. The Minute Book of the Anti-Slavery Association is preserved in KCL. For Knibb, see P. Wright, *Knibb the Notorious*, 1973, *passim*, and 4 Sept 1903 (Knibb centenary). For the reference to Kettering as 'the Holy land' see *NM* 6 Mar 1875 and the 1828 census is ar NRO YZ 4233. The date of the obituary of the Rev. Corrie in the *Citizen* is 1 December 1846.

7   *Late Stuart and Georgian Kettering, pp.67-92*

Landowning: For the Sawyers, *see Bull* Supplement, 48-59, and for the sale of their property, *Bull*, History, *31*.

Market town: The Compton Return is in N.R.O., Fermor Hesketh Baker 708. The statistics of baptisms and burials calculated by Janet Meads from the parish registers are in an unpublished essay by her. For the new fair of 1662, see Bull, *History*, p.22. The new fair of 1748 is recorded in *NM* 30 May 1748 and 8 May 1750. Eayre's map is to be found in Bull, *History*. The quotation from Bridges is in volume 2. For the Eayre family, see Patrick King, 'Thomas Eayre of Kettering and other members of his Family', *NP and P.*, Vol.1, No.5, 1952, pp.11-23. Details of fires are found in Bull, *History*, 32, 36 and 37. The plan of the market place is in Bull *History*, 160. Viscount Torrington's account of Collis's bookshop is in *The Torrington Diaries*, Vol.3, ed., C. Bruyn Andrews, 1970 reprint, p.208.

Wayfaring and Inns: The source of the *George Hotel* sale is *NM* 25 June1825. This section is based on an unpublished research essay by Mrs J. Scouse 'Coaches, carriers and turnpikes: Transport and Kettering 1750 to 1858', and on the collection of 18th-century newspaper cuttings in the Local Studies collection, NCL. Nineteenth-century newspapers have also been worked through. On turnpikes, see *'Milestones', Northamptonshire Roads and Turnpikes*, a collection of documents published by NRO in 1972.

Georgian Kettering as a Social Centre: A valuable source is an unpublished piece of research by Janet Meads, 'Some Aspects of Social Life in 18th century Kettering'. Information on the races in 1727 is given in Bull *History*, 35, but the *NM* reports them in subsequent years. Again, the NCL newspaper cuttings collection has been extensively used in this section.

Woolcombing and Weaving: A. Randall, 'The Kettering Worsted Industry in the 18th Century', *NP and P*, Vol.IV, No.6 and 7, 1971, pp.312-20 and pp.349-56, is informative but not comprehensive. Oter published sources are indicated in the text. Again, cuttings from *NM* are invaluable.

The Arrival of Footwear: The essential source is Roy Church's 'Messrs Gotch & Sons and the Rise of the Kettering Footwear Industry', in *Business History*, 1966, Vol.8, pp.140-9.

Local Government in the 18th century: An unpublished piece of research by David Moseley, 'The Kettering Parish Officers 1671 to 1789' based the Account Book of the Vestry preserved among the parish records is a principal source. Information about weather, fires, poverty and the price of bread are taken from this and reports in the *NM*.

8 *Kettering in Crisis, pp.93-110*

Collapse of the Cloth Industry: The quotation about the cloth trade at its peak is from James Donaldson, *General View of the Agriculture of the County of Northampton*, 1794, pp.11-12. The quotation from John James comes from his *History of the Worsted Manufacture in England*, 1857, pp.231. The report on the state of the poor in 1795 by 'J.T' is a printed sheet in the cuttings collection in NCL. For the terrible winter of 1813-14, see *NM* 5 Feb 1814, and for banks in the district collapsing, see *NM* 29 Oct 1814. For the Yeomanry, Volunteers and Militia, see Bull *History*, pp.42-43, for the history of the Militia, *NM* 31 May 1873 and for the Yeomanry after the Napoleonic War, *NM* 12 Apr 1828, 17 Sept 1870 and 19 Feb 1898. For the last Bishop Blaise procession, *NH* 12 Feb 1870. The information about silk comes from frequent references to it in the newspapers from 1826 to 1870.

The Enclosure of Kettering 1804-5: Numerous papers relating to the enclosure are in NRO. Mr R.A. Martin made use of them in his 'Kettering Inclosure, 1804-5', *NP and P*, V, No.5, 1977, pp.413-24.

Wayfaring 1790 to 1850: The main sources are as in Chapter 7. The railway quotation is from the *Citizen* for August 1847 (NRO). For the railway projects in the 1840s the *NM* and *NH* are the sources.

Politics: Charles Dickens's account of the 1835 election is in the *Morning Chronicle*, 16 December 1835. The account of local Chartism is based on information in the *Northern Star* newspaper, together with the local sources mentioned. Jenkinson's *'Our Rights'* is to be found in NCL. The quotation 'I take my stand ...' is from *Kettering Observer*, 6 Feb 1885.

Local government: church-rate contests were reported regularly in the *NM* and *NH* in the three decades from 1836. For battles between parish Improvers and Economisers the best source is the handbills preserved in the Bull Collection in KCL.

9 *The Rise of Industrial Kettering, pp.111-22*

This chapter is a re-working of this author's 'The Rise of Industrial Kettering', *NP and P*, Vol.V, No.3, 1975, pp.253-66. Most of the material comes from reports in the Northampton and Kettering newspapers from 1850 to 1914, though an important source on the Gotch bankruptcy is a collection of legal papers relating to the hearings in the court of bankruptcy salvaged by the late Fred Moore after the closure of a local solicitor's office. The main developments in Kettering in the years 1834 to 1884 are outlined in 'Kettering – Past and Present', 14 articles in the *Kettering Observer* from 29 August 1884 to 27 Feb 1885.

10 *The expansion of Urban Kettering, pp.123-8*

Sources for this chapter are, again, the local newspapers, together with Ordnance Survey and other maps, and documents relating to estate development and the sale of properties. Chief among these are 'Particulars of Sale' and 'Abstracts of Title'. These are to be found in KCL, NCL and NRO; others in private hands were also consulted.

11 *Victorian Local Government Developments, pp.129-41*

For Mr and Mrs Owen Robinson's golden wedding interview, see *Kettering Leader* 16, 23 and 30 June 1905, reprinted and sold as a booklet. Much of the chapter is based on the Bull Collection (much concerned with local government) preserved in KCL. The context of these documents was has been established from local newsapers. The 'crochetty' remark is from the *Kettering Observer* 23 Jan 1885, and 'Is Kettering built on a Cesspool?' is in *NM* 5 May 1885, supplement p.11.

12 *Religion and Education, pp.142-52*

The Church: Education and other Issues: For the local religious census, see *Kettering Leader* 13 March 1903. On the School Board battle, 1870 to1871, there are over 20 handbills in the Bull Collection in KCL and others in NCL.

The School Board Era: See *Kettering School Board Final Report*, 1903 (KCL) for a summary of the work of the Board. See also *Kettering Leader*, 3 Jan 1903. For a full obituary of Canon Lindsay, *Kettering Leader & Observer*, 6 May 1892.

Local Authority Education: On the Grammar School, see *Kettering Grammar: Past, Present and Future. An Historical Outline*, reprinted from the *Kettering Observer*, 1884, and F.W. Bull, *History of Kettering Grammar School*, Northampton, 1907, and B.A. York, 'Public Opinion and the Kettering Grammar School Question 1883-88', *NP and P*, Vol.VI, pp.329-39. For Canon Smyth's departure, *Kettering Leader*, 20 June 1911.

Late Victorian Nonconformity: Bull *History*, pp.99-113, p.194 and *Supplement*, pp.26-31. F.C. Goodman, *The Great Meeting. The Story of Toller Congregational Church*, 1962. Most of the details are from newspapers. For the Toller Centenary, *NM*, 2 Oct 1875. For the split at Toller, *Kettering Leader & Observer*, 4 Nov 1892. *Baptist Missionary Society, The Centenary Celebrations at Kettering June 2 and 3 1892* (pamphlet), 1892. For the Baptist Forward Movement *NH*, 9 Nov 1898. The Calvinist chapel, Wadcroft, *NM*, 22 Aug 1868. Wesleyans, *Kettering Leader*, 29 June 1917 (the jubilee of Silver Street). Foundation Stone of Rockingham Road church, *NM*, 30 Sept 1892.

13   *Party Politics and the Rise of Labour, pp153-66*

Conservatism and the triumph of Liberalism: On the 1859 Reform meeting, *NM*, 26 Mar 1859. Governor Eyre and Jamaica, *NM*, 16 Dec 1865. J.T. Stockburn's memories of Liberal campaigns, *Kettering Leader*, 29 Nov 1907. For Channing's first election, *Northamptonshire Guardian*, 9 Jan 1886.

Conservatism 1880 to 1914: Opening of Conservative Club, *NM*, 20 Apr 1889. Liberal Club, *NM*, 4 May 1889. Primrose League, *NM*, 12 May 1887.

The Anti-vaccinationists: many references in the newspapers and in the Bull collection. For a history of smallpox vaccination, *NH*, 14 Aug 1891.

The Rise of Labour: For the history of NUBSO in the district see *Kettering Leader*, 9 Apr 1915 (Bradley's retirement speech). For the Trades Council, see *Kettering Leader & Observer*, 29 Aug 1890. On Co-operation, the story of the Kettering Working Men's Self Supporting Co-operative Society is told in *NM*, 26 Nov 1859, and in *NH*, 5 May 1860 and 17 Aug 1861. For KCIS, see W.Ballard, *A Brief History of the Kettering Industrial Co-operative Society 1865-1896*, 1896, and S. York, *The Diamond Jubilee of the KCIS 1866-1926*, 1926. On productive co-operation, W.H.Brown, *An Industrial Republic 1889-1909*, 1909 for the Boot and Shoe Co-op, and for the 'Union' Society, George Stanton, *The Story of an Industrial Democracy, 1896-1917*, 1919. For the start of the ILP, *NM*, 31 May 1895, for the Keir Hardie meeting, *Kettering Leader*, 4 Aug 1905, and for the 1909 candidature difficulties, *Kettering Guardian*, 17 and 24 Dec 1909.

14   *Industrial Culture: Association, Leisure and Sport, pp.167-84*

Virtually all of the information in this chapter comes from the newspapers of the time.

Temperance: Bird's 'twenty-first teetotal birthday' is reported in *NM*, 21 Mar 1874. Pollard's obituary is in *Kettering Evening Telegraph*, 5 Dec 1898. Plummer's letter is in *NH*, 27 June 1863. See also Frederick Smith, *Fifty Years' Reminiscences of Teetotalism*, 1900.

Working Men's Clubs: For early initiatives, *NM*, 28 Jan 1865 and *NM*, 15 Jan 1870. Formal opening of Kettering WMC *NM*, 29 Sept 1888. North Park club, *NH*, 5 May 1893.

Friendly Societies: *NH*, 6 Apr 1850. Foresters' procession, *NM*, 9 July 1842. Church parade *NH*, 27 May 1893. Freemasonry, *NM*, 2 Sept 1871.

Rifle Volunteers: Inspection by Capt. Eden, *NH*, 27 Feb 1969. Retirement of Capt. Warren East, *NM*, 15 Feb 1890.

Festivals and Holidays: Inkerman Bonfire, *NH*, 10 Nov 1855. Christmas Waits, *NM*, 29 Dec 1888. The Feast is fully reported each year. For the Trades Council attempt to amalgamate it with the August bank holiday, *NM*, 6 Oct 1888.

Music, Entertainment and Bands: *NH*, 30 June 1894 carries a history of Kettering brass banding. Many accounts of band contests in the 1880s press. For Thomas Seddon of the Rifles, see *Kettering Leader*, 24 Feb 1899. For the Charles Lawrence/ Harry Bailey concert, *NH*, 18 Apr 1896. The first annual Amateur Art exhibition is in *NH*, 13 July 1896. **Sport:** almost all the information is drawn from newspaper sources. For football, see also D. Buckby and Mick Wood, *Kettering Town Centenary Handbook*, 1976. For the start of football, *NM*, 9 Nov 1872. For the re-founding of the rugby club, see cutting in KCL dated 28 Nov 1902.

15   *The Great War and After, pp.185-202*

This chapter is very largely based on the *Kettering Leader* newspaper. On economic developments between the Wars, Kelly's *Directories* for 1914 and 1914 and the *Kettering & District Annual* for 1935 are useful, as is Tony Ireson's multi- volume *Old Kettering – A View From the Thirties*. For Charles Wicksteed, see Hilda Wicksteed's not uncritical biography of her father (1933) and the guide book *The Wicksteed Park Kettering* (?1955).

16   *The Second World War and After, pp.203-12*

Based almost entirely on *Kettering Leader* and *Evening Telegraph* files. *Barrett's County of Northampton Directory*, 1956, is valuable on Kettering business in the Fifties. *The Guardian* newspaper carried an informative article, 'The Long Walk', on Loake Bros. and their Indian suppliers in its issue of 26 Feb 2002. For post-War Wicksteed Park, the *Evening Telegraph* supplement celebrating 75 years of the enterprise is informative.

17   *Kettering Since 1974, pp.215-24*

This chapter is based on information in the remarkably full collection of press cutting in NCL, particularly good on post-1974 developments.

INDEX

Numbers in **bold** refer to illustration page numbers.

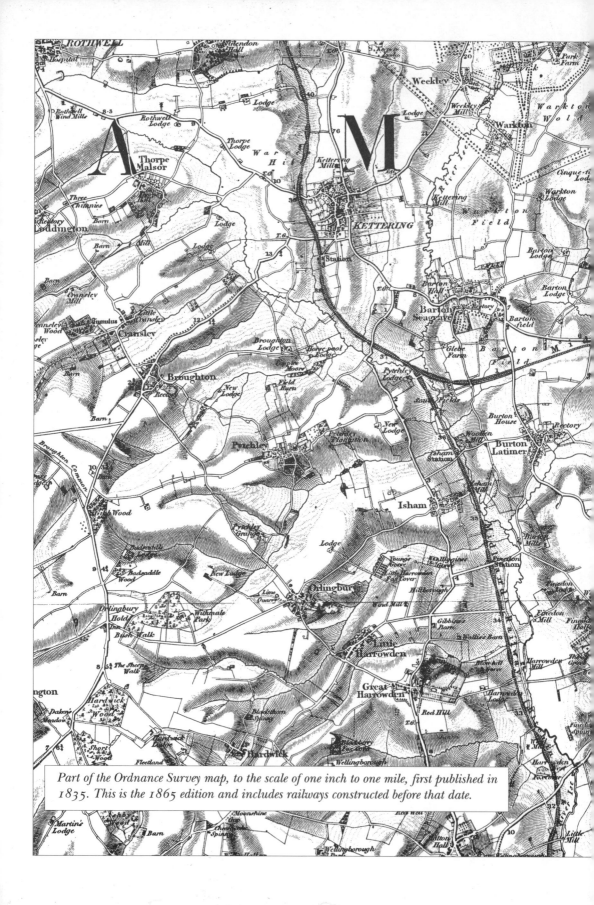

Part of the Ordnance Survey map, to the scale of one inch to one mile, first published in 1835. This is the 1865 edition and includes railways constructed before that date.